The Revelation of

GOD

A N D / A S

Human Reception

IN THE NEW TESTAMENT

The Revelation of

GOD

AND / AS

Human Reception

IN THE NEW TESTAMENT

Dan O. Via

TRINITY PRESS INTERNATIONAL
Harrisburg, Pennsylvania

The substance of portions of this work has been published previously in the following articles: Dan O. Via, "Matthew's Dark Light and the Human Condition," in *The New Literary Criticism and the New Testament*, JS-NTSup 109, ed. E. S. Malbon and E. V. McKnight (Sheffield: Sheffield Academic Press, 1994); Dan O. Via, "New Testament Theology: Historical Event, Literary Text, and the Focus of Revelation," *Perspectives in Religious Studies* 19, no. 4 (1992): 369–88; Dan O. Via, "New Testament Theology: Historical Event, Literary Text, and the Focus of Revelation," in *Perspectives on Contemporary New Testament Questions*, ed. Edgar V. McKnight, 21–47 (Lewiston, N.Y.: Edwin Mellen Press, 1992). These articles are gratefully used by permission of the publishers.

Trinity Press International, P.O. Box 1321, Harrisburg, PA 17105

Trinity Press International is a division of the Morehouse Group

Library of Congress Cataloging-in-Publication Data

Via, Dan Otto, 1928-
    The revelation of God and/as human reception : in the New
Testament / Dan O. Via.
      p. cm.
    Includes bibliographical references and index.
    ISBN 1-56338-198-2 (pbk. : alk. paper)
    1. Revelation – Biblical teaching. 2. Bible N.T. – Criticism,
interpretation, etc. I. Title.
BS2545.R49V53 1997
231.7'4'09015 – dc21
                                         97-1716
                                           CIP

Printed in the United States of America

97 98 99 00 01 02   10 9 8 7 6 5 4 3 2 1

For
Margaret
Dan and Susan
Forrest and Nathan
Carter and Amy
Rebecca

CONTENTS

PREFACE

My purpose in this book is to draw out the New Testament's understanding of the divine-human transaction and to explore some of its implications for a constructive doctrine of revelation. While I shall employ a number of hermeneutical approaches and methods, the substance of my pursuit is theological interpretation and not hermeneutical reflection.

In chapter 1 I shall comment on the title as a way of getting into the point of view to be developed, but here a word should be said about the subtitle: *In the New Testament*. A glance at the table of contents quickly reveals that I have dealt not with the whole of the New Testament but rather with four of its major witnesses — Paul, Mark, Matthew, and John. Had I discussed other New Testament writers my grasp of the New Testament's understanding of revelation would probably have been more richly nuanced, but the basic structure would not, I think, have been changed. What I have tried to show is that the four writers discussed display a common structure in their understanding of revelation but with significant variations from writer to writer.

Three colleagues at Duke Divinity School gave helpfully critical readings of parts of the typescript — Tom Langford, Moody Smith, and Richard Hays. The comments of Richard Hays were especially full and useful. I thank these friends for their help and take full responsibility for the final product. I also wish to express my gratitude to Duke Divinity School for inviting me to deliver the Clark Lectures in the spring of 1993. It is from those lectures that this book has grown. And again, as has been the case before, it was the careful and conscientious typing of Gail Chappell that brought the typescript into existence. I am grateful to her. And finally I want to thank Trinity Press International, and especially Hal Rast, for their support and encouragement in bringing this project to completion.

My family has been a constant source of joy and stimulation. It is to my wife, sons, daughters-in-law, and grandchildren that the volume is dedicated.

Chapter 1

INTRODUCTION

The purpose and direction of this book can be indicated provisionally by a brief and general exposition of the title — particularly of the "and/as." To speak of God's revelation *and* human reception is to suggest that God's self-disclosure is independent of — or something other than — human action and is the initiating factor in the communication between God and human beings. God's revealing action is prior in principle and elicits the human response. To speak of God's self-manifestation *as* human reception is to suggest that the human response is not merely passive and devoid of its own content but is a positive and constitutive factor in the actualization of revelation. Revelation does not occur apart from the specific ways in which it is received by human beings.

To ask what several New Testament writers understand by the revelation of God to humankind is to presuppose some understanding of what revelation is. Therefore, I acknowledge the operation of the hermeneutical circle by stating at the beginning a provisional definition of revelation that will enable me to identify revelational concepts in the New Testament, but that will also be filled out, varied, and made more specific by my exegetical and reflective studies. My definition is broad enough to include both theological and nontheological senses of the term. Put very simply, *revelation* is the unveiling of what has been veiled, the uncovering of what has been hidden. In religious terms it is God who is disclosed (Bultmann 1960, 58–59; Barth 1954, 205; Baillie 1956, 19; Wilckens 1969, 58 — curiously misspelled as Wilkens in the work cited). The question of the sense in which God is unveiled is something to be explored.

In this introductory chapter I have the following objectives: (1) to discuss two New Testament theologians who have dealt explicitly with the topic of revelation; (2) to summarize my conclusions about the New Testament as a guide to the substantive interpretations of four New Testament authors; (3) to contextualize my work theologically by assessing several systematic interpretations of revelation that seem to be in tension with the New

Testament and/or internally problematical and several that seem to be in continuity with the New Testament; and (4) to display the nature of revelation as it occurs in the concrete, everyday lives of two fictional characters. In the book as a whole my discourse will be close to the border between New Testament theology and systematic theology. Or perhaps more accurately: while working more on the New Testament side of the border, I shall work also on the constructive side.

New Testament Theology

Consideration will be given here to two New Testament theologians who have addressed directly the question of the understanding of revelation in the New Testament. Their approaches are quite different.

I begin with Ulrich Wilckens, but since he works self-consciously within the Pannenberg school, something needs to be said about the latter. Wolfhart Pannenberg states that his interpretation of revelation is implicitly critical of both Karl Barth and Rudolf Bultmann. The idea of the word is not to be excluded but is to be moved to a more modest and subordinate role within the context of revelation as history (Pannenberg 1969, ix). Revelation is more something that has happened than something spoken, although both speech and activity belong to the history brought about by God. In the totality of this history God's self is indirectly — not directly — revealed (13). In the Israelite tradition the glory of God is indirectly revealed in God's historical acts. With the rise of apocalyptic eschatology the final and ultimate self-vindication of God is projected onto the end event with the manifestation of God's essence being reserved for the end of history. At the same time the course of history is also revealing, for history receives its unity from its end (125–33). For early Christianity God is still only indirectly revealed in Jesus although in him the apocalyptic event came to pass ahead of time (2 Cor 4:6).

Wilckens states that early Christianity proclaimed the eschatological self-revelation of God in the appearance and fate of Jesus. There is a strong interest in what happens in the historical situation of giving revelation — in the interrelationships among Jesus, the people whom he addressed, and the future Son of man (Mark 8:38; Luke 12:8–9; Wilckens 1969, 73–75). The matter of chief importance to Wilckens is the participation of the early Christian witnesses in a salvation-history theology oriented to apocalyptic eschatology. He wants to show how the New Testament witnesses deal with the historical interests of Jewish apocalypticism — the relationships of past, present, and future (82–90).

It seems then that Wilckens is more interested in the content of revelation than in the manner of it. Also while he stresses the historical element in revelation, he acknowledges that what happened came to expression in the word. How exactly are event and word to be related? And while he affirms that the early church saw the revelation of God in the fate of Jesus, Wilckens concedes that much of the synoptic tradition about Jesus is not historical. In what sense can history be the vehicle of revelation if it did not happen? What really is the locus of revelation? These are questions that I want to consider in the next chapter.

I turn now to Bultmann, the second of the New Testament theologians to be discussed. I will mention three of his essays that deal directly and provocatively with the question of revelation. The three display a certain shift of position, and I will discuss them, not in the order of their composition, but in an order that moves from more "conservative" to more "liberal."

In "The Question of Natural Revelation" published originally in 1941, Bultmann took the position that knowledge of God apart from Christ is only a concept of God that belongs to the state of human inquiry about God. It is merely the opposite of humankind's knowledge of itself, of its limitations, of what it is not. Human beings can know on their own that they are powerless, lacking in holiness, transient, and finite and can conceive of a being who would be the opposite — omnipotent, holy, transcendent, and eternal (Bultmann 1955b, 92–98). It is this conceptual knowledge given with human beings' knowledge of their own existence that Paul is talking about in Rom 1:19–20 (114). For Christian belief, only on the basis of the gracious manifestation of God's self in the forgiveness of Christ do human beings have a knowledge of God's self as distinguished from having a concept of God (98, 109). The significance of this conceptual or natural knowledge of God is that it refers us to the forgiving grace of God in Christ. It is only in doing so that it is revelation for us. Apart from Christ it is not revelation (118).

These issues are touched upon in "The Problem of Hermeneutics" published originally in 1950, and here Bultmann's point of view seems to have changed somewhat. In order to recognize an event — the Christ event — as an act of God, there must be a prior understanding of what may be termed an act of God. And this awareness of who God is may very well be available in the human inquiry about God (Bultmann 1955a, 257). Thus it appears that the knowledge stemming from human self-understanding is a necessary point of contact for recognizing the Christ event or Christian proclamation *as* an act of God. Moreover, here Bultmann refers to the knowledge of God available in the inquiry into the meaning of human existence as *existentiell* and not merely as conceptual (257). *Existentiell* knowledge is that which comes from active existing, as distinguished from *existential* knowledge, which is analytical or theoretical.

In 1929 Bultmann had published "The Concept of Revelation in the New Testament" in which he dealt more fully, explicitly, and positively than he would in "The Problem of Hermeneutics" with the knowledge of God given with the living of life. Bultmann proposes that the proper question to put to the New Testament is which of two possible understandings of revelation determines the New Testament view. The first understands revelation as the communication of informational knowledge. In religious terms it is doctrine. The second grasps revelation as an occurrence that puts one in a new situation as a self with the possibility of understanding oneself in the new situation (Bultmann 1960, 58–60).

Bultmann argues exegetically that the second understanding prevails in the New Testament. Revelation is the occurrence of life that overcomes the fundamental human limitation — death. What is revealed is not the idea of life or the doctrine that death does not exist. Rather the actual abolition of the reality of death occurs. This event breaks into human life from beyond it (Bultmann 1960, 71–72). Bultmann can refer to the medium of the revelation as either the fact of Jesus Christ (75) or the proclamation of the word (76). There is a knowledge based on this revelation, which is the opening of a person's eyes concerning his or her own existence. One is given to understand oneself now as qualified by the proclamation. A person understands herself as coming out of a sinful past and standing under the judgment of God but also as freed from the past by the grace encountered in the word (85–87). Bultmann is obviously interested in this article in the content of revelation in the New Testament. But there is also an implicit concern about the manner or how of it. The latter is visible in his raising the question of how an understanding of revelation is possible at all. What is the relationship of the occurrence of life given in the gospel to the living of ordinary existence? How does the latter affect the former? In this piece, as in the later "The Problem of Hermeneutics," Bultmann holds that we can ask about the meaning of revelation in the New Testament at all because we already have a vague, preliminary knowledge of revelation given in the inquiry into human existence. As in the other article this knowledge is conceptual. But here he makes a move that develops more explicitly the hint given in the word *existentiell*. To know something about the concept of revelation means I have knowledge of revelation itself (Bultmann 1960, 60–62).

We know about revelation because it belongs to our lives. We know it, and yet this knowledge is a peculiar nonknowing. To know about revelation is to know our authenticity and at the same time to know our limitations that make us dependent on revelation. The preunderstanding of revelation understands that our limitations are provisional and can be broken through (Bultmann 1960, 61–62). But if as human we know revelation *itself* while not knowing it, as Bultmann has said, then our limitations must to some degree have been broken through or could be broken through independently of the Christian revelation.

My own project is to develop in a way somewhat different from Bultmann's the role of the naturally human element in the constitution of revelation — without neglecting the divine initiative. I shall seek to expand on the various ways in which several major New Testament witnesses affirm the place of human reception in the actualization of revelation.

The New Testament Understanding of Revelation Anticipated

Here I want to state very briefly the conclusions that I shall reach from my interpretation of four New Testament witnesses, conclusions about the nature of what may be called the "revelation situation." This summary should help orient the reader to the direction that the discussion is going to take. The revelation situation is composed of four elements: (1) the word of God as content or meaning; (2) the word of God as power, or the action of the Holy Spirit; (3) the imaginative reception and configuration of the word by human beings; (4) a historical-cultural situation in which the received word is meaningful. For example, within the first two chapters of 1 Thessalonians, Paul refers to the gospel (1:5; 2:4) or word of God (2:13) as rational content or *logos* (1:5a) and as empowered by the Holy Spirit (1:5b). He also speaks of the way in which the Thessalonians have received the gospel (1:6; 2:13) and of the historical circumstances in which he had worked and they have received the word (1:6; 2:2, 4–7, 14–17). These four factors recur regularly in the New Testament witnesses, although not with the same emphasis or degree of explicitness. My argument will be that for the New Testament, revelation is actual only when all four elements are operative. Only the four together are sufficient. Sometimes I shall use an expression such as "linguistic tradition" to refer to the word of God, the human language in which the word of God is received, or both of these inclusively. One of the questions to be pursued is how to relate word of God and receiving human word if the former appears only in the latter.

My reference point will be the New Testament in the situations in which the texts were produced. Account will occasionally be taken of the linguistic tradition available to an author — as when Paul is considered as an interpreter of the Old Testament — but more attention will be paid to the creative composition of the author with regard to both form and interpretive content. As pertinent texts are discussed, I will attend to the four constitutive factors of the revelation situation: (1) the word of God as content, (2) the power of the Holy Spirit, (3) the way the historical-cultural situation seems to influence a given representation of the gospel, and (4) the place of human reception, which will be observed in what the writers say in principle about the role of natural human understanding and imagination in grasping the gospel, in what they say about specific instances of their own or their addressees' response to and shaping of the word of God, and in what is implied about the human construction of the gospel or word of God by the writers' actual employment of human linguistic, literary, and thought forms that are used by other religions or in secular speech and writing.

While I believe that these four constituent factors of the revelation situation really are present in the New Testament witness, I do not claim that my interpretation of the concept of revelation in those texts is the only possible one or that my understanding of these factors' relative significance and interrelationships is the single one required by the New Testament. I continue to find basically convincing Wolfgang Iser's view that authors produce texts that contain gaps and tensions and that manifest the potential for multiple meanings. At the same time a text also imposes some constraints on interpretation that prevent an interpreter's making it mean anything at all. From this complex of potentiality, interpreters produce works that may seek to achieve congruences that did not exist in the text. Since these interpretive works reflect the interpreter's subjectivity and social-cultural world, many (legitimate) interpretations of the same text emerge (Iser 1978, 9–10, 14–15, 17, 19–25, 27, 30, 38, 92, 135, 141, 150, 152).

While the commonsense value of Iser's distinction between text and interpreter seems difficult to gainsay, Jonathan Culler has shown that the actual situation is more complex and that well-grounded distinctions between text and interpretation are impossible to establish. Culler takes a clue from Sartre for a more paradoxical position: rather than trying to specify what the text does and what the interpreter does, this position claims it is more accurate to acknowledge that the reader does everything and the text has already done everything. For the reader the text is already complete, and she can never exhaust it. On the other hand, apart from the reader's creative reading, the text is only marks on the page (Culler 1982, 75–76). The two points I want to derive from this discussion are these: (1) text and interpretation are distinguishable, even if problematically so; (2) there is a multiplicity of legitimate interpretations. The angle of vision from which my interpretation grows is constituted — at least in part — by my choice to interpret the New Testament theologically (some would say anthropologically), my continuing debt to existential interpretation (although considerably modified), and my subscription to various types of literary and historical criticism.

It is obvious that the word "reception" in the expression "human reception" is not being used in the passive sense of merely accepting what is given. The language in which human beings receive the gospel is not an empty tube through which flows the pure water of God's word. It is not a sheer transparency. I rather mean reception in the active sense of what human beings do to constitute in part the content of the divine revelation. I intend for reception to include human volition, reflection, and imagination. The main thrust of my project is not to argue that there is a certain range or scope of knowledge of God that is available to human beings independently of the biblical tradition and proclamation. That is a part of the picture, however, and one could make that argument from certain New Testament texts. What I do want to propose is that the revelation present in the tradition stemming from Israel, Christ, and the early church is itself affected in form and content by human categories that are independent of what comes from God through the biblical tradition and proclamation.

It will be noticed that the theme probably most stressed by neo-orthodox and salvation-history theology — the history of Israel and the Christ event as the primary media of revelation — has not been present in my formulation. The reasons for this will come to light in chapter 2.

Systematic Considerations

The sketches in this section will be brief but will be expanded and more fully debated in the appendix.

Interpretations in Tension with the New Testament

First I discuss several interpretations of revelation that seem to me to be in tension — in different ways — with the overall New Testament position. I begin the presentation with Karl Barth, who contributed so much to giving revelation a central place in Christian theology. Barth argued that revelation comes wholly from the divine realm and not from the human (Barth 1954, 207, 209, 211). He apparently will not allow that the structure of human language contributes anything to the content of revelation (Thiemann 1985, 94–95), although he obviously acknowledges that it occurs in human language. Yet it is not a word that we can speak to ourselves (Barth 1949, 156–60). Nor will Barth concede (1959, 26–29) that human (non-Christian) religions contain any natural knowledge of God independent of the revelation in Christ that could serve as a point of contact for assimilating the gospel.

For the Barthian theologian T. F. Torrance the word of God has absolute priority over all the media of its communication and reception. It is what it is in its own reality. Its identity is independent of our recognition of it, and its truth, independent of our acknowledgement (Torrance 1982, 13–14). Torrance seems to deny that any strictly human preunderstanding of what revelation and God might be is necessary as a point of contact that would make the world of the Bible accessible to us. Rather the Bible itself is able to bring us under the power of its word. If one begins with self-understanding, one ends with it (102–3).

Here I simply mention, but in the appendix shall discuss more fully, the lingering Barthianism of what I shall call the "Yale school" (Frei, Lindbeck, Childs). These scholars tend to deny both the inevitability and the fruitfulness of the operation of the hermeneutical circle in interpretation, or what more recent interpreters might call the "impact of the social location." At this point I offer three brief criticisms of the Barthian tendency. First, it is opposed by the New Testament, for the New Testament affirms the operation of the hermeneutical circle. The measure of understanding that one brings to the hearing of the gospel defines the measure of meaning that one receives from the hearing (Mark 4:24). Chapters 3–6 of this book will show that it is pervasively the case in the New Testament that cross-religious and cross-cultural categories that have no peculiar relationship to the Bible shape the content of the New Testament revelation. Second, no one could expound the content of a revelation that was totally prior to human structuring. And it is not possible to argue that a revelation that has been actually received is completely independent of the human categories in which it is grasped. Third, as I shall seek to show in the appendix, the Yale school's theological project cannot be carried out, for their interpretive practice is inconsistent with their programmatic position.

I turn now very briefly to an approach that is at the opposite end of the spectrum of theological possibilities from Barth. James Barr wants to understand the Bible as the classic model for the faith related to Jesus and the God of Israel. He seeks, however, to do this without any use of the concept of revelation. The formation of tradition and the choice of certain books to form the Scripture are human acts, but the Christian doctrine of revelation has characteristically claimed a movement from God to humankind, often by means of supernatural acts and direct verbal communication in human language. Barr seems to have two primary objections to the traditional understanding of revelation. First, if revelation is thought to be focused in an almost exclusive way in the Christ event as attested in the Bible, then revelation must have come to an end long ago and could no longer be a reality for us. Second, we have no access to and no means of comprehending a communication or revelation from God that is antecedent to the human tradition about God (Barr 1973, 118–22).

In Barr's view if the concept of revelation is to be used at all meaningfully, then it should not refer to a past event but to ever new situations in which tradition and Scripture are used to illuminate some person's or community's present (1973, 122). Thus revelation can continue into the indefinite future. I appreciate Barr's criticisms of the traditional view of revelation, but I believe that the idea — whatever terms are used for it — is far too important in the New Testament to be abandoned. I shall try to show that the New Testament understanding of revelation does not fall under Barr's criticisms.

From a constructive point of view Ronald Thiemann has argued, against the position of Barr, that revelation and associated notions are essential for the internal logic of Christian theology. He especially questions whether the prevenience of grace can be maintained apart from a doctrine of revelation (Thiemann 1985, 2–3). Thiemann's own project is to replace the prevailing modern concept of revelation, which he sees as based on foundationalist epistemologies, with a doctrine of revelation that focuses instead on the identity of God as the one who promises (7, 81, 84, 101).

Thiemann wants to exclude epistemological issues from his construction of revelation and to center rather upon the gospel as narrated promise and God's identity as the one who promises (1985, 69, 72–77, 80, 101–2, 109, 112, 137). My response to this is that while promise is certainly a biblical motif, Thiemann's move shifts attention away from the questions of *how* does God manifest God's self and *how* do human beings receive that revelation to the questions of *what* is the identity of God — God is the one who promises and fulfills (111, 137) — and *what* is revealed — God's intention to save (132–33). This is good theology, but the shift from *how* to *what* in constructive terms leaves unattended the important question *how* God is made known. And in exegetical terms the vocabulary of manifestation, revelation, and enlightening activity as applied to God (Matt 4:12–16; Mark 4:21–22; John 1:4–5, 9; 3:19–21; 8:12; Rom 1:17; 1 Cor 1:18; 2 Cor 3:14–4:6; Gal 1:12, 16; 4:4–5) and the vocabulary of knowing, understanding, seeing, and hearing as applied to human beings (Matt 6:22–23; 13:14–16; Mark 4:18, 23–25; 8:17–21; John 9:41; 17:3; Rom 10:19; 2 Cor 2:14) are far too basic and pervasive in the New Testament to dismiss the question of how knowledge of God is made available. Clearly the questions of *how* God is known and *what* God makes known are not discrete issues in the New Testament. This book, therefore, will give a certain attention to the content of revelation, but its focus will be on the manner or how of revelation.

Interpretations in Continuity with the New Testament

I move now to a summary discussion of five interpretations of revelation that seem to be — in a broad sense — in continuity with the New Testament position. I do not suggest that they belong to the same "school." But each of them in its own way affirms both the intervening self-manifestation of God in human life and the constitutive shaping of the word of God by human reflection and imagination.

Paul Tillich by means of his famous principle of correlation posits an analogy between doing theology and the occurrence of revelation: each of them involves a relatively objective given that must be subjectively received (Tillich 1953, 3–4, 6, 40, 43–44, 68–69, 123–24, 140, 152). Tillich also makes an evaluative distinction between original revelation and dependent revelation (140), with the latter obviously including the activity of theology. This distinction will be critically assessed in the appendix.

For Tillich religious revelation is the extraordinary unveiling of a mystery without the mystery's ceasing to be a mystery (1953, 120). The meaning of revelation for a specific religious community is derived from a "classical" example, and not from an abstract generality. In the case of Christianity the defining example is the reception of Jesus as the Christ, the bringer of new being, by Peter (55–56, 120). Something objectively happened to Peter, and Peter received it so that the reception is a part of the revelation (123–24, 140, 152). The reception always entails the questions that the receiver is asking and seeking answers to, questions that arise from the receiver's existential and cultural situation (4, 44, 92). Since the situation has an impact on the constitution of revelation (68–69, 72), revelation is always changing during the course of the historical process (140), and thus God in God's self-manifestation, although not in God's depth, also undergoes change (68).

Ray Hart gives a focal place to the human imagination in the constitution of revelation. For the Christian faith, revelation is a given foundation — the mediation of the word of God by the tradition — although revelation is not there in Scripture in the same way that Scripture is there. Revelation has to find its own tongue from Scripture (Hart 1968, 36–37, 40–41, 44, 104). Theology is a response to this given in the light of present history and in whatever language is at hand (34, 44). Theology cannot say what the tradition said without saying it in another way (306).

Formally speaking revelation covers the spectrum of language from the mythopoetic and imaginative to the explicative and conceptual, but imaginative language is nearest to the event of revelation. It inverbalizes the event (Hart 1968, 12–14, 48). The function of revelation is to solicit human beings in their situation to their own potential wholeness, to the neighbor's well-being, and to the glory of God. It is a solicitation to see ourselves as existing out of the potency established in the Christ event (122–23, 182, 216).

Revelation is a continuing process as it interacts with theology in the hermeneutical spiral. There is movement from imaginative immediacy through interpretive schematizations to new immediacy (Hart 1968, 85, 94–97). The language of revelation and the language of theology are imaginative at their optimum (255, 275, 277). The imagination rends and dissolves the patterns from the past and recreates them in new configurations by placing the "thing" in a new and alien context. Imagination is not just a way of knowing but a participation in emergent becoming, as the self expands through new interpretations and the unfinished human being moves toward wholeness (165, 167, 184, 196, 198, 200–201, 205).

I turn now to two Roman Catholic theologians. According to Karl Rahner God manifested God's self to human beings at the outset in creation, communicating both the gift and the capacity to accept it (1994, 117–19, 128). This original revelation was/is given to all human beings and to all times in view of and in God's absolute willing of Jesus Christ (123, 127, 129, 172). The structure of the self-communication is that God creates emptiness in human beings in order to communicate God's self to this emptiness (123). The universality of the revelation does not mean that all accept it, as Rahner observes by reference to Rom 1:18 (54, 128). However, the knowledge given with the original revelation is always inevitably present in the depths of human existence, whether in the mode of acceptance or rejection (52, 57, 77). Since there is salvation, and hence faith, everywhere in history, then a supernatural revelation must have been at work everywhere in history and not just in the biblical history of salvation (147–49). Yet this universal revelation, however real, is provisional and is made ambiguous by human guilt (155).

At times Rahner can say that because the universal knowledge of God is given by grace, it is not "natural" (1994, 127, 149). But he can also say, I think more circumspectly, that the original knowledge is both natural and the result of grace (57). For Rahner the knowledge given in creation is qualitatively an unthematic awareness oriented to the holy, nameless, indefinable mystery (44, 52–53, 61, 65, 76, 123). At the same time it is mediated to us by our concrete encounter with the world of persons and things (52). This unthematic knowledge of God is the permanent ground out of which thematic knowledge is given with a specific religion such as Christianity (53, 132, 161). Every real intervention of God in the world is the becoming historical and concrete of God's embedding

God's self in the world at the outset (87). And the particular history of revelation in the Bible is the valid, fulfilling self-interpretation of the original, universal revelation in creation (158–61).

I shall now discuss David Tracy by reference to his orientation to the concept of the classic. A *classic text* is one that has an "excess of meaning" that demands constant interpretation. It is not timeless but rather permanently timely. It is rooted in its own historical time but appeals to the historical situations of later times (Tracy 1991, 102). A religious classic brings to expression the sui generis character of religion — the experience of the otherness of the whole as holy mystery (155, 159, 168–69). And this expression is an event of revelatory power (173, 193, 202–3). The event of Jesus Christ, which comes to expression in Christian classics (248, 254), is then understood as the manifestation of the power of the whole that is normative for the Christian community (233–34). The revelation in Christ, then, is a specification of the disclosure of the divine that occurs in religious classics generally (235).

The manifestation of the holy frees the human receiver to respond (Tracy 1991, 175, 202); therefore, the role of the receiver is not autonomous or initiatory. However, the one who receives the tradition and creates a revelatory classic text does have a constitutive role in the occurrence of revelation. The receiver, who is, of course, an interpreter, gives expression to his or her preunderstandings and nonpassive critical freedom (118, 124–25, 171, 194, 199, 235, 255–56). Moreover, the producer of a text of revelation, in order to bring the revelation to expression, must seek the appropriate genre, style, and form (199–200). As a result the expression of revelation makes use of the "secular" (209–10).

The final theologian to be discussed here is Gordon Kaufman, who rejects the idea that theology works with a deposit of revelation given directly, objectively, and authoritatively by God. In Kaufman's view all theology is an imaginative human construction, historical through and through and subject to criticism and revision (1981, 30–31, 53, 94, 99–100, 250, 254). Theology's notions about God, humankind, and the world are our ideas, not God's (Kaufman 1993, 31, 56). Moreover, what Kaufman says about human constructedness applies as much to the Bible as to later theological formulations (1981, 250; 1993, 21, 47, 58).

Kaufman, however, is prepared to argue for a reconstructed understanding of revelation that does not regard it as an authoritative given that can be used to legitimate particular doctrines or claims (1993, 48, 464). Emphasizing the human constructedness of theology can deepen our consciousness of the mystery of life and open us to what has traditionally been called "God's grace and mercy." Clearly identifying our sphere of activity points indirectly to that which lies beyond our knowledge and control and ultimately constitutes us (57–58). What we can claim is that in our talk about God, in our imaginative and reflective constructing of images of God, God could be said to be making God's self known to humankind. The Bible's formulations are a significant subjective feature in God's movement toward humanness (351–54). In fact our groping efforts to understand the cosmic grounding of our move toward humanization are not just our unfounded imaginings but represent the proper human response to the self-revealing of God (487).

Revelation in Life

In the last section of this chapter I want to give two fictional examples of how revelation may occur in real-life situations. Since here I am dealing with fiction, I shall refer to the concrete situation in which a revelation is received as a life situation rather than a historical situation. My first text is Flannery O'Connor's "Revelation" (1966; hereafter cited by page number only). O'Connor understood herself as a Christian writer, and this story of hers — with its own nuances and imaginative power — manifests the fourfold pattern I have outlined in such a way that it may be regarded as an instance of revelation in the New Testament mode.

In this story a religious revelation in Christian terms occurs for and is received by Mrs. Turpin. Mrs. Turpin gazes down into the pig parlor "as if through the very heart of the mystery ... as if she were absorbing some abysmal life-giving knowledge" (217). There is a hint of irony here. The religious mystery is connected with her intent gaze at the hogs on the farm. It is "as if" she were gazing through the heart of the mystery and absorbing the knowledge. Yet however ironical the mysterious knowledge may be, it is real and life-changing. The final scene is a vision of salvation for herself and others.

The story begins in a doctor's office where Mrs. Turpin has been engaged in a stream of egregiously complacent, bigoted, and self-congratulatory conversation, at which an ugly female college student has been seething. When at a certain point Mrs. Turpin cries out — because she is grateful for having been given a little of everything — "Thank you, Jesus" (206), the girl, overcome with rage, hits Mrs. Turpin in the face with a book and grabs her by the neck shaking her and howling. In shock Mrs. Turpin said to the girl, as if she were waiting for a revelation, "What you got to say to me?" (207). And the girl answered, "Go back to hell where you came from, you old wart hog!" (207).

Back at her farm Mrs. Turpin continues to be in a state of considerable agitation. She could not believe that these words apply to her and yet could not escape the suspicion that they do. She rails against God for sending her such an undeserved message and wonders incredulously how she can be both a hog and the saved paragon that she is. Her questions to God are at the least aggressive: "What do you send me a message like that for?" (215). "Who do you think you are?" (216). Then comes the vision of salvation in which she is included in a very surprising way.

Let us now look at the story in the light of the four elements constituting the occurrence of revelation. First, the life situation is composed of Mrs. Turpin's social world as perceived by her and the events in the doctor's office and at the farm. Mrs. Turpin is an imposing person who is used to giving orders and who thinks of herself as a respectable, churchgoing woman, morally and socially superior to most of the people around her. One of the most formative patterns of her mind is the habitual placing of people in a hierarchical class structure. On the bottom are most blacks, and alongside them, poor white trash. Just above are common whites and perhaps good blacks. On the next rung belong homeowners, and the level above them is occupied by home-and-land owners. This is where Mrs. Turpin placed herself and her husband. At the top are the big home-and-land owners. Mrs. Turpin recognizes with some frustration that not everyone fits into this scheme, but it nevertheless provides her essential security.

The book was thrown at Mrs. Turpin by Mary Grace — an ugly, scowling, ill-mannered, acne-faced student from Wellesley College. The incident is physically traumatic, and the spiritual-psychological wound has several dimensions. Mrs. Turpin's identity and status are challenged, and this challenge is underscored by the fact that it comes from someone ugly and ill-mannered, the opposite of what Mrs. Turpin takes herself to be. She is given a very threatening message that she cannot escape, by someone beneath her. And yet Mary Grace has a nice, stylish mother, and she herself goes to Wellesley. So perhaps Mrs. Turpin feels at some level that she is being attacked from above as well as from below.

Back at the farm Mrs. Turpin denies that the hog identity belongs to her and yet does not believe her own denial (210). As we have seen, Mrs. Turpin aggressively attacks what she sees as the injustice of God, but in the process of accusing God she does tacitly acknowledge that God has in fact effected a thorough rearrangement of her hierarchical world. God has put the bottom rail on top. Mrs. Turpin is now on the bottom and therein lies her salvation.

Immediately after her most defiant question to God — "Who do you think you are?" — comes the vision of salvation. Mrs. Turpin sees — here is the life-giving knowledge — a giant swinging bridge stretching from earth to heaven and passing through a field of fire. On it is a horde of souls rumbling toward heaven. At the head of the procession are the white trash and blacks along with assorted freaks and lunatics. Bringing up the rear are people like her and her husband. And yet they, too, are on the way to the starry beyond, even if they are a little shocked at having their virtues burned away.

Second, in order for this life situation to be revelation it must be understood in light of the biblical tradition. That makes the present occurrence an enactment of the biblical stories and images. Several echoes of the New Testament are present in Mrs. Turpin's understanding of her situation although some were probably more explicit than others. The reference to God's liking trash reflects the gospel picture of Jesus' concern for sinners (Matt 11:19; Mark 2:17; Luke 15:1–2), and the motif of putting the bottom rail on top as well as the arrangement on the swinging bridge echoes the gospel saying that the first will be last and the last, first (Mark 10:31). The size and mixture of the horde on the bridge to heaven are reminiscent of the motley throng gathered into the feast of the kingdom (Matt 22:10; Luke 14:21–23). The passage of the bridge through the field of fire echoes the purging fire of 1 Cor 3:13–15, which will burn up the builder's inferior works but leave the builder herself or himself saved. There could also be an allusion here to the grass of the field that is thrown into the oven (Matt 6:30; Luke 12:28).

Third, the merging of life situation and biblical word is imprinted on the heart of the recipient of revelation by the present action of God or the Spirit or the power of the word. This is not terribly explicit in the story but is nevertheless present. Mrs. Turpin experiences the unnerving message from Mary Grace as directed precisely at her and no one else (210), and she consciously understands it as a message from God (215). Were the power of the Spirit not operative, how could Mrs. Turpin's very considerable resistance to the message have been overcome, and why would Mary Grace's very human angry outburst have been seen as word from

God? This transaction reflects the biblical theme that in revelation God is present as hidden. That is, there is no necessity for seeing the human events and meanings as acts of God. That Mrs. Turpin is brought so to see them suggests that the Spirit was active. Even so Mrs. Turpin could have rejected the believing interpretation of her experience. As Paul acknowledges to the Thessalonians, even though he preached the gospel in the power of the Spirit (1 Thess 1:5), they could have received it simply as human word (2:13).

Fourth, thus in order for Mrs. Turpin to recognize Mary Grace's human act and word as God's word, there is something that Mrs. Turpin must do. She must be actively receptive. She must have a measure of understanding to bring to the occurrence, a measure that affects the measure of understanding she finally receives (Mark 4:24–25). Of the four revelational factors, active human reception may be the least thematized in the story, but it must be presupposed to account for what does happen in Mrs. Turpin's experience. In order for her to see Mary Grace's message as God's message, she must already have some understanding of what God's word would be. Where does Mrs. Turpin's prior understanding come from in the story's perspective? Probably nothing in the story explicitly suggests that it was natural to her. Perhaps it comes from the residue of the Christian tradition present in her symbolic world. She does see herself as a Christian before her final revelation. And we have seen that the way in which she subjectively experiences the life situation of the story gives expression to certain New Testament motifs. At the same time Mrs. Turpin's Christian self-understanding until the final event is so deformed that it is difficult to distinguish it from simply natural self-understanding.

We have considered the factors that constitute Mrs. Turpin's experience of revelation within the story. The story then becomes a part of the linguistic tradition that encounters the reader in his or her historical situation. Whether that encounter becomes a revelation for the reader depends on what the Holy Spirit and the reader do with it.

It is worth mentioning that the biblical word element could be richer for the reader than it was for Mrs. Turpin, for the reader may make connections that the character in the story did not make. There is an allusive reference to Job (210), but it is difficult to tell whether this belongs solely to the narrator's discourse or is also a part of Mrs. Turpin's self-awareness. In either case the reader could take a further intertextual step. There is a certain parallel between Job's vigorous effort at self-justification (Job 23:10,

12; 27:5–6; 31:35–37) followed (after some chapters) by God's vision-audition to Job (38:1; 42:5) and Mrs. Turpin's assertive self-defense followed by her vision. In some sense — even if ironical — Mrs. Turpin recapitulates the experience of Job. More substantively one may notice the intertextuality — apparently unobserved by Mrs. Turpin and the narrator — between Mrs. Turpin's experience of salvation and Paul's preaching about the word of the cross in 1 Cor 1:18–30 (see further, Via 1990, 47–48). The word of the cross is the power of God although in its lowliness it is foolish to human beings. It is an offense to the Greek, who seeks wisdom, and to the Jew, who desires miracle. The cross as interpreted by Paul's preaching is an ambiguous combination of power and weakness, wisdom and foolishness. This unexpected combination shows that things are not what they seem. God, showing God's power in weakness, brings to nothing those who think they are something (1 Cor 1:27–28). But those brought to nothing may have their lives refounded on a new ground — the wisdom and righteousness of Christ (1:30).

Mary Grace, because of who she is, is an offense to Mrs. Turpin, but it is precisely the incursion of this offense into Mrs. Turpin's life world that brings to nothing the something that she thinks she is. In the shocking action and words of Mary Grace this story fuses the grace of Mary with the scandalizing grace of the word of the cross. As a result the woman who believed that she has been given a little of everything good is reduced to a wart hog from hell. The bottom rail is on top, and she is at the end of the line. But she is on the bridge to heaven, not because of her virtues but because her virtues are being burned away.

O'Connor's "Revelation" is full of biblical-Christian imagery, and the occurrence of revelation is the dramatic focal point. While it is not easy for Mrs. Turpin to receive the message, the issue is clear-cut, and she does in the end accept it. My second text is quite different from the first. In genre it is a novel rather than a short story, and its narrative world is far indeed from the rural South, stretching as it does from urban Chicago to various exotic and far-flung places. In Saul Bellow's *More Die of Heartbreak*, the revelational pattern is definitely there, but it is more ambiguous, more subject to different interpretations, and the difficulties of receiving revelation and the tensions generated by doing so are complexly drawn. As the title suggests, the novel is concerned with the heart — here the seat of love and feeling. More die from heartbreak than from atomic radiation, but there are no demonstrations against heartbreak in the streets. If people were more aware of their feelings, there would be a real march on Washington, and the capital would never hold all of that sorrow (Bellow 1987, 197, 315; hereafter cited by page number only).

A major theme in the novel is that when a man of fundamentally academic interests and humane sensitivities gets involved with people who are basically oriented to money, he gets corrupted and deformed, becomes persuaded to do things that contradict his character (285–87, 298, 300–301, 306–8, 325–27, 333–35). The protagonist, Uncle Benn, is a distinguished senior botanist who has been a widower for fifteen years. During these years he has had a few unsatisfying sexual relationships but is looking for the right woman. The narrator is Uncle Benn's nephew, Kenneth, who believes his uncle's intuition to have been that plants functioned as sense organs, collecting cosmic data for the earth. Finally Benn marries a younger woman from a scheming, avaricious, monied family that wants to use him to make more money.

He lets himself be sucked in. The scheme involves his suing a wealthy uncle of his, who had defrauded him at an earlier time, for $2 million. His uncle asks him what he needs $2 million for, and he has no answer. He comes to recognize that he has been disoriented. He says, "I moved over into a kind of life I haven't been able to manage" (298). The great joy of his life has been his rapport with plants, his instinct, his connection. But now in his disorientation he discovers with shock that he has been fooled into thinking that an artificial azalea is real (300). He has lost his bearings and feels like a phony, an imposter, in the household of his new wife's parents (327).

It is a painful irony for Benn to realize that prior to his marriage he had received a revelation warning him not to marry this woman but had gone against the message and done it anyway. Benn comes to believe that his refusal of the revelation was a sin (240, 298), but, as he says, a man trained in science cannot go by revelation and cannot be rational and also hold with sin (298). One cannot surrender to a brain fit (240).

The revelation occurred one night when Benn and Matilda, his wife-to-be, went to see the old Hitchcock movie *Psycho*. At a certain point in watching the movie when he sees the transvestite murderer, he instantaneously identifies that figure with Matilda. He is shocked that his mind has made this connection. The association was immediately so fixed that it could not be cast off. It was especially the shoulders of the *Psycho* character that reminded him of Matilda. That this is not for Uncle Benn just a psychological event is suggested by his belief that he has been warned practically from on high (although Alfred Hitchcock and Tony Perkins were the effective agents) that Matilda is not the woman of his heart (240, 298).

Revelation occurs for Uncle Benn when a message from an unexpected external source in his present life situation becomes internally relevant and inescapable. The four defining features in the New Testament view of revelation are present, although one of them only in an allusive way.

First, the life situation is composed of the impending marriage and the effect of the movie. Given the social and ethical context, the message is more than a warning that Matilda is not really the woman of Benn's heart. It is a call not to abandon intellectual and humane values for material ones. It is revealing that when Benn was looking at the world from the standpoint of his love of plants and dedication to science, he saw the far-off places where he conducted his research as Indian forests, Chinese mountains, and the sources of the Nile. But having been corrupted by the attraction of more money, Benn saw the faraway places as "nothing but the Third World, squalid, misgoverned by the kleptocrat military, scenes of famine, filth, AIDS, mass murder" (330).

Second, the divine initiative, or word as power, is seen in the note that the message came practically from on high (240) and that eternity itself had warned him (277). Moreover, the power of the word is suggested by the overwhelming inescapability of the association that has laid hold on him — Matilda as the murderer (233). The scandal of the revelation (1 Cor 1:18–30) is reflected in Benn's chagrin that this movie — this trash, this box-office crap — should have released this message from his heart (234): a Jew who seeks wisdom is still a Greek (1 Cor 1:22). In some tension with the element of divine initiative is the notion that what gave him the message was his instinct (261, 326) or his sensations as he watched the movie or even the outrages of his mind (233, 277). At times Benn sees the occurrence as revelation, but because in revelation God is hidden in the ordinary — or in the mean — this experience can always be interpreted in another way: as instinct or an aberration.

Third, the message from the life situation, grasped as a revelation from God, is actively received by Benn. His own prophetic soul had sent him a special message (326) or the message came from his heart (234).

Fourth, the biblical tradition, or the word as content, which interprets the present in the light of the divine initiative and personal, imaginative reception is not present in any very concrete way. However, it is alluded to broadly in the reference to Benn's "prophetic" soul (326) and in the implied author's preference for justice, truth, and humane values over material ones as well as in the association between human love and divine love (277).

It might be worth pinpointing the reasons why Uncle Benn resisted taking the revealed message as one he should heed. (1) To believe in revelation would be contrary to his scientific training (240, 298). (2) The revelation occurred through a mean and inferior medium — a movie he did not like (234–35). (3) To accept the revelation would have violated his personally appropriated aesthetic values. That is, it seemed like an attack on Matilda's beauty, which in his mind was a justification for the marriage (298, 306). She was so beautiful. (4) Finally, to heed the revelation would have seemed like a personal offense against Matilda, a breach of love (234, 277). Benn wanted to thaw two hearts (279). This violation of love was especially painful for him because he understood human love as the source for humankind of the warmth of heaven (277). Therefore in the end there was a conflict of religious values — the truth of the revelation versus love.

The underside of Benn's marrying for love is that in deciding to marry this woman he was opting for her parents' penthouse, the silks and satins, the carpets deeper than forest moss, the tremendous force of the taps in the bathroom, the whirlpool tub (277–78). The reasons for rejecting the revelation all appeal to values of a humanistic society, values that are necessary to some degree for living in our world. The conflict between revelation and necessary humanistic values shows that appropriating revelation is always an "in spite of." It is living out of a reality that will always be to some degree over against the world in which we must also live.

Because the message that laid hold on Benn — do not marry Matilda; Matilda is a murderer (298) — is in conflict with humane values, he can see the revelation as an atrocity committed by his mind (233), as a result of his being out of his mind (234), or as an act of partial understanding, perhaps worse than being an out-and-out nut (240). To heed the message is an attack on Matilda, love, and humanistic values. To reject the revelation is a sin against the Eternity that sent it (277, 298).

Benn does, as we have seen, go against the revealed message, and the result is personal deformation and loss of orientation (300–301). The revelation, though rejected, is real because all of the requisite factors for actualization are present. The message is experienced as from God (at least for Benn's religious side) and as subjectively understandable and pertinent to his situation. And even though he disobeys the message — real revelation can be rejected — it remains with him as a sense of sin.

I have been interpreting a novel by a writer who is Jewish, a novel that makes virtually no use of New Testament images, as an instance of the New Testament understanding of revelation. On what grounds? While it is difficult to make out specific echoes of the New Testament, some parts of the Jewish tradition broadly alluded to in the novel certainly overlap with early Christian themes — the loving God, for example. But more importantly the fourfold structure of revelation as it appears in the New Testament is present in the novel: (1) a specific present situation, (2) personal reception, (3) the divine initiative, and (4) a religious tradition applied to the present situation. I conclude from this that what the New Testament means by revelation can occur apart from the specifics of the Christian tradition, and at least one significant chapter from the New Testament supports this idea.

In Romans 4 Paul seeks to show that the Christian gospel of justification by faith does not overthrow the law of Moses by portraying Abraham, who belongs to the law, as already having Christian faith. That is, Paul defines Abraham's faith as *resurrection* faith. The fact that Paul describes the God in whom Abraham believed as the one who gives life to the dead and calls into existence the things that do not exist (Rom 4:16–17) shows that Paul is interpreting Abraham's experience of God in the light of the Christian experience of the God who raised Jesus from the dead (4:24). We could say that Paul posits a "resurrection situation" in Abraham's history and a corresponding faith arising from it. The resurrection situation is what the Christians' and Abraham's situations have in common — the promise of life in the midst of death.

The broader import of Romans 4 is that for Paul the death-resurrection-faith situation is a possibility — in principle and in actuality — at any time during the history of God's saving acts. Not only Abraham but also other Israelites had the kind of faith Abraham had (Rom 4:11–12). Romans 4 constitutes a certain modification — or deconstruction — of Paul's customary position. Generally faith in Christ (Rom 3:22; Gal 2:16) or in his death and resurrection (Rom 10:9; Gal 2:20; 3:1–2; Phil 3:9) is the condition for salvation. For Paul, being in a right relationship with God comes through faith in Christ (Rom 10:10). Faith in Christ is *in itself* the way to, or the consequence of (Phil 1:29), salvation. But in Romans 4, faith in Christ is not itself the way to justification. Rather faith in Christ has become a paradigm or model for analogous situations that are not specifically faith in Christ but are qualitatively similar to it. If that were not Paul's real point, he would not be able to show that the faith of justification was present in Abraham and thus does not overthrow the law.

The medium for this shift in Paul's position is the hermeneutical move of interpreting X as Y; that is, interpreting Abraham's faith in God's promise (X) *as* the Christian's faith in the death and resurrection of Jesus (Y). The substance of the shift is that faith in Christ has ceased to be the focus and has been replaced in the center by the category of having righteousness reckoned to one. This is what happened for both Abraham and the Christian believers — the reckoning of righteousness. What the two have in common is that faith is reckoned as righteousness (Rom 4:22–24a).

The focus, or fundamental category, is having faith reckoned as righteousness, and the faith in which righteousness — a right relationship with God — becomes a reality has a certain character. Having this faith is the content of salvation, and this content is what Paul wants to define here. But the faith in which righteousness becomes a reality does not have to be faith in Christ. It has to be *like* faith in Christ. It has to be holding in hope to God's promise of life in the face of the impossible. Faith in Christ is the paradigm for faith as righteousness but is not the only actual access to the right relationship.

So just as there can be a right relationship with God that is like faith in Christ but is not specifically faith in Christ, so there can be a revelation situation that manifests the structure of the New Testament understanding of revelation — and thus is real revelation — but whose linguistic element is not specifically or peculiarly Christian.

Chapter 2

EVENT AND WORD: THE HISTORICAL JESUS

This chapter will deal primarily, but not exclusively, with two of the factors that compose the revelation situation — the word as content and the elusive historical element. A certain attention will be given to the place of the historical Jesus in the occurrence of revelation.

For the purpose of this discussion I am using the terms "word" or "kerygma" and "literary text" as more or less equivalent. It would not be legitimate in all contexts to equate spoken and written language, but I believe it is in this one for two reasons. First, New Testament scholars regularly speak of the written interpretive or theological dimension of the Gospels as kerygmatic. Second, proclaimed word and literary text in their common distinction from historical event both come under the category of linguistic representation. While I want to maintain a relative distinction between event and linguistic representation, I am also very much concerned to probe their mutual interpenetration.

Neo-Orthodoxy and Salvation History

In chapter 1 Karl Barth and T. F. Torrance were considered from the standpoint of their emphasis on revelation as coming exclusively from God. Here in chapter 2 neo-orthodoxy will be more broadly analyzed from the viewpoint of its emphasis on history as the fundamental medium of revelation. I think that it can be plausibly maintained that neo-orthodox theology affirmed the centrality of God's self-revelation in history, and I should like to look at characteristic examples — from Old Testament, New Testament, and systematic theologians.

G. Ernest Wright stated that the biblical presentation of faith, which can properly be called "biblical theology," is a recital or proclamation of the acts of God together with the inferences drawn therefrom. These acts are themselves interpretations of historical events (Wright 1952, 11). Wright appears to be talking about the Bible itself rather than the contemporary scholars dealing with it. According to Wright, the Bible makes history the arena of the divine activity. God has revealed God's self in a striking series of historical events. Biblical theology is thus a confession of these events: Israel's understanding of revelation derived from the initial event in which God graciously delivered the people from slavery (38, 43–44). The New Testament sees Christ as the climax of God's revelation in history, inaugurating a new epoch, and interprets the Old Testament typologically. That is, Old Testament events are taken to have been real in their own time but also to have been used by God to point to greater facts in the future. What the New Testament confesses is the act of God in the life and death of a historical person (60–61, 66–67).

Notice that our problem — the relationship between event and language in revelation — has already emerged. Wright oscillates between saying that revelation occurs in the historical events and saying that it occurs in the interpretations of events, interpretations that are the expression of faith. This tension is not reflected upon by Wright, though it comes inadvertently to expression.

In 1931 Sir Edwyn Hoskyns and Noel Davey had already published their influential *Riddle of the New Testament*. They affirmed that the New Testament proclaims the suffering of a certain man — a historical event of the recent past — as a model to follow and a bearing of human sin. Great significance was attached to the event, and the question is whether that significance was added from some outside source or was embedded in the concrete historical life. Hoskyns and Davey conclude that the christological significance lies behind, and not ahead of, all parts of the synoptic tradition and the remainder of the New Testament. There is no point at which literary or historical criticism can identify a stratum of material where the Christology has been imposed upon a nonchristological history (Hoskyns and Davey 1931, 52–59, 144–45). Thus for Hoskyns and Davey the event happened as interpreted. The significance of the story is in the events, and no tension between word and event is acknowledged.

Similarly, for Emil Brunner revelation in the Bible is held to be God's mighty acts (1946, 118). Revelation took place in the indissolubly linked words and acts of God to form a chain of historical events in the history of Israel. Both word and act together constitute the fact of historical revelation. This history reaches its completion and finality in Jesus Christ (84, 95). Thus for the Bible the word of God is the living event. The written word of the Bible is not *the* word of God and to regard it as such exclusively is idolatry (119–20). Yet the act of historical divine revelation is completed only where in the spoken word of the apostle it becomes the knowledge of faith. The Bible is word of God insofar as God uses it to make God's saving purposes known. And the believing witness of apostle and Scripture is necessary to make Jesus effectively known as the Christ (122, 135).

Thus for Brunner the event is the basis of revelation, but revelation is effective only through the word of witness — linguistic representation. Word and event are organically united. The work of Torrance shows that the neo-orthodox position extended beyond the 1960s. Torrance maintains that in Jesus Christ word and deed were inextricably interwoven, and he speaks of the New Testament forms of thought and speech making factual reference to Jesus Christ (1982, 89, 94) and appeals to the "objective reference" of biblical statements (114). At the same time Torrance acknowledges that the Bible's reference to a reality beyond itself is not a matter of isolated statement but of a coherent pattern of statements, and he recognizes that the correlation between linguistic pattern and external reality is not a perfect coincidence (66, 114).

Wolfhart Pannenberg, as we have seen, sought to distance himself from neo-orthodoxy in both its Barthian and Bultmannian forms, but in Pannenberg the emphasis on the importance of history continues and is probably intensified as the role of the word is diminished. According to Pannenberg the proclamation of Christ presents a fact that in the fate of Jesus of Nazareth God has been revealed to all. The hidden eschatological meaning of the prophets' words has been actualized as a historical fact in the cross of Jesus (Rom 3:21), and in the death-defeating reality of the resurrection life has dawned. Jesus is the final revelation of God already present, yet there is still a revelation of God to come in the return of Jesus Christ. The proclamation cannot indicate that the facts are in doubt but must assert that they are reliable. Faith does not need to worry that knowledge of God's revelation in history has been altered because of shifts in the history of research just as long as the current image of the facts of history allows one to reassess and participate in events that are fundamental to faith. Faith transcends its own picture of the events (Pannenberg 1969, 138; 1988, 208–13).

But does not Pannenberg deconstruct his contention that revelation is in the historical facts? He acknowledges that research changes our view of the facts, and it turns out that it is really our image of the facts — our construal of them in language — interacting with faith that is the ground of salvation.

Continuing his emphasis on revelation as factual event, Pannenberg declares that the kerygma is not itself revelatory speech but is an aspect of the event of revelation in that it reports the eschatological event. The kerygma is to be understood solely on the basis of its content, on the basis of the event that it reports and explicates. We should not think of the kerygma as bringing something to the event. The events in which God demonstrates God's deity are self-evident as they stand within the framework of their own history. It does not require any kind of inspired interpretation to make the event recognizable as revelation (Pannenberg 1969, 155). Indeed, Pannenberg states in *Revelation as History* that the truth lies before our eyes and its appropriation is a natural consequence of the facts. The action of the Holy Spirit is not an additional event without which the event of Christ could not be known as revelation (136). However, Pannenberg explains in his *Systematic Theology* that he was not directing this against the function of the kerygmatic word and its interrelationship with the Holy Spirit. Rather he was presupposing the latter. The eschatological revelation does not need to be manifested by an outside supplementary inspiration as a principle of interpretation, for the reality of the risen Lord itself sheds forth the Spirit (Pannenberg 1988, 249–50).

We have seen that Pannenberg tacitly acknowledges (1969, 138) that the image of the events is more far-reaching as a vehicle of revelation than are the events. And he has stated that the events are understandable within the framework of their own history. What is that framework if not a linguistic interpretation? In fact, he affirms in his *Systematic Theology* that the gospel "report" of the history of Jesus Christ makes the history a present reality to those who hear it (Pannenberg 1988, 253–54). Language event threatens to deconstruct factual event.

Neo-orthodoxy and salvation-history theology raise questions that they do not satisfactorily answer. If event and word are organically united, does that mean that word must be an *accurate* representation of event? Or might the word be revelation even if it were an inaccurate representation, if it were severed from the event? If criticism shows that the (alleged) events do not match the word, what do we make of the validity of the word? If the history did not happen, what is the vehicle of revelation?

According to James Barr, the kind of theology that we have been discussing had not really sensed the implications of historical criticism (Barr 1973, 5–6). Historical criticism's throwing into question the historicity of certain events of salvation history — the giving of the law at Sinai, the immediate conquest of Canaan, the virgin birth, the nature miracles, the physical resurrection of Jesus — challenges the claim of historical revelation. If the act of God is a theological interpretation of history, a history much of which did not happen, then what really *is* the act of God? Where does revelation occur? Langdon Gilkey raised this issue in 1961, and we are still dealing with it.

According to Gilkey, neo-orthodoxy accepted the liberal affirmation of the causal continuum in nature and history and so rejected belief in God's literal intervention in the processes of the world — the miracles that constituted God's acts in the Bible and in theological orthodoxy. The only event left is an east wind blowing back the Red Sea. When biblical writers and orthodox theologians spoke of God's acting, they used the category "acting" univocally: God acts in the same way human beings act. Neo-orthodox theology still speaks of God's acting but now only in an analogical sense: God acts (and so is somehow like human beings) but not in the same way human beings do. Neo-orthodoxy, however, has not clarified what the analogous "act" means or to what it refers. It has no content, so the language about God's acts is merely equivocal (Gilkey 1961, 195–99).

Gilkey stated that neo-orthodoxy found it impossible to say what God has done. Most of the acts or events turn out to be symbols, interpretations, or expressions of faith. An act of God may be epistemologically like other events, but if we are to give the concept any content, we must be able to say how it is ontologically different. We need something to replace the old signs and wonders. If we are going to say what God has done, how God has revealed God's self, we must give credible and intelligible meaning to our analogical category (Gilkey 1961, 200–203).

The Nature of the Historical

I have been talking about history in a rather provisional and unreflective way, but it is now time to raise the critical question about what history is, a question to which we are pointed both by the difficulty of the biblical material and by contemporary reflection on the nature of the historical. Each of these spheres points us finally in the same direction. In separate sections I will deal with the following topics: (1) the character of the historical past and (2) the problems of history writing or historical scholarship. But it should be kept in mind that these two topics inherently overlap and cannot be separated in principle. The first topic in this context has the purpose of providing a position from which to give a critique of several ways in which New Testament theologians have employed historical criticism. The second topic intends a position from which to make a positive statement about the locus of revelation.

I have used the vague and imprecise term "the historical" in order to include under it three more specific and interrelated dimensions, all of which can be embraced under "the historical." As Hayden White has pointed out, historical theory has conventionally distinguished (1) past reality; (2) historiography, the historian's written discourse about his past object; and (3) philosophy of history, the study of the possible relations between the object and the discourse (White 1989a, 21). In this section the focus will be on the past reality as understood by a certain type of contemporary historical thinking.

Traditional historiography has predominantly held that history happens as lived stories and the task of the historian is to discover these stories and tell them. The truth in history is the correspondence between the lived story and the told story, and there is held to be a principled difference between historical narrative and the inventions of fiction. But this difference has recently been vigorously questioned on the ground that history and fiction both use signs to create meaning and both substitute signifieds (conceptual contents) for the referents that are presumed to exist outside of discourse. There is no such thing as a real or lived story. Stories are told or written; they are not found (White 1990, ix–x; 1989a, 27).

However, the fact that history does not happen *as* narrative does not mean that nothing happened or that we can know nothing about the past. Historical events are events that really happened, or are believed to have happened, but are no longer directly accessible to perception (White 1989b, 295, 297). An account is properly historical if it deals with real, not imaginary, events and handles evidence in a judicious way, being careful to observe the chronological order in identifying causes and effects (White 1990, 4–5). Thus we can have relatively objective knowledge about past events and even about sequences. It is when we try to define the nature of the sequences, to determine the character of the relationships between events, when we establish continuities, that the literary and imaginative factors enter in a determinative way. And we must remember that this real past is accessible to us only in language (White 1989a, 19), as textualized. The ramifications of this must still be considered.

My own response to this line of thinking is to agree in considerable part but to refrain from denying all narrative quality to the historical past itself. In an earlier work I sought to give a philosophical argument for the position that while history does not happen as explicit, clearly discernible stories, historical existence does have an incipient, inchoate narrative quality (Via 1985, 219–22). This incipience is made explicit, is elaborated and manipulated, in history writing.

In the next section, I will briefly survey several ways in which New Testament scholars have used knowledge of the historical past in the service of New Testament theology. Then in the section after that, I will elaborate on how historical writing — or the relationship of the written discourse to the past reality — makes problematical the employment of knowledge about the past and also turns the discussion in a different direction.

The Use of Historical Criticism in New Testament Theology

New Testament theologians have pursued knowledge of the historical past for different reasons, with different goals in view, and I deal with this only selectively. I begin with William Wrede, who called for a New Testament theology that is strictly historical and objective, carried on without regard for the doctrine of inspiration and not limited to canonical sources (1973, 69–70, 101). In Wrede's view the method and results of the study are to be determined wholly by the nature of the historical object. The historian need not be influenced by his or her own contemporary viewpoint and should not be concerned to serve the interests of the church or systematic theology. That would be an untenable breach of objectivity (69–70, 72–73).

In Wrede's judgment, New Testament theology should be understood as the history of early Christian religion and theology, and its proper subject matter is not the texts of the New Testament but what was taught, believed, hoped for, striven for, in the historical process itself. Wrede was interested in historical knowledge for its own sake. New Testament theology, like every science, has its goal in itself, and it must be guided by a disinterested concern for knowledge (Wrede 1973, 69–70, 84–85, 116).

Wrede in certain ways deconstructs his objectivist position. The New Testament theologian must distinguish the essential from the secondary, the significant from the insignificant (Wrede 1973, 77, 81). But how can one do that apart from some degree of intervention by one's own subjective set of values? Similarly Wrede calls on the New Testament theologian to do more than display a mere succession. One must make connections and demonstrate order and development. And yet Wrede acknowledges that the evidence is fragmentary (92, 95, 98). How can one turn fragments into an orderly development apart from the employment of the imagination and literary construction? (It might be observed in passing that Helmut Koester's *Introduction to the New Testament*, vol. 2, comes close to fulfilling Wrede's prescription for New Testament theology as a scholarly history of the religion and theology of the early Christian communities without regard for the distinction between canonical and noncanonical sources.)

Heikki Räisänen in his recent work praises the historical goals of Wrede but has his own nuances. He regularly assumes and asserts that texts from the past are amenable to definitive interpretations and that the number of legitimate interpretations of a text is severely limited (Räisänen 1990, 42, 63, 74–75, 107). Räisänen believes that New Testament theology has historically been dominated by theological concerns but should be much more historical (63–64, 74, 90). He concedes that complete objectivity is not attainable, but a high degree of it can be achieved, and a high degree is far superior to a low degree (106). Räisänen's proposal is that New Testament theology should and can make a principled distinction between the historical meaning and actual significance of a text, between history-of-religions work and theological work, between original meanings and later dogmatic usurpations (75, 90, 107). However, it should be remembered that the basic distinction between meaning and significance has been called into question by the hermeneutical tradition of Wilhelm Dilthey, Martin Heidegger, Rudolf Bultmann, and Hans-Georg Gadamer and rejected by most schools of recent literary theory.

For Räisänen historical knowledge serves the purpose of giving definitive interpretations of texts. This historical knowledge is not, however, for its own sake but paves the way to understanding. It is a question of the roots of our religion and culture (Räisänen 1990, 98–99).

Ben Ollenburger believes that biblical theology has been largely a historical discipline — due in significant part to the influence of

J. P. Gabler and Wrede — but that it should be understood as a form of theological activity or inquiry (1985, 37–42). And yet Ollenburger preserves a place for historical knowledge. He disagrees with the opinion that what is general or universalizable is theologically superior to the historically particular and relative. That which is theologically normative need not be distinguished from the historically contingent. Scripture is theologically useful not because it is generalizable but because in conversation with the historical particularity of its stories and discourse, the church can sustain its identity (49–51).

Ollenburger has neglected to address an issue that Robin Scroggs has recently raised. Since social-scientific criticism has succeeded in making New Testament situations and texts ever more sharply discrete in their particularity, we are faced with the question whether there can be any analogy between the New Testament text and our own faith situation that would make the former useful (Scroggs 1988, 19). Unless there is an analogy of some kind between the New Testament text and our situation — a point that is generalizable to some degree — then the biblical text cannot be useful to us theologically. In simply positing a direct connection between the particularity of the Bible and our own particularity, while denying the importance of generalizability, Ollenburger begs the question of how the church understands its identity with elements so culturally distant.

In any case Ollenburger has affirmed the importance of the Bible's particularity, and we must recognize that such particularity cannot be identified apart from historical criticism. He has in fact grounded the Bible's usefulness and normativity on its particularity, thus implying the necessity of historical-critical knowledge for constituting the content of revelation — however much Ollenburger may not have intended that result. The next two scholars I wish to discuss have made the connection between historical knowledge and revelation or normativity more explicit.

For Joachim Jeremias the historical Jesus is the primary object of New Testament study. We cannot confine ourselves to the kerygma because the gospel sources themselves show us plainly that the origin of Christianity lies neither in the kerygma nor in the resurrection experiences of the disciples but in the man who was crucified under Pontius Pilate and in his message, which antedate the kerygma. Moreover, the kerygma points us back to the historical event that it interprets. And in theological terms the incarnation implies that the story of Jesus demands historical research and criticism (Jeremias 1964, 12–14). Thus we need to know who the Jesus of history was and the content of his preaching. It matters whether Jesus spoke of his impending death and what significance he attached to it (Jeremias 1964, 13, 15; 1971, 276–99). We need to know this because only the Son of man and his words can invest our message with full authority (Jeremias 1963, foreword). Jeremias understands and accepts that this position sees the object of faith as historical knowledge with its dubious hypothetical character (1964, 15).

According to Oscar Cullmann, revelation in the New Testament resides in real facts, historically datable events, and for Cullmann one of the primary facts is that Jesus had an explicitly messianic self-consciousness. He conferred upon himself such titles as Son of man, Servant of God, Son, and Messiah (Cullmann 1959, 8, 316–18, 327). More than that, Cullmann maintains that the early church believed that Jesus was the Messiah only because it believed Jesus believed himself to be the Messiah. And it is an illusion for us to think that we can believe in him as the Messiah if he had no self-consciousness of being what we confess him to be (8).

Jeremias has stated in effect that historical criticism is the means for *constituting* the content of revelation — the phenomenon of the historical Jesus. The content of revelation thus actualized in the Jesus of history then becomes the authorization of all other revelations in the life of the church. And Jeremias has accepted the consequences of this at the level of formal principle: the object of faith is subject to change since it depends on historical construction. Jeremias's own specific picture of the historical Jesus, however, is quite conservative of the tradition. Would he also agree that Bultmann's historical Jesus as nonmessianic eschatological prophet (Bultmann 1951, 9, 26–32, 42–44) or Dominic Crossan's historical Jesus as a peasant Jewish Cynic (Crossan 1991, 421; 1994, 114–22) is the only source of our authority? Jeremias has not dealt with the multiplicity in our pictures of the historical Jesus. This is probably because he believed that historical scholarship had established his picture as correct. But if revelation is grounded in the historical Jesus and there are fifty historical Jesuses vying for our allegiance, where does authoritative revelation lie? And Jeremias has tacitly — deconstructively — conceded that each historical Jesus is an interpretation when he attaches the adjectives "dubious," "subjective," and "hypothetical" to historical knowledge (Jeremias 1964, 15). So where does revelation reside, in the event or in the interpretation?

It is worth noting that while Crossan's historical Jesus has a content very different from that of Jeremias, Crossan's theological stance toward the historical Jesus is virtually identical with Jeremias's theological posture. For Jeremias the historical Jesus is the real object of Christian faith, and for Crossan Christian belief is (1) an act of faith (2) in the historical Jesus (3) as the manifestation of God (1994, 199–200). While Jeremias is tacitly aware that all reconstructions of the historical Jesus have a certain subjective and dubious character, Crossan is more clearheaded about the uncertainty of our historical knowledge and about the fact that all portrayals of the historical Jesus are bases for divergent Christologies (1991, 423, 426; 1994, 200).

I find puzzling Crossan's claim that Jesus was neither the broker nor the mediator of the kingdom of God because for Jesus the kingdom had neither broker nor mediator (1994, 198). It seems to me consistent with Crossan's position to argue that for Jesus God's presence could not be institutionally *brokered*. But it seems just as clear that for Crossan the kingdom was *mediated* by Jesus' word, healing, and communal meals (1994, 198). Was there no vehicle for the kingdom's coming? What could that mean? That there were mediating vehicles seems required by Crossan's claim that religious faith is dependent on scholarly reconstructions (1991, 423–26).

Cullmann is just as problematical as Jeremias. He does not so much state a formal principle as make a specific historical judgment about causality. But like Jeremias he uses historical reasoning both to constitute revelation and to legitimate it. Jesus' interpretation of himself by means of messianic titles (content) causes the messianic faith of the church and thereby legitimates it, since without that particular cause, the church's faith, then and now, would be an illusion, would be without foundation. This is a theological judgment on Cullmann's part that creates a dilemma with equally unattractive alternatives. If Cullmann remains a Christian believer, his exegesis is dogmatically constrained to find in the Gospels a historical Jesus who self-consciously attributed messianic titles to himself. If Cullmann, on the other hand, acknowledges that the problematic of historical construction brings his messianic historical Jesus into question, he can no longer in good faith remain a Christian, for his faith would lack a justifying basis.

One cannot help but think that the effort to constitute or legitimate revelation by historical work participates in the belief, widespread in modern intellectual life, that history has an objectivity that somehow transcends the theorizing and limiting conceptual categories employed by the other human sciences. But that is a false hope. As Mark Cousins has pointed out, history is involved in the same kind of theoretical problems that affect the other human sciences; thus historical investigation must hang with other forms of inquiry in a tissue of uncertainty (1989, 127–28). For example, history writing involves a level of irreducible theoretical decision making with regard to identity and difference. What objects have sufficient difference to be regarded as different, and which ones have enough identity to be regarded as the same (127–28)?

New Testament scholars as historians regularly engage in this kind of evaluative decision. For example, Bultmann makes an identity/difference decision in favor of difference when he declares that the historical Jesus tradition is merely *historisch* (confined to the past) while the kerygma is eschatological (extended to later generations; Bultmann 1962, 17; 1964, 30).

Burton Mack makes a similar theoretical decision in dealing with the relationship of the historical Galilean Jesus to the death of Jesus in Mark's passion narrative. In Mack's view there is no necessary cause connecting the former to the latter. The Jesus group for which Mark wrote was confused about its purpose in the wake of its failure to reform the synagogue. Mark's story of Jesus' death has little to do with the historical Jesus but much to do with the rejection of Mark's group by the synagogue (Mack 1988, 6, 10, 56, 355). Mack has decided that the historical Jesus and the Jesus of Mark's passion are too different to belong to the same history.

Mack believes that historical developments, imaginative literary creations, and theological conceptions can all be thoroughly explained by the social settings involved. In accounting for the emergence of Christianity, one has no need to appeal to miracles, resurrections, divine appearances, unusual charismatic phenomena, or revelation (Mack 1988, 12–15, 23, 322). I would agree that Christian origins can be accounted for in historical and social terms. The question is whether that is necessarily an exhaustive explanation. Mack consistently gives the impression that he is presenting an objective historical account of the emergence of Christianity. But his work contains a tissue of evaluative decisions and displays as much use of the imagination as he attributes to the early Christian writers. The problematic of history writing is as much a challenge to the claim to write objective history as it is to the attempt to give certainty to the constitution or legitimation of revelation by the appeal to history. However, before turning to a more systematic look at that problematic, I want to consider one more New Testament scholar.

Robert Morgan has insightfully addressed the question whether historical information about Jesus should be included in New Testament theology. Jeremias and Cullmann have obviously made the historical Jesus an integral part of New Testament theology, while Bultmann, of course, made Jesus only a presupposition for, rather than a part of, that theology (Bultmann 1951, 3). New Testament theology itself interprets the theological thoughts of the New Testament, which unfold faith's self-understanding, which is awakened by the kerygma (Bultmann 1955c, 237–41, 251). There is no New Testament theology apart from the resurrection faith of the believing community. Ernst Käsemann was critical of Jeremias's program (Käsemann 1969, 24–35) but also broke with Bultmann by making the historical Jesus the criterion for later kerygmatic interpretations of him (52, 63–64) and by according to the historical Jesus a place within New Testament theology (Käsemann 1973, 244).

Morgan believes that information about Jesus should be included in New Testament theology but not in such a way that a religiously indeterminate historical presentation becomes a substitute for or stands in competition with the christological evaluation of Jesus in the Gospels and in historic Christianity. Rather, the christological framework of the Evangelists and their soteriological concerns should be retained, but the Gospels should be interpreted critically in light of modern scholarly knowledge about Jesus (Morgan 1987, 191–98).

This seems to me to be a live option, but I think I would slightly prefer separate treatment of the historical Jesus if that were done under certain conditions. First, the historical Jesus material would not be presented as religiously indeterminate but as Jesus' theological interpretation of his own mission. This would relativize the difference — at least in principle — between the historical Jesus and the Gospels' Christology. The difference would be relativized further by recognizing that kerygma or christological interpretation is also a historical phenomenon subject to critical inquiry. Second, New Testament theology would be understood as resting on a hermeneutical position from which questions are directed to both the Jesus material and the Gospels' Christology. Approaching the Jesus material and the Gospels' interpretations and other New Testament literature from the same hermeneutical perspective also relativizes the difference between Jesus and kerygmatic interpretations. My primary interest here, however, is not the place of the historical

Jesus in New Testament theology but the place of the historicity of Jesus in the New Testament understanding of revelation.

The Problem of History Writing in Postmodern Theory: Event and Text

The earlier discussion of the historical focused on the problematical nature of the past but could not avoid the related issue of history writing. This section will focus on the latter but will not escape the former. I shall cite a systematic theologian who has confronted head-on in an insightful way the contemporary problematic of history.

Recall that Gilkey's essay of 1961 discussed the challenge to the claim that God reveals God's self in history, the challenge that comes from historical criticism's demonstration of the nonoccurrence of certain historical events that the Bible takes as God's revealing acts. Peter Hodgson's book addresses postmodernism's challenge to the very existence of history (1989, 30–39, 42–43), to the claim that there is such a thing as a coherent structure of events with meaning, purpose, and inherent discernible connections. He wants to rethink the relationship of God to history in light of postmodernism's attack on history.

Hodgson argues that God and history are correlative and co-constitutive of each other. God is self-actualized in the historical process, and the latter is shaped by a gestalt that transcends it. The point of congruency between them is liberating, transfigurative praxis (Hodgson 1989, 44, 191). This means that God appears and works in history as a gestalt that guides, lures, and shapes the process. This shape through which God works is hidden within a plurality of discernible, worldly shapes of freedom. On the one hand, liberation praxis is the bearer of God's redemptive gestalt. On the other, God's shaping, saving presence transfigures and empowers the human emancipatory project (49, 208–9). For the Christian community the transpersonal structure of praxis is composed of Jesus' proclamation of the kingdom and his death and resurrection along with the associated images of Israel, the church, and possibly other religions (208–9, 215). While Hodgson is arguing against the tendency of postmodernism to eliminate all center or structure from reality, he regards making praxis primary as a characteristic of postmodernism (235).

Hodgson is not claiming that we can establish a single, triumphant history of salvation, but neither does he acquiesce in a tragic view of history. What we can affirm is a plurality of momentary configurations or clearings of freedom throughout the course of history (Hodgson 1989, 47, 128, 233).

Hodgson's work and my own complement each other but have different objectives. His concern is to analyze the interaction of God and human beings in the historical process from a contemporary Christian theological standpoint. My question is, How does the recital of God's acts in the Bible, naively portrayed as historical, function in the revelation situation — primarily for the New Testament writers but by implication also for us? In representing the human side of revelation, I give more attention to the hermeneutical than to the ethical, while he probably reverses the emphasis. Hodgson focuses on the historical while not ignoring the other elements in the revelation situation (Hodgson 1989, 39, 42, 49, 52, 83–88, 194–95, 209). I, on the other hand, focus on the configuration of four elements that constitute the revelation situation, of which history is one.

Perhaps the point of contact between Hodgson's work and mine can be put succinctly in the following way. His project is to give a philosophical-theological analysis of the possibility and character of the moments of freedom that occur in the historical process through liberating praxis. His moments of freedom are what I am calling the actualizations of revelation that occur in the historical situations in which revelation is actively received. My project is to describe and interpret the New Testament's understanding — or understandings — of how these moments occur. What are the factors that compose — in their varying interrelationships — the actualization of revelation?

I should now like to make my own observations about several historiographers-philosophers whose views will suggest a certain way to answer the question of how God reveals God's self in history. The relationship of event to written text becomes especially problematical when history writing takes narrative form. Pursuing this issue will get us into the question of the character of historical knowledge. What is historical knowledge about?

The writing of history properly entails two moments, not sharply separable. (1) There is the research effort intended to discover the truth about the past. (2) The events from the past are then transformed into a narrative, and narrating requires the use of the same linguistic figurations and rhetorical strategies employed by imaginative writers (White 1989a, 25; 1990, 4–5; 1989b, 295). As a matter of fact the research moment is based on source materials already subject to imaginative figuration. There are no data that have not been culturally processed (White 1989b, 297; Kellner 1989, vii). New Testament scholars have often not recognized this. Willi Marxsen, for example, seems to assume that the historical is in fact the uninterpreted. There was an uninterpreted Jesus, but unfortunately we cannot reach him (Marxsen 1990, 16, 22–23).

Louis Montrose has articulated a now emerging poststructuralist orientation to history in a concise chiasm: historical study is reciprocally concerned with the historicity of texts and the textuality of history. The historicity of texts means that all texts are embedded in a specific social and cultural setting. The textuality of history means that we have no access to a lived, material past that is unmediated by textual traces and that these traces are subject to further textualization (figuration) when the historian uses them in constructing a narrative (Montrose 1989, 20). The historicity of texts correlates with the research moment's quest for fact, and the textuality of history correlates with the figurative character of source materials and the intensification of this in the narration.

With textuality having been introduced, we need to take a selective look at recent thinking on the nature of a text. We have a solid beginning point with Paul Ricoeur's definition of a text as a sequence of signs larger than a sentence (some would not impose the quantitative limit) having the following characteristics. (1) A text has a certain "objective" propositional content that may be identified and reidentified as the same thing. (2) Texts enter into relationships with other texts, but a text may be distinguished from its context by its internal structure (Ricoeur 1971b, 135, 138–39; 1971a, 538–39, 546, 555).

The definiteness of meaning in a text has been challenged in various ways, and I cite the most radical ones. Stanley Fish has claimed that there is no meaning embedded in a text and that its formal features are the creation of the reader's interpretive acts, guided by an interpretive community (Fish 1980a, 172, 176–79; 1980b, 12–14). Jacques Derrida challenges the distinguishability of a text from other texts. All boundaries or borders separating one text from another have been removed so that a text is no longer an enclosed segment but a differential network of traces referring endlessly to other differential traces (Derrida 1979b, 83–84). This unbounded totality is not to be thought of reassuringly as having any ordering form or center (Derrida 1970, 247–49; 1980, 7, 12–13, 73).

I have three responses to Fish. (1) His position seems to unravel from within when he concedes that no one, neither he nor anyone else, can say what an interpretation is an interpretation *of* if the reader creates the form and meaning of the text (Fish 1980a, 177). (2) The words on the page are not just meaningless signs (ciphers) waiting to be given meaning by the reader. A text or utterance is a particular manifestation of a language system in which words and structures have a meaning *given* by the society that uses it. While any text may stretch and modify the given meanings, it does not escape them. Otherwise there would be no intelligibility (de Saussure 1966, 14–18; Scholes 1985, 152, 154, 159–62). (3) I do not believe that a text has one determinate meaning. Any text has gaps and is likely to contain tensions. But it is a potential, a set of clues, for meaning and imposes some constraints on what an interpreter can make out of it. The meaning is constituted by the mutual interaction of text and reader (Iser 1978, 9–10, 13–15, 17, 19–25, 27, 30, 38, 92, 135, 141, 150, 152). Recall my observation in chapter 1 that Iser's position needs to be nuanced (see p. 6).

My position against Derrida is that while the boundaries of a text are not hard and fast, there are relative borders imposed by internal structures. Texts react reciprocally with each other and with society. Thus we should speak of *inter* textuality (Scholes 1985, 16, 31). I distinguish this from Derrida's *textuality* in which all boundaries are erased and all internally organizing forms are denied, leaving us with one totalizing (non)text.

I turn now to consider how recent reflection on the nature of the textuality of history writing has exploited the literary and imaginative dimensions of history's linguistic character and narrative structuring. The narrating moment extends and deepens the figurative-rhetorical-literary features found in the sources. Most nineteenth- and twentieth-century historians believed that the narrative form was a part of the content in the sense that the events happened in the narrative form in which they were represented (White 1990, 27–30; Kellner 1989, vii, 7). But recent historians and theorists, to the extent that they employ the narrative mode, hold the narrative form to be a content in a different sense. The form is not just a container for contents to be taken from sources. Rather the narrative form already is a content prior to its use in a particular narrative. This content is a meaning that the narrative substitutes for a straightforward copy of the events. It is a secondary referent, which is different from the primary one. It is materially the type of plot structure that the historian confers. A set of real events does not intrinsically contain a particular plot type, but the historian by means of a poetic judgment imposes the plot in order to interpret the events. Several histories of the same set of events will have different meanings (contents) depending on whether they are plotted as tragedy, romance, comedy, or satire (White 1990, xi, 2, 43–47; 1978, 58–59, 62, 70; Kellner 1989, 7). The ambiguity of event and language is clearly put by White in his statement that historical discourse is not a matter of matching an image to an extrinsic reality (referent) but of making a verbal image that interferes with our perception of the putative referent while illuminating it (1989a, 24).

That such interpretive literary devices are content means that they constitute in part the only access we have to the historical past. This rhetorical or constructed character of our knowledge of the past is expressed by Hans Kellner in his claim that history is a matter of getting the story crooked, not straight, and in his claim that the rhetorical discourse is one of the *sources* for history writing (vii–viii, 7). The literary rhetoric is actualized in narration in various specific ways. For example, it is a poetic move to break into a succession of events and choose a certain segment to be told as a particular story, to select a beginning, which is believed to generate other events that end at a certain point (Kellner 1989, 59–61). This segment is then periodized as beginning, middle, and end, three parts that have a coherent and logical relationship to each other (7; White 1990, 24). The structure thus imposed confers continuity on what is discontinuous. Our assumption or intuition of continuity can be derived not from the documentary sources nor from our own lives but only from the mythic path of narrative (Kellner 1989, 1, 55, 65). When the continuity is specifically qualified as causality (White 1989b, 295), the literary or fictional nature of the narrative is underscored, for as E. M. Forster argued long ago, it is causality that transforms a story with its temporality into a plot (Forster 1954, 27, 86). It should also be observed that the historian's employment of metaphors — such as life cycles, roots, seeds, flow, gears, crossroads, chains, and so on — is a matter of explanation and not just of adornment (Kellner 1989, 8).

Historians are divided over how to prioritize the research and narrative moments of history writing. One group holds that research in the documentary sources is the infrastructure (prior cause) of history writing, while the narrative text is the secondary superstructure. The other group makes the mental protocols and

literary construction the causal infrastructure and the facts the superstructure (Kellner 1989, 10, 328). Kellner seems to want to
break down any clear boundary between infrastructure (cause)
and superstructure (effect) and to recognize that at every stage of
historical understanding documentary evidence and literary construction are reciprocally dependent on each other (330–31, 333).
Yet Kellner seems to favor giving priority to literary constructedness when he denies that there is any story out there in the
archives and monuments and affirms crooked readings of history
(vii, 7, 10, 23–25). If one follows this line out logically and addresses the question What is history about? the answer will be
that history is not about the past as such but about our ways
of creating meaning from the scattered meaningless debris around
us (10). Historical knowledge is knowledge acquired by making
interpretive meaning.

In What Sense Then Does God Reveal God's Self in History?

I affirm my belief in the possibility of some degree of knowledge
about the real past. But I want here to confront the concerns
of New Testament theology with the conclusion of the previous
section, which represents an important strand in contemporary
thinking. If history is about the creation of meaning, what does
it mean to say that God reveals God's self in history? What is the
import of revelation in history if we have no unmediated access
to the past? The locus of revelation becomes the imaginative construction of history writing, the narrative, the interpretive word,
the kerygmatic proclamation, the literary text. Does that mean that
historical event has simply been swallowed up in the word, in the
language about the event? No. I shall seek to argue that historical actuality, as distinguished from linguistic representation, is in
a certain way a necessary factor in the revelation situation. And
while these two elements are theoretically distinguishable, in the
life process they are dialogically interactive. It should be remembered further that for the New Testament the revelation situation
is constituted by four factors, not just two.

It should also be noted that the shift of emphasis from event to
language and literature is not prompted solely by recent reflection
on the nature of the historical but also by reflection on the New
Testament.

The Biblical Material
in Recent Theological Discussion

I will look at two contemporary scholars who directly address —
in both a critical and theological way — the question of the nature of the revelatory event. Then I will move to a statement of
my own. I will be especially interested in the related question of
how much history must we be able to identify as the real historical
past in order to justify the biblical claim that revelation occurs *in*
history. If this question cannot be finally answered, it is still worth
pursuing for two reasons. First, historical critics of the Bible continue to make unrelenting efforts to acquire knowledge of biblical
events, ideas, and symbols in their contexts. Second, the pursuit of
the question may help us gain some purchase on the nature of revelation in the New Testament even if the question cannot be finally
answered. I now look selectively at two theological interpreters.

Recall that Gilkey in his 1961 article stated that we should
strive for an ontological understanding of an act of God in order
to clarify in what sense these acts are analogously but not univocally like human acts. More recently Gilkey has claimed that
it was the factuality of the revelation — the belief that God was
in fact encountered in the history of Israel, Jesus, and the work
of the Spirit — that established these events as vehicles of revelation for the believing community. Revelation is constituted by
objective event and creative linguistic interpretation (Gilkey 1979,
46–48). But without making an explicit and articulated transi-
tion, Gilkey seems to move the emphasis from event to word. The
event of revelation is God's creative, redeeming action in Israel and
Jesus, this action understood as symbols. The biblical symbols relate the dynamic, ontological structures of history to their ground
in God, and through the Holy Spirit the symbols become effective.
The event of revelation is the symbols as power (53–56; 1976,
149, 153).

In a more recent article Gilkey displays the impact of the present
situation on his grasp of the Christian revelation. According to
Gilkey's analysis our own social-cultural epoch is characterized by
two opposing tendencies. On the one hand, the political and religious right has produced a dangerous and oppressive idolatry
centered on the nation and capitalism. On the other hand, the radical relativism of postmodernism will not allow that there is any
center or reference point at all (Gilkey 1985, 721–24).

In Gilkey's view in order to have the identity, courage, hope, perspective, and power for liberating praxis against the idolatory, we must have some kind of ground or center from which to move (1985, 722–23, 728–29). But how can we claim such a center when our time has recognized the relativity of Western culture? This entails acknowledging that we have a plurality of religions existing in some kind of parity, each with only an approximation of truth and grace (724–26).

The solution for our present theological task is to achieve a dialectic or paradox of combined absoluteness and relativity. We neither absolutize nor abandon our own standpoint. We begin with the absolute as relatively present in the relative. We acknowledge relativity in order to avoid the errors of the idolatry we oppose. But we affirm a center because of the injustice and heteronomy that we face and because this center is pressed upon us by the empowering experience of liberating praxis. In the Christian symbols there is that relative manifestation of absolute meaning. The Christian revelation is final but is not the only revelation. Our time is one of many centers (Gilkey 1985, 729–33).

We see here that the present historical situation as interpreted by Gilkey has had a constitutive effect on the word of God. The linguistic fund of Christian revelation is understood as true but not as the only final truth.

Paul Hanson explicitly took up Gilkey's 1961 challenge, stating that what we need is an ontological account of how an ordinary looking event can be confessed as an act of God. If we cannot explain the connection between observable event and confession, we have no right to claim a historical basis for the confession (Hanson 1978, 24, 26). Given Hanson's stated interest in event and ontological explanation, we might have expected that he would explain how events from the past generate the confession and/or new redemptive events in the present. But what he does is to articulate how the *confession* of the exodus — a past event — provided *interpretive* motifs that enabled the deliverance under Cyrus to become a new redemptive event in the present for 2 Isaiah. Moreover, the exodus in its own time — an event — was empowered to become an act of God for early Israel because it was interpreted in the light of earlier traditions about God's deliverance of the patriarchs (37–38, 48–49, 51–52).

Thus it seems that for Hanson it is really the exodus as confession or interpretive story, not as past event, that functions as revelation. The event character belongs to the new event interpreted by the confession and not to the old event described in the confession. Clearly for Hanson revelation is a fusion of word and event. But the event is the present situation of the interpreter, and what encounters us out of the past is the interpretive word by means of which the present is made revelatory event.

I turn summarily to a brief, illustrative look at the New Testament. For the New Testament, by means of the historical ministry, death, and resurrection of Jesus — an event that happened — a new possibility for human beings with God was opened up (Mark 1:15; John 1:14; Rom 4:24–25; 5:18–19; 2 Cor 4:6; Heb 9:12, 24). At the same time this event remains fixed in the past, and salvation occurs through the proclamation of the event, the word (Mark 1:27–28, 45; 3:8; John 5:24; 17:8, 20; Rom 1:16; 1 Cor 1:18; 2 Cor 5:18–20; 6:2). The New Testament portrays Jesus as both acting and acted upon and as speaking, but it does not tell us how to connect event and word. The nature of the relationship will be constructed in various ways by different interpreters, based on their own reflection and on clues from the New Testament. It is tempting simply to say that event and word are equally important and that the event reaches us through the word, but that is too easy because we do not know whether the event in the interpretation is the same as the event that happened. So what event reaches us in the word?

While the Gospels have much in common, each one is a different interpretation of Jesus, and the non-Gospel literature of the New Testament interprets his significance in different ways as well. The Gospels manifest in an intense way what contemporary historical theory says about the imaginative constructedness of history, and obviously the Gospels are much more intentional than modern history in presenting an interpretive — theological — point of view. The differences in the portraits, some large and some small, often amount to tensions and sometimes to contradictions. I mention one among many possibilities as an example.

In Mark Jesus' last words on the cross are "My God, my God, why have you forsaken me?" (15:34). But in Luke this is missing, and rather we have "Father, into your hands I commend my spirit" (23:46). In both Gospels Jesus suffers physically. But in Mark he also suffers the spiritual pain of estrangement from God, while in Luke he suffers no abandonment and dies serenely trusting. Both cannot be history as past event. In view of many such differences, the implicit position of the canon is that not all of the "history" has to be real history of the past in order to justify the claim that revelation occurred in history. Given the nature of the New Testament evidence and the fact of the varying social locations and theological positions of modern scholars, the picture is always changing, and there can be no general agreement on the content of the history of Jesus. We do not know exactly what the history of Jesus is, nor do we know exactly how much has to be history of the real past in order to justify the belief that God actually intervened in history. Nevertheless, the New Testament appeals to a real event and makes salvation dependent on it.

Given the imaginative constructedness of both the Gospels and modern historical scholarship, it seems to me that a construal of the New Testament understanding of revelation should not make a history of Jesus the ground element. The New Testament itself suggests that it is both enough and also all that can be managed to say that *some* statement about the history of Jesus is necessary in order to make the claim that God acted in his history. Some theologians will also want to understand the historical Jesus as a criterion for the legitimacy of later developments in the early church. Because the believing community has experienced the power of the interpretive word to change lives and social situations, it trusts that word. If we also believe the historical Jesus is the authoritative criterion for testing later developments, we find ourselves in a paradoxical situation. We trust the interpretive, kerygmatic word while keeping it under scrutiny in light of the history of Jesus, the content of whose self-interpreted history we can never be unequivocally certain about.

When we turn to our assessment of the actual content of the revelation in the New Testament, we find that it is so materially constructed from theological intentions and imaginative decisions (to which we have access only through our own imaginative, theological, and theoretical decisions) that I am inclined to reverse the neo-orthodox formula that God's revelation occurs basically in historical acts that are then interpreted and communicated by symbolic language. I would want to retain the connection between language and event and say the following: God reveals God's self in the language, the word, the text — language as the event of revelation — and the historical events narrated are a set of symbols for the event character of the word and for the capacity of a present situation to be a new, redemptive event under the impact of the word. That is, it is not so much that the word interprets the event as that the event narrated interprets the narrative word about the event *as* event. I seem to have let the revelatory event of the past be absorbed in the language event and in the capacity of the present historical situation of the receiver of revelation to become a new revelation situation. Yet that past historical event retains a theological importance.

What then is the nature of the claim — whether made by the New Testament or by us — that God was eschatologically active in the historical ministry of Jesus? That claim is a *theological* affirmation derived from the *faith* experience or existential experience in which the merging of the Jesus tradition and one's present situation is experienced powerfully. Since the story of the event has the power of revelation to liberate and transform, then the event narrated must have had the same power. One may reflect further that there is an ontological connection between the event and the story. The narrative's power does not rest just on its linguistic qualities. This is where the New Testament's proclamation of Jesus' resurrection becomes significant. We may understand the resurrection of Jesus as the power of his earthly mission extending beyond its moment in time and manifesting itself in the church's proclamation as well as in sacrament and in acts of faith and love. There is no logical reason why the historical event of Jesus must have corresponded exactly with the event narrated in the Gospels in order to understand the former as empowering the latter, with Jesus' resurrection being understood as the power. Nor do we know how much factual correspondence there must have been in order to justify the claim of an ontological relationship between event and narrative.

So what is the event that reaches us in the experience of the word? It is the word itself. And through the word the present situation is so interpreted that it becomes an element in the occurrence of revelation. And yet the position to which I have come is not thoroughly neat and free of (il)logical loose ends, for the linguistic text as revelatory event trails behind it a set of events from the historical past that are not completely confined to or absorbed in their value as symbols of the event quality of the word, historical events whose relationship to the revelatory word needs to be reflected upon. The concept of language event lost its currency unfortunately when the new hermeneutic, with which it was closely associated, went out of fashion in the theological marketplace. But it has been recaptured, at least in part, in the application of reader-response criticism to the Gospels (Moore 1989, 87). Wolfgang Iser has been insightful in pointing out the power of the text to be an event by drawing the reader into participation. (1) The reader's response is elicited to deal with the fact that the text both reveals and conceals. (2) What the text reveals is a multiplicity of perspectives whose reconciliation is not formulated in the text and which can be made to converge, if at all, only by the reader. (3) The reader is summoned to order the text's images and make their meaning explicit. (4) A literary text will make the everyday world unfamiliar without offering an explicit philosophical alternative to the ordinary. The reader must find the motive for this questioning of everyday reality (Iser 1978, 22–25, 27, 35–36, 38, 43, 45, 47–50, 74, 132, 141, 152, 155, 157, 169). The events narrated in the New Testament text symbolize this power of the text to be an event (see Tracy 1991, 113–15, 173, 193, 199–200, 209), to engage readers and do something to/for/with/in them in their own situations. We have seen that it is not possible to discuss the content of the word in the New Testament without also moving into a tacit recognition of its power.

Chapter 3

PAUL

The discussion of Paul will largely take the form of a running commentary on 2 Cor 2:14–4:15 with special reference to the four elements of the revelation situation. Some may not take 2:14–4:15 to be an internally connected and coherent segment, but I argue that it is because the ending (4:7–15) returns to the theme of the beginning (2:14–17) although with a variation. These two similar paragraphs frame the whole, each focusing on the theme of manifestation (*phaneroō*) — whether it be the manifestation of knowledge (2:14) or life (4:10–11).

The Historical Occasion and Purpose of 2 Corinthians

The historical setting needs to be dealt with only briefly since my purpose is primarily theological interpretation, but it cannot be ignored because the historical bears on the specificity of meaning and is, theologically speaking, an element in the revelation situation. This historical context is presupposed in the text to be interpreted and is allusively referred to in 2 Cor 2:17; 3:1; and 4:2.

Paul wrote 2 Corinthians (or 2 Corinthians 1–9) after a painful visit (2:1) and a harsh letter (2:3–4; 7:8–10) and with at least a threefold purpose. (1) He wants to promote the collection for the saints in Jerusalem. (2) He wants the Corinthians to understand the nature of his apostleship and especially that it was based on Christ's own mission of suffering (4:7–12; 6:4–10; 13:3–4). (3) A perhaps more comprehensive purpose is his desire to bring consolation and salvation to the Corinthians (1:3–7).

The intentions of the letter result from the presence of opponents of Paul who have come to Corinth from elsewhere and have brought into question Paul's personal authority and integrity (10:2, 10; 12:16–17) and the validity of his gospel (11:3–4). The opponents make use of letters of recommendation and also commend themselves (3:1; 10:12). In Paul's opinion these people enslave and mistreat the Corinthian Christians (11:20). The opponents claim to be Hebrews, Israelites, and servants of Christ (11:21–23), and evidently they put great store in their visions, revelations (12:1–2), and speaking ability (11:6). Paul refers to his opponents as super-apostles (11:5; 12:11) and as false apostles (11:13). Probably these two appellations refer to the same group. They are super-apostles in their own opinion and from Paul's ironical viewpoint. They are false apostles from Paul's straightforward position.

What are the history-of-religions connections of these Christian preachers with whom Paul finds himself in conflict? Paul seems to indicate that they were Jewish (11:22), but there is no evidence that they wanted to impose circumcision or the whole law on Gentile Christians. Perhaps they sought to require something like the fourfold minimal cultic provisions cited in Acts 15:20, 29 (Barrett 1973, 6–7). It is not possible to determine whether their origins were in Palestinian or in Hellenistic Judaism (Murphy-O'Connor 1991, 12; Furnish 1984, 53–54). The value that they evidently placed on visions, revelations, and rhetoric would suggest that they had accommodated to or had assimilated certain Hellenistic tendencies resident in the Corinthian church (Barrett 1973, 10; Murphy-O'Connor 1991, 12–15), although visions and revelations could also point to Jewish apocalyptic.

It seems that the opponents have effectively disturbed Paul's relationship with the Corinthians. He is afraid that the latter have been or are being led astray to accept another Jesus or a gospel other than the one he preached (11:3–4). Whether at the prompting of the opponents or from other causes, the Corinthians have accused Paul of being crafty and taking advantage of them (12:16–17). Evidently they feel that he has commended himself in unfitting ways (3:1; 5:12; 6:4). In addition they consider him vacillating for not returning to see them after his visit to Macedonia — as he has promised he would (1:15–17). Paul explains that he canceled the plan to return because he wanted to spare them another painful visit (1:23; 2:1).

Paul's response to this situation is to interpret what others may take as his inferiority, insufficiency, or weakness as his participation in the death — and resurrection — of Jesus (4:7–12; 6:4–10). His apostolic ministry is a presentation of the gospel, the word of God (2:17). What Paul says in 2 Corinthians 10–13, whether written shortly before or after chapters 1–9, may be taken as bearing on the situation reflected in the latter. He will concede no inferiority to his opponents; in fact, he claims superiority. He is as much a Hebrew as they and is a better minister of Christ, precisely because of his suffering, hardships, and weakness (11:21–29; 12:11–13). Paul acknowledges that his boasting is foolish (11:21; 12:1) but stresses that he boasts only of his weakness (11:30; 12:5, 8–10). His strength is in his weakness, for through his weaknesses Christ's power is active (6:3–10; 12:5, 9–10; 13:3–4).

My concern is with *how* the word of God — the gospel preached and enacted by Paul — is revealed. What are the elements that are necessary for the word of God to become actual in human life? What is the mode of the divine self-disclosure?

Divine Initiative and Human Vehicle: 2 Corinthians 2:14–17

Paul begins this paragraph by giving thanks to God who leads him (Paul) in public procession (we will return to this) and manifests the fragrance of knowledge about him (God) through Paul in every place. Here fragrance (*osmē*) is the image for knowledge of God. Immediately Paul connects this image to himself, though with another word — aroma (*euōdia*). Paul then is the vehicle of knowledge of God imaged as fragrance. He is the aroma of Christ. More literally Paul is a part of the linguistic tradition that is an element in the revelation situation. He *speaks* the *word* of God. And what Paul says here about the effect of the word as fragrance parallels what he says about the effect of the word of the cross in 1 Cor 1:18–21. The message works life in some and death in others, depending on their response.

In some degree all the elements in the revelation situation come to expression in this paragraph. The emphasis is on God's word as a *power*, on what *God* does in and through Paul's mission. It is God who makes manifest knowledge of God's self; God is the active one. But this word of God has a content, for it is something spoken. This means that it is also a word humanly shaped. It is a word that Paul — and others, we — speaks. The same image — aroma, fragrance — is used of both the knowledge of God and Paul's preaching. How are the divine and human related in this paradoxical and ambiguous preached word? There is also an allusion to the situation created by Paul's opponents. He denies that he — like them — is a huckster of God's word. The content of the canonical word is thus seen to have been affected in its specificity by the historical context.

A further word needs to be said about the verb translated in 2:14 as "leads in triumphal procession" (*thriambeuō*). God is here described as the one who leads Paul in triumphal procession in Christ. The usual meaning of *thriambeuō* with a direct object (as here) is "to triumph over someone" or "to lead someone as a prisoner of war in a shameful and humiliating procession." It can hardly mean "to cause someone to triumph." Despite these customary usages C. K. Barrett argues that the context calls on us to see Paul as sharing in the victorious general's triumph and not as humiliated (1973, 98). However, if we take the more expected connotation, which would represent Paul as put to shame, then the sense would parallel Paul's statement in 2 Cor 4:11 that he is always being given up to death for Jesus' sake (Murphy-O'Connor 1991, 29–30). If we read this way, then in 2:14–17 the primary vehicle of Paul's message is his word, but his life is also, allusively, a vehicle. In 4:7–12, on the other hand, it is his life, his participation in Jesus' death and resurrection, that receives the major attention.

The Corinthians as a Letter:
2 Corinthians 3:1–3

Paul again makes an allusion to the historical situation precipitated by his opponents. They evidently need letters of recommendation, but he does not. The letter of recommendation was a technical category, and such letters were a well-established form in Paul's day (Furnish 1984, 180). Starting from this historical reference, Paul takes up the letter image to describe the Corinthians: You Corinthians are a letter of Christ. The letter image functions to express the accomplished reality of revelation in them. As letters they are those in whom revelation has occurred.

While the general theme of this paragraph is evident, the details are difficult to make clear sense of. The person of the possessive pronoun modifying "hearts" in 3:2 is a textual problem. The Corinthians are the letter, but is the letter written on Paul's heart (our hearts) or on the Corinthians' heart (your hearts)? The manuscript evidence seems to favor "our" (*hēmōn;* that is, Paul's; P[46] ABCD and others) rather than "your" (*humōn;* ℵ and others; Furnish 1984, 181). But what could it mean to say that the Corinthians are a letter written on Paul's heart? Is it a way of expressing his concern and affection for them? They are in his heart (7:3). Or does it mean that since they are his commendatory letters (3:2a), and since they are written on his heart (3:2b), the core of his being, what they make known to the world (3:2c) is who he really is?

Rudolf Bultmann (1985, 71) argues that despite the manuscript evidence only the reading "Your (*humōn*) hearts" makes sense. And probably the idea of the Corinthians' hearts is more intelligible in context. The difficulty with reading "Paul's heart" is that in 3:3 the Corinthians are a letter written on their own hearts, for Paul is the one whose ministering has somehow helped this to come about — through his preaching and life. This would support the "your hearts" reading in 3:2. That is, it would if we should expect Paul's imaging to be logically consistent, but perhaps we cannot. In any case the idea of the Corinthians as a letter written on their own hearts is less awkward than the Corinthians as a letter written on Paul's heart, but it is still not thoroughly clear.

What does it mean that they are the letter and that the letter is also something written on their hearts? Perhaps Paul's point is that they are constituted in the totality of their being by what they are in their hearts, the center of their being. And they are formed at the center by a letter. Thus they confront the world as a letter, as something written and readable. That means that they are constituted from the core outward by language. The allusion to language looks back to the reference to preaching in 2:14–17 and forward to the reference to the reading of the old covenant in 3:14–16 and the preaching of the gospel in 4:3–6. The Corinthians are formed by the language in which are unified the reinterpreted old covenant and the gospel. They are Christ's letter: they belong to him and are his means of communication — and they are Paul's letter of recommendation.

Furthermore, while ink gives life to a literal letter, the power that gives life to the letter that constitutes the Corinthians is the Spirit of the living God. They are written by or in the Spirit. Thus in context the Spirit is interpreted as the power of the language of the gospel (or tradition) to rewrite the heart, to reshape existence. The Spirit is the power of the gospel to shatter an old understanding of existence and generate a new one. It is the Spirit that enables the language to imprint the heart, to turn the tradition into a revelatory event. What happens when the language of the gospel is empowered to imprint the heart is an occurrence that is at once the manifestation of knowledge of God (2:14; 4:6) and a new self-understanding (3:14–17) that is a transformation of existence (3:18).

A few other details deserve consideration. Paul's role in the writing of the Corinthians as a letter is expressed by the verb "to minister" (*diakoneō*). They are a letter of Christ "ministered" by Paul and written by the Spirit. He uses the verb elsewhere only of his work in gathering the collection for the Jerusalem church (2 Cor 8:19–20; Rom 15:25), but the cognate noun represents his apostolic mission generally (2 Cor 4:1) or Christian service at large (Rom 12:7; 1 Cor 12:5; Barrett 1973, 108). Here both Paul's preaching and his life conformed to the death-resurrection pattern are the content of his ministry.

The tablets of human hearts on which the Corinthians as letter are written are contrasted with tablets of stone. The human hearts point to Jeremiah's new covenant in which the eschatological time will bring a change of heart (Jer 31:31–34). They also point to Ezekiel's hearts of flesh, which will replace the hearts of stone in the new time as a result of the work of the Spirit (Ezek 11:19; 36:26–27). The tablets of stone in 2 Cor 3:3 then refer both to the hearts of stone in Ezekiel and to the tablets of stone on which the law of the old covenant was written (Exod 24:12; 31:18; 34:1; Deut 9:10–11). The interplay between these passages in 2 Corinthians, Jeremiah, Ezekiel, Exodus, and Deuteronomy suggests a connection between the Spirit and a new heart, on the one hand, and between the law and a stony heart, on the other hand.

The New Covenant: 2 Corinthians 3:4–6

The implicit allusion to the new covenant in the previous paragraph has become an explicit reference in this one. The revelation that has occurred creates a new covenant, which can in this context be called the ministry (*diakonia*) of righteousness whose splendor or glory surpasses the splendor of the ministry of law (3:9). The new covenant establishes a right relationship with God, and it is grounded in the Spirit — the power of the language of the gospel tradition — not in the letter. The term "letter" (*gramma*), in its contrast with Spirit, represents the law as human, not divine, and as having the power to kill (Bultmann 1985, 77; Barrett 1973, 113; Furnish 1984, 189).

The law kills in that it generates a misunderstanding of itself (Rom 7:10–11), according to which obedience to the law is the way to a right relationship with God (Rom 9:30–10:4; Phil 3:8–9). In our context this self-generated misunderstanding of the law is imaged as a veil that conceals the proper understanding of the old covenant (2 Cor 3:14) or law (2 Cor 3:15) and thereby negates the life that the law in principle might have given (Rom 7:10; Via 1990, 21–29, 38–44).

The Removal of the Veil: 2 Corinthians 3:7–4:6

To have the heart rewritten by the power of the linguistic tradition is to have the veil of misunderstanding removed and to be given a new understanding, to have the hardening of the mind erased (3:14–15). It is specifically the old covenant that was misunderstood (3:14), and only in Christ is the veil of misunderstanding abolished. Thus in context the new covenant is the old covenant given a new reading from the standpoint of the gospel (3:14–16). Clearly a part of the linguistic tradition that is one of the constitutive factors in the revelation situation is the Old Testament. The latter is not optional for the Christian, but neither is the hermeneutical key optional by which the old covenant must be read to gain the proper understanding. Being in Christ is the hermeneutical key, and the relationship of the new understanding of the old covenant to Christ is dialectical.

The close link between the old covenant (text) and the gospel (hermeneutical key) is underscored by the fact that Paul speaks of both the old covenant (3:13–16) and the gospel (4:3) as veiled. The two are misunderstood together or understood together. The gospel is the proper interpretation of the old covenant. Being in Christ opens up the real meaning of the old covenant. This conviction undoubtedly is what prompted Paul to find his specific gospel in the Torah (Rom 3:31; 4:3–8; 10:6–9). The Old Testament and the gospel tradition together are the language with which the Spirit writes its letters. Paul's employment of the Old Testament would have apologetic force, for as W. D. Davies has suggested the appeal of Paul and other New Testament writers to the Old Testament is part of a widespread tendency in the Graeco-Roman world of the time to search for ancient authority and to appeal to tradition (1993, 22–23).

Keep in mind that in this passage Paul makes Christ and the Spirit functionally equivalent (3:17–18). The Lord is the Spirit. It seems to me more probable that the Lord is Christ (Bultmann 1985, 89–90) than that the Lord is God (Furnish 1984, 234, 251) since Paul has just referred to Christ as the divine factor in the revelation situation (3:14), will momentarily explicitly identify Jesus Christ as Lord (4:5), and elsewhere can speak of the Spirit, the Spirit of God, the Spirit of Christ, and Christ in a functionally interchangeable way (Rom 8:9–10).

And while the term "heart" characteristically refers to the core of a person and "mind" to the perceiving and discriminating function, in 3:14–15 both heart and mind are the instruments of understanding; moreover, in 3:18 "face" is the virtual equivalent of "heart" (Furnish 1984, 207, 214; Bultmann 1985, 86). But we shall see that in our passage understanding and being are not discrete dimensions of a person.

The relationship between *Christ* = *Lord* = *Spirit* and the new understanding is dialectical in that Christ — or the Spirit — is both the origin and the result of the human effort to understand. On the one hand, the Spirit is the life-giving, generative source of the whole renewal process (3:3, 6, 18), and it should be noted that the Spirit is both the power of language to change the heart (3:3) and also the power prompting the person to act (3:6, 18). On the other hand, human initiative is predicated of the revelation situation. Having already spoken of the life-giving initiative of the Spirit (3:3, 6), Paul can then speak as if the situation is, nevertheless, undetermined. Whenever — or if — a person turns to the Lord, at that point the veil of misunderstanding is removed (3:16). It is human turning to the Lord that effects the lifting of the veil. And the use of the subjunctive mood for the verb "turn" in 3:16 shows that it is uncertain whether the person will turn — despite the activity of the Spirit. Thus something rests on human effort, and if one does turn to the Lord, then the Spirit is there, for the Lord is the Spirit (3:17). The Spirit's presence, then, is the result and not just the source of the human move to new understanding. And yet the use of the passive voice for the removal of the veil — the veil *is removed* (by God: divine passive) — shows that the divine and human merge and cannot be neatly separated.

Through 3:15 the dynamic of veiling and unveiling has been attributed to Israel in its entanglement with the law. However, at 3:16 Paul begins to broaden the scope of his view and to include all people in the veiling and unveiling (Furnish 1984, 234). That move is indicated by the use of an implied indefinite subject in 3:16 — whenever *anyone* should turn to the Lord. The inclusiveness is enforced by the use of the pronoun for "all" in 3:18. Thus the situation of the mind veiled in misunderstanding yet open to the possibility of illumination is for Paul the universal human situation. Moreover, the presence of the veil concealing the truth is God's work — the divine passive again. Their minds *were hardened* — by God (3:14). That this notion of the fatedness of misunderstanding is present in Paul is supported by the fact that it is God who does the hardening in Rom 9:16–18; 11:7–10 and the god of this world who causes the blinding in 2 Cor 4:4. In view of the universality and fatedness of human blindness, it is significant that Paul attributes any degree of initiative and resolve to the human side.

The Place of Human Reception in Constituting Revelation

This is an appropriate point at which to look more comprehensively at Paul's view of the role of human reception in constituting the revelation situation. Paul assumes that all human beings in principle have knowledge of God (Rom 1:19–20) and moral awareness in some sense (Rom 2:14–16), though in actuality these have been lost, and it is only through the Spirit that one can gain knowledge of God and God's purpose. The merely human (*psychikos*) person is unable on her or his own (fully) to understand and receive the things of the Spirit. These come only from the activity of the Spirit itself and from being given the mind of Christ (1 Cor 2:11–16).

However, the merely or specifically human capacity to know God is not totally lost, but neither is it the case for Paul that what human beings can know about God as human, or "naturally," is radically independent of the divine initiative. The human capacity that I am inquiring into is natural in that it is something that a human being has as his own and brings to what comes from word and Spirit. It is her act of receiving. It does not come from word or Spirit. Yet it is not in the deepest sense one's own, for it is a capacity that one has as a creation of God. For Paul the human act of reception, while in some degree independent of word and Spirit, independent of the event of the gospel, is nevertheless what people can do because they have been created by God with knowledge of God. As we have seen, this capacity to know God has been deformed by the fall into sin — the refusal to acknowledge God (Rom 1:18, 21–23) — but it has not been totally obliterated. It is still sufficiently available to serve as a justification for holding all people — regardless of culture or religion — accountable to God, without excuse (Rom 1:20).

The question then is what the person as a creature of God brings to the reception of God's decisive revelation in Christ. What is the evidence in Paul that the person as created with knowledge of God, but fallen and deprived of the original knowledge, still has a vestige of the original knowledge, which functions as an organ of human reception that has a constitutive role in shaping the final revelation in Christ?

1 Cor 15:10 shows that the human capacity to contribute to the constitution of revelation by receiving the word actively is a positive human effort, though paradoxically so. Leading up to 1 Cor 15:10, Paul has cited several persons and groups as witnesses to the resurrection of Jesus — Cephas, the Twelve, more than five hundred brothers and sisters, James, all of the apostles, and finally himself (15:5–8). Then he states that he worked much more than all of these people (15:10). Paul claims action of his own in this work, and yet what he did was not his doing but the grace of God working with him. It was both.

Clearly Paul's claim here of significant work is nonspecific, but by that token it is also comprehensive and thus includes his work as a receiver and interpreter of tradition about Jesus. No matter what Paul specifically did as receiver of tradition and proclaimer of the gospel, his interpretive work contributed to the actualization of effective revelation, for the result of his preaching, and the preaching of the others, was that people believed (1 Cor 15:11).

The chain of human interpretation in the ongoing process of revelation is unending, for if the one who preaches engages in hermeneutical work (and the preacher, of course, was also a receiver), so must the hearer of the preaching hear interpretively if the preaching is to be believed as word of God. The hearing-reception of the gospel is an act of understanding and evaluation. In 1 Thess 2:13 Paul commends the Thessalonians because receiving the word of God that they heard from him, they accepted it not as human word but as the word of God that it truly is.

The very fact that Paul mentions human words shows his awareness that he was in fact speaking human words and that the Thessalonians could have taken his message as nothing but human words. That they did not was an act of interpretive evaluation on their part. Their reception displayed the as-structure, which, according to Heidegger (1962, 188–93), interpretation always takes. X (something to be understood) is understood as Y (something already understood or better understood). The Thessalonians understood Paul's human words (X) *as* (*kathōs*) word of God (Y). Note that the Y that they have and bring to the hearing "naturally," simply as human beings, is a sense of what word of God is that is sufficient to interpret Paul's words as word of God. The Thessalonians can interpret — recognize — Paul's gospel *as* word of God only because in some sense they already know what word of God is. Nothing is said here about the activity of the Spirit. Taking Paul's preaching as word of God is a matter of human reception and interpretation. Paul thanks God for something that the Thessalonians did, the way they received his word.

While 1 Thess 2:13 does not tell us what specific hermeneutical moves Paul thought the Thessalonians made so as to understand human words as word of God, Paul's writing as a whole enables us to grasp something of his governing position. This discussion has to do with how word of God as content is received by assimilation, or as Jonathan Culler puts it, by naturalization (Culler 1975, 114, 116, 137–39, 159–60). For Culler, to naturalize a text or something heard is to interpret or contextualize this new or strange thing by bringing it within a structure of conventions that the reader/hearer already regards as natural or familiar. This cultural pattern to which a text is related in order to make it natural is learned from experience and reading (121). The *natural* is what one already knows that makes possible the naturalization of something new by assimilating the new thing to the already familiar.

Keep in mind that for Paul in 1 Thess 2:13 that which is already known, which Paul's preaching is seen *as* so as to make the preaching natural, is word of God. Thus here it is the word of God already in the person before she hears the gospel, the word of God that receives and assimilates the preached word, that is natural. As we have observed from Romans 1, that prior natural word of God is a vestige of the knowledge of God that God made available in creation. But since for Paul the full, decisive revelation in Christ is in part constituted by human reception, so that natural word of God that receives the word of God in the Christian proclamation must also be in part constituted by human learning.

And it should be remembered that while the prior word of God that naturalizes the preaching and makes it assimilable is a necessary constituent of the revelation through Christ, this natural word is at the same time a deformation of God's original revelation in creation (Rom 1:21–23) and is incapable on its own of giving full knowledge of God (1 Cor 2:14). The latter comes only when natural word is a means of access for preached word and Spirit (1 Cor 1:18; 2:9–10; 2 Cor 3:3, 6). The prior word then naturalizes the preached word and makes it assimilable, but the preached word transcends and explodes the natural or prior word.

Although it is generally the case in Paul that the preached word has Jesus Christ as its content, there is a Pauline subtext according to which the proclaimed word that makes a right relationship with God fully actual is not limited exclusively to the preaching of Jesus' death and resurrection. That proclamation is paradigmatic for the fully saving word but is not the only expression of it. The saving word of justification by faith is already found in the Torah in Deut 30:11–14 (see Rom 10:6–11, 17). Paul is in fact also speaking christologically here. Since he replaces the near Christ (Rom 10:6–7) with the near word (10:8), the word represents Christ, and the risen Christ is interpreted as the power of the proclaimed word. Paul then is trying to persuade us that both the saving word of justification and its christological empowerment were adumbrated in Deuteronomy — although Deuteronomy used other words. And Paul also takes it that the word of the Lord to Abraham in a vision (Gen 15:1–6) evoked in Abraham a righteousness by faith (Rom 4:3, 9, 11–12) that is qualitatively the same as the faith-righteousness of those who are justified by their faith in Jesus' death and resurrection (Rom 4:17–25; Via 1975, 49–66; 1994b, 1142–43).

The reception of the preached word as word of God takes on a more specific character in terms of the tragicomic genre — to be discussed below — with its death-resurrection motif. Although the death and resurrection of Jesus as revealing and saving event is not foregrounded in 1 Thessalonians, it is nevertheless present (1 Thess 1:10; 2:15; 4:14; 5:10), and the tradition that Paul inherited focuses on this content, whether Jesus' victory over death be expressed as his coming again (1 Cor 11:23–26) or his resurrection (1 Cor 15:3–4). Paul makes the motif of Jesus' death and victory undergird his characteristic themes of justification by faith (Rom 4:3, 5, 23–25) and participation in Jesus' defeat of the demonic powers (Rom 6:3–8; 8:2–3, 9–11) as well as sustain his reflection on the conflict between human and divine wisdom (1 Cor 1:18–31). Paul speaks of the content of the gospel with equal facility as the righteousness of God (Rom 1:16–17) or the cross (1 Cor 1:18).

My proposal here is that the word of God as the message of Jesus' death and resurrection is naturalized in human beings by means of the tragicomic genre with its death-resurrection structure. Human beings receive and assimilate the gospel by shaping it according to this generic pattern. It is probable that both tragedy and comedy emerged in the Greek world out of a death and resurrection ritual that was widespread in the Mediterranean sphere, and then they diverged as tragedy put the emphasis on death and comedy, on resurrection (Via 1975, 45, 99). Death and resurrection here should be understood to have both literal and figurative expressions. In very broad and nontechnical terms, tragedy has a plot moving toward destruction and ruin, while the plot of comedy moves toward well-being. As Susanne Langer put it (1965, 123–24), the comic pattern is the life rhythm of upset and recovery, with the upset and recovery representing the death and resurrection of the ancient ritual.

Tragicomedy moves toward life and well-being but places a certain emphasis on the death — literal or figurative — that must be overcome to reach well-being. Tragicomedy may alternate death and resurrection episodes, but more penetratingly it portrays some situation as tragic and comic at the same time (Guthke 1966, 6–12, 18, 43, 45). We can see this point of view in Paul: his strength and power, which emanate from God (comedy), come to expression precisely in his weakness and suffering (tragedy; 2 Cor 6:3–10; 12:9–10; 13:4). Paul represents both the ministry of Jesus, as we have seen, and the life of the believer as shaped by the rhythm of upset and recovery, the overcoming of death by life, or perhaps better the interaction of death and life (2 Cor 4:7–12; 6:3–10), for death is not simply left behind in a triumphalist way. My interpretation of 2 Cor 4:7–15 will show in some detail how Paul adapts the tragicomic pattern to his particular Christian concerns.

Jesus' death and the early disciples' experience of his power transcending death and laying hold on them were probably historical events. The tragicomic generic pattern, by which Paul and the Evangelists represent and interpret Jesus, did not create the basic events. But how these historical realities were related to each other and to the human world, how they were given significance, owes something to the interaction between the religious-theological imagination and the tragicomic genre.

We may imagine that the proclamation of Jesus' death and resurrection reverberated in the mind of Paul, and other early Christian thinkers-writers, and activated the tragicomic genre, which became the structuring pattern for the spelling out of the gospel. The tragicomic plot as a narrative form already has an incipient content. Plot form itself implies an emerging understanding of the human reality in history — as comic, tragic, romantic, ironic, et cetera (White 1978, 58–59, 62, 70; 1990, xi, 2, 43–47). Paul then would have taken this nascent content and developed it in light of the early Christian tradition and in light of his own input as qualified both by his historical-cultural contextualization and by his unique individuality.

The pertinent point here for the issue of the human reception of revelation is that the tragicomic genre through which and to which the gospel is assimilated by the receiver is not an exclusively or peculiarly biblical formation but is rather a cross-cultural and cross-religious phenomenon. It is a human way of grasping reality that the receiver brings *to* the gospel and by which she makes sense of it. The same thing is true in principle for metaphor, irony, parallelism, and other literary forms that are used to articulate the gospel.

Ronald Thiemann in speaking more broadly about the employment of narrative in theology has observed that theologians are divided on the question of the precise status of narrative. Some take narrative to be a transcendental quality of experience, a universal form of consciousness. Others understand narrative simply as a literary form that requires appropriate literary approaches (Thiemann 1985, 83).

My use of tragicomedy in relation to Paul and the Gospels does not fit exactly into either of these positions. I take tragicomedy to be more than a literary form. It is a mode of experience, an interpreted pattern of historical existence. But my point does not depend on being able to assert that it is universal. Just the fact that it is cross-cultural and cross-temporal shows that it is a natural human way of grasping experience and is not peculiar to the Bible.

The use of cross-cultural and cross-religious categories does not mean that the various interpretations of the good news do not have their own specifically and distinctively Christian meaning. Paul and the Evangelists, for example, by the way in which they receive the word of God and produce their texts leave their own unique and Christian imprint on the revelation. That is also true of those who through the centuries receive the New Testament texts and apply them to their own situations. At the same time the formal and the incipient material similarity between the New Testament texts and various cross-cultural texts that belong to the tragicomic genre discloses a continuity between the New Testament and a broadly human way of grasping the human reality. It is because the gospel is a variation on a fundamentally human way of apprehending reality that human beings can naturalize it and live in it. Or it is because it has been naturalized in this way that it can be grasped. The *human* capacity to shape existence in a tragicomic way is one factor that enables people to receive the gospel. But it should not be forgotten that for Paul the preached word of God as content and power redirects the natural meaning of the tragicomic genre into unanticipated channels. The capacity to receive constitutively is by itself only a potentiality for revelation, a necessary cause but not in itself a sufficient cause. Revelation actually occurs only from the confluence of the four constitutive elements.

The consideration of another human category that is pertinent to the discussion returns us to our 2 Corinthians text — the category of conscience. Paul states that in manifesting the truth he commends himself to every conscience of human beings in the sight of God (2 Cor 4:2). Conscience is a point of contact for receiving the gospel, for constituting revelation. The proclamation of the gospel is sufficient only if it touches the conscience. Bultmann suggests that for Paul the gospel is understood when it effects a resolution of the problems of conscience (1985, 74, 102–3). Thus to some degree the gospel is shaped by the particular way conscience functions.

The idea of conscience emerged in popular Greek wisdom some centuries before Paul's time, and according to the understanding current in the first century A.D., conscience could be defined as a human being judging herself or himself in light of a standard of right that is independent of this judging function itself. This judgment may have reference to past actions or actions contemplated for the future (1 Cor 4:4; 8:10; 10:25–27). Conscience was held to be a universal human phenomenon belonging to human beings as human, and its normal function was pain. The latter could be spoken of in terms of (1) being pain, (2) inflicting pain, or (3) feeling pain (Pierce 1955, 15, 17, 40–41, 45–46, 50, 77; Davies 1981, 674; Bultmann 1951, 217–18; Stacey 1956, 206–8; Jewett 1971, 425). Conscience then is a structure of human beings that belongs to humans as human. It is something that they bring to the reception of the gospel. It is universal according to popular Greek philosophy, and that is also the case for Paul because, as he says in 2 Cor 4:2, his appeal is to *every* conscience of human beings. At the same time his appeal is *before God*. Recall that conscience is not the source of the standard of right and wrong, but rather it judges according to a norm outside of itself. The conscience that Paul wants to engage is one that judges with reference to a standard that takes account of the divine will.

The concept of conscience (*suneidēsis*) assumes that a person has a relationship with herself. Conscience is human being as a whole and not just an instruction on this or that. It is not something one has but what one is as self-related (Ebeling 1963, 411, 417). It is knowledge (*eidēsis*) that one has with (*sun*) oneself. It is knowledge that one has acted, or contemplates acting, against one's own standard of right. (Or it might be knowledge that one has not so offended.) But more than that it is the self questioning itself about whether it accepts its own past deeds and affirms its own future potentiality (418). Thus conscience generates self-accusation. This is the pain of conscience. It is the pain of self-division, of self against self. The person holds a certain normative position but acts contrary to it, or one fails to identify oneself with one's own past or future, and this self-contradiction causes or is pain. For Paul the painful tension that results from the accusation of conscience is destructive of a person (1 Cor 8:10–11). To maintain the position that self-division is destructive is to assume that well-being or salvation resides in wholeness or the accord of self with self.

If the gospel is to be effective revelation actually received, it must conform to the nature of the universal human phenomenon of conscience. I maintain this despite the strictures of Krister Stendahl (1963, 200, 202, 204, 206–7, 209–10, 212) against those who fall into the peril of modernizing Paul by interpreting him in light of "the introspective conscience of the West." I addressed his position earlier (Via 1971, 208–11) with an argument I would still stand behind and here slightly expand. In addition to saying that the gospel must conform to the structure of conscience, one also needs to turn it around and say that the receivers of the gospel do shape it so that it speaks to their being as conscience. If the gospel does so speak, it will intend the human wholeness whose painful absence the accusing conscience attests.

Paul's gospel does appeal to conscience by justifying the sinner, acquitting the guilty (Rom 3:21–26; 4:3–5). The person who has taken a hostile stance toward God and God's claims is placed in a relationship of peace (Rom 5:1, 10–11) by this unconditional acceptance without regard to merit. Being at peace with God enables one to be at peace with oneself, no longer self-divided. Knowing that one is accepted by God despite one's lack of merit or moral achievement, a person can honestly acknowledge her flaws rather than deceive herself into believing that they are nonexistent. At the same time the person will not be pained by his violations of the right because God's unconditional acceptance of him overcomes his own self-accusation, and the future is thus opened up (Rom 8:33–34, 35–39). Freed from the painful self-accusation of conscience that was generated by the conflict between responsibility to God and actual response, a person is at one with his or her own flawed past and new future possibilities.

In discussing Paul's view of the role of human reception in constituting revelation, I have sometimes referred to this capacity as "the naturally human." As such it includes the knowledge, structures, and moves that people can have or make because these things are familiar to them from nature and culture. But I have also referred to the capacity to receive and assimilate God's self-disclosure as the prior word of God, the word of God that exists in people prior to their encounter with the gospel of Jesus Christ. I believe that this dual way of speaking about human reception is faithful to Paul's position. One can make a connection or an identification between, on the one hand, the natural human capacity to make sense out of God's revelation in the gospel and, on the other hand, the knowledge of God with which God has endowed all human beings by placing them in a creation that speaks of God. As we have seen, this original knowledge of God has, in Paul's view, been deformed. But at the same time it still functions in some kind of positive way, and this positive functioning can be seen in such factors as Paul's claim that he *himself worked* more than the other witnesses of the resurrection, his acknowledgment of the hermeneutical move made in grasping his human preaching *as* word of God, and his assimilating of the gospel to such broadly human structures as the tragicomic story-form and the phenomenon of conscience.

Understanding and Participation

In 2 Cor 4:4, 6 Paul refers to actualized revelation — the confluence of the four constitutive factors — as the illumination of the heart by the light (or enlightenment) of the knowledge of the glory of God. In the Bible *glory* is the way God exists and acts, the way God is in God's self-disclosure (Barrett 1973, 132). The biblical presentation often symbolizes God's manifestation or glory as light (Isa 60:1; Acts 22:11). The motif of light coming out of darkness could echo a number of Old Testament texts (Gen 1:3; Job 37:15; Ps 18:28; 112:4; Isa 9:2; 42:16; 60:1-2; Furnish 1984, 223-24; Murphy-O'Connor 1991, 41-43). These passages use light as a symbol of revelation in three different dimensions or contexts — the original creation of the world, the illumination of everyday existence, and the eschatological renewal of the world. The light of the gospel is then associated with all of these. The word that

Paul here uses for "light" or "illumination" (*phōtismos*) has an active sense that connotes a radiating, shining brilliance (Bultmann 1985, 106, 108). This suggests the active, penetrating power of the gospel.

Paul can refer interchangeably to the illumination as the manifestation of God's glory (4:6) or the manifestation of Christ's glory (4:4). It is precisely *God's* glory that is manifested in Christ — in the face of Jesus Christ (4:6) — because Christ is the image (*eikōn*) of God (4:4). In Jewish (Wis 7:26) and early Christian (Col 1:15) sources an *eikōn* is not just a faint copy of something but that by which the original is truly represented (Furnish 1984, 248). The knowledge of who God really is — God's glory — symbolized as light occurs specifically through the gospel of Jesus Christ, the proclamation of his death and resurrection. Paul speaks of *gospel* and *knowledge* interchangeably as the means of access to the reality of God. Notice the parallelism between the important chains of words in 4:4 and 4:6. Illumination-*gospel*-glory parallels illumination-*knowledge*-glory.

Knowledge of God's glory does not come about because the human spirit has unmediated access to the Spirit of God (as in mysticism), although, as we have seen, actual revelation does require the work of God's Spirit. Nor is the content of the knowledge a matter of the true heavenly origin and status of the human spirit and how this was lost and can be regained (as in gnosticism). The knowledge comes through the proclamation of Jesus' death and resurrection and the entailments of the preaching for living out this pattern in the historical world.

We have seen that actualized revelation is a matter of coming to *understand*. Nowhere is this more explicit than in 2 Cor 4:4–6 where God's light shining in our hearts overcomes the blinding of the *mind* (*noēma*) by the god of this world. Salvation for Paul, however, is not just a matter of a new relationship with God effected by understanding. Salvation is also portrayed as participation in Christ; therefore, it is a new kind of being. And we shall see that new understanding and new being are not discrete categories, but rather they overlap and interpenetrate each other.

Let me briefly illustrate these two modes of salvation, that is, these two actualizations of revelation — (1) understanding and (2) being through participation. In Phil 3:4–16 to know the significance of Christ and to have the new relationship with God that is righteousness is to have a new understanding of oneself. We come to understand that God is the ground of our being and not we ourselves. In Rom 9:30; 10:3, 6–8, 10, 17, 19 righteousness is manifested in Christ, who is then interpreted as the preached word, which, if it is believed and understood, makes the one who understands it righteous (Via 1994b, 1153–55).

The mode of new being through participation in Christ can be seen in Rom 6:3–10. We who have been baptized into Christ Jesus participate in his death with the result that our old self (*anthrōpos*, humanity) has died. And while Paul refrains from saying that the resurrection life has emerged now in the present, he does say that it is assured for the future. And even now we walk in a new quality of life and in a new dimension of freedom. In 2 Cor 5:17 Paul is less reticent in his language about the present fullness of salvation. He still does not use explicit resurrection language but does affirm that if anyone is in Christ that person *is* a new creation.

What is the relationship between the understanding-relationship language and the participation-being language? E. P. Sanders has seen these two ways of understanding salvation in Paul as having a problematical relationship with each other. Sanders believes that the real thrust of Paul's theology is the participation language. Paul uses understanding-relational language to express participation meanings but not vice versa. Sanders seems to hold that while there is an inescapable incompatibility between the two sets of terms, Paul nevertheless imposed participation meanings on relational language. Sanders is uncertain about what category might be used to make the participation motif intelligible to us, but in his view it cannot be reduced to the existential construct of new self-understanding creating a new relationship (Sanders 1977, 502–3, 506–8, 519–22).

I want to argue that for Paul the two modes of salvation interpenetrate each other in that Paul himself interprets participation-being *as* a new relationship with God through Christ, grounded on a new self-understanding, and does so without any sense of "reducing" the former. We have already seen that in 2 Cor 3:1–3 Paul speaks of the hearts of believers as a letter written by the Spirit with the language of the gospel. The very employment of the motifs of letter and writing necessarily suggests understanding and language, and Paul in fact explicitly associates reading and knowing with believers imaged as letter. At the same time the letter is a rewriting of the heart, the core of a human being. Thus the new understanding written on the heart engenders a new kind of being. The same is true in 4:4, 6.

Nowhere do understanding and being penetrate each other more deeply than in 2 Cor 3:18. This verse is closely connected to 3:14–16 by the motif of the veiling/unveiling of the mind, which obviously carries the theme of understanding. The hardening of Israel's mind (*noēma*), which prevents its proper understanding of the Old Testament, is imaged as the veiling of the heart (*kardia*). Notice that mind and heart are here used synonymously. But in *Christ = Lord = Spirit* the veil is removed: understanding is initiated. 2 Cor 3:18 describes the state of the person who has turned to the Lord and whose heart has been unveiled. Quite interestingly, however, Paul actually refers to the unveiling as the unveiling of the face (*prosōpon*), a move probably prompted by the prominence of Moses' face in Exod 34:29–35, which Paul is here interpreting. Thus while it is the heart that was veiled, it is the face that is unveiled. Clearly *face* is the equivalent of *heart* (2 Cor 3:15) or *mind* (3:14) in this context, although in other contexts, including Paul's letters, *face* can be opposed to *heart* as outward appearance to inner reality (1 Sam 16:7; 2 Cor 5:12). Yet the way in which Paul can use either *heart* (inner core) or *face* (outward appearance) to represent the real person in 2 Cor 3:15–18 shows how naturally he assumes that the inside and outside of a person are *in principle* two connected sides of the same reality (Via 1990, 68–73), however much they may have come apart under the conditions of actual fallen existence.

The person in Christ has been given to understand — whether the object of understanding be the Old Testament (2 Cor 3:14) or the Lord (3:18; 4:4). Understanding the Lord (the removal of the veil) is amplified as seeing the glory of the Lord. Recall that the glory (reality) of Christ is available in the gospel (4:4). The verb translated here as "seeing" (*katoptrizō*) (3:18) in "seeing the glory of the Lord" should be taken to mean "to behold as in a mirror" or simply "to behold" and not "to reflect." This translation is required both by the middle voice and by the context. The connection with the glory of the Lord leads to transformation, and transformation through beholding is more intelligible than transformation through reflecting (Bultmann 1985, 90–95). Yet one might want to argue that both connotations could be at play here. Metaphorically speaking one may reflect what one sees.

Beholding the glory of the Lord, we are being transformed into the same image from glory to glory. The verb "to transform" (*metamorphoō*) is used elsewhere in the New Testament only of the transfiguration of Jesus (Matt 17:2; Mark 9:2) and the transformation of the believer by the renewal of the mind (Rom 12:2).

The historical context is provided by the Jewish apocalyptic hope for future transformation (Dan 12:2–3; *2 Apoc. Bar.* 51:1–10; *1 Enoch* 38:4; 50:1) and the Hellenistic belief that beholding a deity could have a transformative effect (Apuleius *Metamorphoses* 11.15.23–24; Furnish 1984, 214–15, 240).

To be transformed (*metamorphoō*) is to be given a new form (*morphos*), and form suggests shape. However, the shape connoted by this term is not just an outward appearance but an expression of the reality of the thing itself (Bultmann 1985, 95; Beare 1959, 78–79). What is the believer transformed into? In broad terms Paul's meaning seems to be that one is transformed into Christ in some sense, for *Christ = Lord* is prominent in this context (2 Cor 3:14, 16, 18; 4:4–6). But Paul's precise meaning is difficult to discern. What he actually says is that the believer is transformed into the same image (*eikōn*), and one of the reader's first questions is The same as what? One may wonder until continued reading directs the attention to 4:4, where image (*eikōn*) appears again: Christ is the image of God. Thus if the believer is transformed into the *same* image, she must be transformed into the image of God that Christ is. As we have seen, Christ as image (true representation) of God is where (4:4) the glory or reality of God (4:6) is manifested. Paul seems to be saying something very like the believer is transformed into the divine.

There are other movements of thought, however. In the Priestly creation story, image of God is what human beings *as human* are created as — in their sexual differentiation (Gen 1:26–27). And Paul's language clearly echoes this. Thus Christ as image of God is the human being as intended in creation, and that is what believers are transformed into.

If the context of 2 Cor 3:18–4:6 tends to associate divine glory with Christ as image of God and to suggest that the believer participates in that divine glory in that the believer is transformed into the same image, in another passage Paul employs the term "image" to create more distance between the believer and Christ. In our 2 Corinthians passage the believer is transformed into the image of God, who is Christ. But in Rom 8:29 the term "image" stands *between* Christ and the believer so to speak. God has predestined believers to be conformed (*summorphos*) to, to be formed with, not Christ but the *image* of Christ. Having the same form as the true representation of Christ is not the same thing — exactly — as having the same form as Christ. Something — however fine — stands between Christ and the believers.

This tendency to create a distance between Christ and the believer brings us again to 2 Cor 3:18 and "the same image." We saw that the context directs the attention forward by and to the use of "image" in 4:4. But the term "same" also makes us look back. When Mark 14:39 says that Jesus prayed the "same" word, it means the words prayed just before. So when 2 Cor 3:18 mentions "the same image," we are a little puzzled because no image has been previously mentioned. Our attention is directed back, but to what? We are looking for what the image into which we are transformed can be the same as, and the best candidate is "glory" in the immediately preceding "glory of the Lord." Image can be the same as glory because in this context Paul makes *image* and *glory* virtually synonymous by interpreting Christ with both categories. He is the manifestation of God's glory because he is the image of God. The association of image and glory is also supported by Jewish sources (Wis 7:25–26). The image into which we are transformed is Christ the Lord as the glory of God. Thus we seem to be back where we were: the believer is transformed into Christ, who is the manifestation of the divine. But not quite. Paul could have said that we are transformed into the same glory. We in fact expect him to have said that, but he does not. The substitution of *image* for *glory* creates some distance between the human believer and Christ as divine glory.

And yet Paul does use the term "glory" to qualify the status of the believer. We are transformed into the same image from glory into glory (2 Cor 3:18). In Paul's theology *glory* is the nature of Christ's heavenly resurrection existence (body; Phil 3:20–21), and believers' bodies of humiliation will be changed into the same or similar form (*summorphos*) as his body of glory at the eschatological moment in the future (Phil 3:20–21; 1 Cor 15:50–56). Glorification with Christ is a future possibility (Rom 8:17). Nevertheless, Paul can speak of the believer as already glorified in the past by God (Rom 8:30). Eschatological glorification is in some way already really anticipated, but it is not literally and fully actualized, for Paul is still pushing toward the full sharing in the resurrection of Christ (Phil 3:10–14). That press into the future Paul describes in 2 Cor 3:18 as being transformed from glory into glory. What one will be, one is already in process of becoming. A central aspect of this process is a sharing in the suffering of Christ (Rom 8:17; Phil 3:10). What this entails will be more concretely and fully explicated in the interpretation of 2 Cor 4:7–12.

It is an elementary Heideggerian theme that self-understanding constitutes human being: "There is some way in which Dasein (being there, human being) understands itself in its Being.... Understanding of Being is itself a definite characteristic of Dasein's Being" (Heidegger 1962, 32). The understanding of Being is a basic mode of Dasein's Being (78, 182–83).

Paul anticipated Heidegger, although Paul's discourse is more nearly at the *existentiell*, ontic or actual, level than at Heidegger's *existential* or formal level. In any case, for Paul the new understanding given with the removal of the veil of misunderstanding from the face (self) constitutes a new mode of being — transformation into the image that is Christ, the image of God (2 Cor 3:18; 4:4) — or into the image of the image (Rom 8:29). The interpenetration of understanding and being is supported by the connection that Paul makes between the transformation of being and the reading of Scripture with understanding. That is, the Lord, the beholding of whom transforms us, is the Spirit who is the key to the meaning of Scripture (2 Cor 3:15–17).

Is the new understanding given with the revelation of the knowledge of God's glory (2 Cor 4:6) *self*-understanding? In this context the most explicit content of the new understanding is the old covenant, God, and Jesus Christ (3:14–16; 4:6). Yet *we* are transformed by this knowledge (3:18), and that implies a new self-understanding. To understand God's dealings truly is to understand ourselves in a new way (Phil 3:8–11). Prior to receiving the gospel we exist in self-deception (1 Cor 3:18; Gal 6:3), falsely believing that our works and wisdom can be trusted to count with God toward salvation (Rom 3:27–28; 1 Cor 1:29; 8:1–2). But the revelation of the gospel also makes us confront the unpleasant secrets that we have hidden from ourselves (1 Cor 4:5; 14:25) and gives us to understand that we have nothing of our own to trust in but can only respond to the God who accepts the ungodly (Rom 3:23–24, 27–28; 4:5; 1 Cor 1:26–31).

Paul as Interpreter of the Old Testament

This section continues in a particular way the discussion of the place of human reception in constituting revelation. The relative length of this description of Paul as an interpreter of the Old Testament has in view two objectives: (1) to place the discussion in the context of contemporary scholarship on the subject; (2) to demonstrate in some detail Paul's own natural interpretive ingenuity as an instance of the human reception that shapes the word of God.

Paul's thought in 2 Cor 3:7–4:6 unfolds in very substantial part as an interpretation of Exod 34:29–35 — Moses' descent from the presence of God on the mountain with the two tablets of the covenant, the Ten Commandments. Moses' face was shining in a way that unnerved the people. We have already touched on Paul's confessional affirmation of the authority of the Old Testament, and that observation needs to be expanded a bit. Paul speaks of the Old Testament — almost globally — as the word of God (Rom 9:6), and he can find the gospel of Jesus Christ, the advent of righteousness, already present in it (Rom 3:31; 4:3, 5; 10:5–10). At the same time Ernst Käsemann was quite right to say that Paul drew a line through Scripture, finding the law on one side of the line (Rom 10:5) and the gospel of righteousness on the other side (Rom 10:6–7; Käsemann 1971, 158–59, 164–66). Lev 18:5 falls on the side of law while Deut 30:11–14 preaches the gospel (a point to which we must return later).

Paul's employment of Exod 34:29–35 in 2 Corinthians is more ambiguous than his treatment of the passages mentioned above. He uses this Old Testament text to give a critique of the law, at least in relative terms, to portray it as inferior to the gospel (2 Cor 3:7–11, 13). At the same time he takes the image of the veil (*kalumma*) from the Moses story and uses it in his explication of the gospel. Paul employs the veil to express the recalcitrant misunderstanding of Scripture on the part of Israel (3:14) and to assert the hidden, impenetrable meaning that both Old Testament Scripture (3:15) and gospel (4:3) take on in consequence of human obduracy. On the other hand, he negates the negative connotation of veiling or concealing with the idea of *un*veiling (*anakaluptō;* 3:16, 18) to express the availability of the Lord and the believer's understanding of and openness to the glory of the Lord. We could say that the veiling/unveiling category affords Paul the language to express both the negative and positive aspects of the human posture toward revelation.

In a still more positive way Paul appropriates the LXX's description of the glorification of Moses' face and makes glory a central category in this passage. True, Paul uses the notion of canceled glory to support his devaluation of Moses and the law (2 Cor 3:7, 9–10, 13). But he also uses *glory* more extensively in a positive way of the true manifestation of God (4:6) in Christ (3:18; 4:4) and of the eschatological existence of believers (3:18). We can conclude that for Paul Exod 34:29–35 is authoritative Scripture. And even if it is ambiguously word of God for him, his method of interpretation is in principle analogous to his method for dealing with Deut 30:11–14 (Rom 10:5–10), an Old Testament passage that he clearly does regard as authoritative. So how does Paul deal with texts that he regards as word of God?

One can identify four positions regarding the question of whether Paul was dependent in 2 Cor 3:7–4:6 on rabbinic or other Jewish interpretations. (1) There were no rabbinic or other Jewish interpretations of Exod 34:29–35, thus Paul's reading is uniquely and creatively his (Barrett 1973, 115). (2) Paul is Christianizing a Jewish midrash. (3) He is modifying a midrash composed by his Corinthian opponents. (4) There was probably no extended midrash on Exod 34:29–35 prior to Paul, but there were interpretive traditions — in the targums, Philo, Qumran, the rabbis, and elsewhere — especially about the glory of Moses. Paul's interpretation agrees with some of these traditions and creatively departs from others, and his originality is seen particularly in his application of them to his situation (on this see Belleville 1993, 165–85).

What does Exod 34:29–35 say, and how does Paul interpret it? Since there is no interpretation apart from the individual and social position of the interpreter, let me give what I regard as a plain reading of the Old Testament text, and then we will consider Paul's interpretation. My reading is, of course, also a conditioned interpretation. The Exodus text, short as it is, contains problems and resists a definitive interpretation. Brevard Childs has pointed to a stylistic-grammatical tension within our passage. He claims that Exod 34:29–33 uses a narrative style and places the action of Moses and its consequences in the past while 34:34–35 initiates a shift in style that relates a continuing practice in the sanctuary (1974, 618). Whatever may be the case with the Hebrew text, the LXX, to which Paul was apparently making reference, stylistically distinguishes only 34:34 from the other verses.

Exod 34:29–33, 35 in the LXX is dominated by the aorist indicative (although that is not the only tense to appear) and thus stresses action considered as a point in the past. Exod 34:34 shifts this to customary or repeated action in the past by the use of the conjunction "whenever" (*hēnika...an*) and by using several imperfects. Surrounding 34:34 with pointed past action accommodates the verse to that style, yet 34:34 in itself by its use of the imperfect still narrates customary action in the past. This stylistic difference may be due to the employment of different traditions. Nevertheless the flow of the narrative tends to relativize the difference and to create a single story, although not a harmonious story.

The story as it stands contains a thematic tension. It seems clear that Moses took the veil *off* when speaking with the Lord (Exod 34:34, 35c-d). It is unclear, however, whether he put it *on* when he was speaking to Israel (implied 34:34–35) or when he was speaking neither with Israel nor with God but was going apparently about everyday activities (34:33; possibly 34:35). If he donned the veil when speaking to Israel, the history-of-religions rationale would perhaps have been to protect Israel from the holy, but if he put it on while going about ordinary activities, the reason might have been to protect the holy from profanation (Oepke 1965, 559–60).

Let us consider the above in a little more detail, dealing first with the suggestion that Moses put on the veil while going about the everyday. Up to 34:33b the veil has not been mentioned. Moses has come down from the mountain with the tablets, and the people have been frightened by his shining (LXX: glorified) face, but Moses has nevertheless talked to them — without any reference to the veil. It is only after Moses finished speaking with Israel (34:33a) that he put the veil over his face (34:33b). Then he took it off when he went into the sanctuary to speak with the Lord (34:34). This is reiterated in 34:35d. Thus he has the veil on only in between speaking with Israel and God. That being the case in 34:34, when 34:35 says that he put on the veil, that could be taken to mean that he put it on in the ordinary in-between time. In this motif the veil is connected with speaking, or more precisely, it is on when Moses is *not* speaking with either of his two partners.

However, we read also in Exod 34:34 that the veil was left off while Moses was speaking with the Lord until Moses came out. This suggests that when Moses came out to the people, he put the veil *on*. And the first thing he did upon coming out was to speak to Israel. He would leave the veil off until coming out, and upon coming out (aorist participle), he would speak to the people. Thus both putting on the veil and speaking with Israel are coincident with coming out of the sanctuary. This implies that Moses put it on when speaking with them. Then we read immediately that the Israelites saw his glorified face, and he put the veil on until he went in to speak with God (34:35). This may imply that it was on both while speaking to Israel and in ordinary times. In any case, the putting on of the veil has now been connected with Moses' glorified face.

If we trace this shining face of Moses through the text, we come upon an implied motive for Moses' donning of the veil. After Moses' return from the presence of God on the mountain, his glorified face makes the people afraid to come near him (Exod 34:29–30). Then in 34:35 Israel saw his glorified face, and he put the veil on. The fact that the people's fear and Moses' putting on the veil are both connected with the glorified face suggests that the fear provides his motive for donning the veil. Moses wants to assuage their fear. We can understand when Barrett (1973, 119) sees consideration for the people as a suggested motive. On the other hand, the fear is mentioned in 34:30, but not until 34:35 is the veil associated with Moses' shining face. Thus we can understand why Carol Stockhausen (1993, 148) can claim that Moses' motive is either unexplained or at most implicit. There is no explicit "Moses did it because." And this is revelatory for the text as a whole. It is a story but does not have a plot. That is, it is structured by *sequence*, but *causality* is absent or weak.

Turning now to Paul's interpretation, we will observe some of the distinct ways in which the apostle changes the meaning of the Exodus text. First, there are enough detailed similarities between Exod 34:34 and 2 Cor 3:16 to justify the conclusion that the latter refers to the former (Dunn 1970, 312–13; Hays 1989, 145–46). Exod 34:34 says that whenever (*hēnika*) Moses entered (*eiseporeueto*) before the Lord (*kuriou*), the veil (*kalumma*) was removed (*periēireito*), and Paul's text says that whenever (*hēnika*) one turns (*epistrepsēi*) to the Lord (*kurion*), the veil (*kalumma*) is removed (*periaireitai*). Most of the key words are the same. N. T. Wright (1992, 183) seems to be correct in holding that here Moses, as distinguished from the rest of Israel, is the model for the believer, for *anyone* who turns to the Lord and is not hard-hearted. But that is true in a kind of external sense, for Paul has considerably changed the key of the melody-discourse. Paul takes the Exodus description of Moses' literal-physical entering into the sanctuary where God is believed to be present and has it mean the Christian believer's personal-inward turning to the resurrected Lord with the understanding of faith. Second, in Exodus 34 Moses' veil is a literal material face cover, but in 2 Cor 3:14–15 it is a metaphorical veil, a covering of the mind, an impediment to understanding. Third, in Exodus the veil covers the object to be seen — Moses' face. But in 2 Corinthians 3 it covers the mind of the seer-perceiver. Fourth, in Exodus Moses' donning of the veil is unmotivated or implicitly motivated by his desire to relieve the people's fear of the divine light in his face. But in 2 Corinthians 3 Moses puts on the veil in order that Israel might not see the end of what was being abolished.

When Paul says that the veil of Exodus 34 is the *same* veil that has covered the mind of Israel through the centuries, he arbitrarily reads into the veil of Exodus 34 a meaning that was quite foreign to it. N. T. Wright raises a "how" question: How can Paul move the veil from Moses' face to the understanding of his own Jewish contemporaries? And to the "how" question Wright gives a "why" answer: Paul does it in order to say that the reading of the old covenant remains a hidden thing. Wright then goes on to say that while Paul's interpretation has moved a long way from the text, it grows naturally out of Paul's reading of the passage (1992, 178, 182). That is just the point I want to raise a question about. Paul's interpretation grows, not out of the text, but out of *his reading* of it. That is true in principle of all interpretation. It manifests the interpreter's interests and location. The question that I want to pursue by looking critically at Paul, a question that I cannot definitively answer, is How much of the reader's reading is too much?

Paul's interpretation of the veil grows out of his belief that the failure to understand the truth about God is something not only chosen but also determined from beyond human choice. God hardens the heart (Rom 9:18; 11:7–10), or the god of this world blinds the mind (2 Cor 4:4). Paul's interpretation uses key words from his text but gives very different meanings to both words and actions in order to assimilate them to his position.

According to Paul's reinterpretation, the Israelites of Moses' time were prevented by the veil from seeing the end of what was being set aside or rendered ineffective. Exactly what was being set aside is obscure. Perhaps the law or the old covenant in some general sense is meant. There is no clear candidate for what is modified by the masculine or neuter participle of *katargeō* (set aside; 2 Cor 3:13). The setting aside cannot refer directly to the old covenant since *covenant* (*diathēkē*) is a feminine noun. But it probably refers to the law since there is a contextual reference to the reading of Moses (3:15).

By giving the story a nonhistorical meaning, Paul establishes an analogy between the situation of Israel in Moses' time and the situation of the Jews in Paul's own time. In both cases there is a failure to perceive something about the law, and the failure is supernaturally caused, but two slightly different aspects of misunderstanding are brought to expression. The Israelites of Moses' day were prevented from seeing the end of the law in the process of being set aside. They did not grasp its limitation. While Paul does not specify here what his own fellow Jews failed to understand, the suggestion is that they took the law to be "letter" rather than "spirit" (2 Cor 3:6). That is, they misinterpreted the law as calling for meritorious works rather than as calling for faith (Rom 9:30–10:3; Via 1994b, 1153). And also now in Paul's time the failure to understand the law and the failure to grasp the gospel are two sides of the same thing. And those who do not believe in the gospel are also supernaturally blinded (2 Cor 4:3–4). Blindness to the real meaning of the law and blindness to the gospel are connected in that only in Christ — only from the perspective of the gospel whose center Christ is — can the law be understood (3:14–15). Law and gospel are either understood together or misunderstood together. The veil is removed from the law when Christ is seen as the *telos* of the law (Rom 10:4): the *telos*-termination of the law as a means of salvation (Rom 4:4; 10:3; Phil 3:9) and the *telos*-fulfillment of the law as a pointer to faith (Rom 9:31–32). *Telos* has both meanings.

Let me recapitulate my analysis of the difference between Paul and his text in somewhat different terms. What Exodus 34 and Paul have in common is the veil motif (and its entailments), but we have seen that Paul gives to the veil a quite different meaning and function. He creates an analogy between the Israel of Moses' time and his own day by assigning to the situation of the former a very different quality than it had according to the Exodus text. In Exodus 34 itself the categories of meaning are the numinous, the physical, and the emotional (fear and its calming). The numinous takes physical form — it shines in the face of Moses — and this makes the Israelites afraid. Moses puts on the veil (perhaps) to calm their fears. But in Paul's account of this occurrence the categories are existential and hermeneutical or epistemological. The veil is not Moses' physical instrument but — metaphorically — the hardening of the mind of Israel, which prevents the understanding of Scripture (2 Cor 3:13–15).

The rabbinic rule *gezerah shava* established that there could be an analogy between two laws if they contained certain expressions in common. The analogy is thus not based on the inner content of the laws (Handelman 1982, 57). Paul's treatment of the Exodus passage is in accord with this principle. His rendition — interpretation — of Exod 34:29–35 contains the key term "veil" from the text. But since he gives the story an entirely different inner meaning than it has in Exodus, he also gives the word "veil" a different meaning.

Paul's exegetical practice carries a hermeneutical presupposition about the location of a text's meaning: the real meaning is not obviously present on the surface of the text but is latent or hidden behind or under it. In this Paul shows himself to belong to the guild of professional interpreters, which characteristically has maintained — as Frank Kermode puts it — the right to affirm and the obligation to accept the superiority of the latent or concealed sense to the manifest sense (1979, x–xi, 1–2). Kermode goes on to argue that the New Testament writers were an important factor in generating this preference for the hidden meaning that has characterized professional interpreters from ancient till postmodern times. The church did this by taking the Hebrew Scriptures as part of the Christian canon and finding the real meanings to be Christian ones rather than the obvious ones (18–19).

Within the guild of interpreters over the years there have been many differences of degree with regard to how the assumed superiority of the concealed sense is understood and actualized in practice. I shall look at several instances — very selectively and without giving them equal time. This will show that Paul's hermeneutical presupposition belongs to a broad human and cross-cultural interpretive tendency, a specifically human way of receiving texts or linguistic tradition.

I begin with rabbinic midrash because it is both an illustrative exemplar of this hermeneutic and a probable influence on Paul. Jacob Neusner has defined *midrash* simply as "biblical exegesis by ancient Judaic authorities" (1987, xi), and he distinguishes three dimensions of midrash: (1) a concrete unit of scriptural exegesis, (2) compilations of such units, and (3) a process or method of interpretation (9, 13). He then differentiates process into three types of exegetical method: paraphrase, prophecy, and parable.

Midrash as *paraphrase* states in other words the plain meaning of the Hebrew text. This is where the translations of Scripture belong, and it should be observed that in translation the boundary between text and interpretation is obscured as the translator joins in composing the text (Neusner 1987, 1, 7).

Midrash as *prophecy* takes Scripture as a prefigurement of the present and near future of the interpreter. The *pesher* exegesis of Qumran was typical of this method (Neusner 1987, 1, 7). In this mode the interpreter believes that he or she lives in the light of a new revelation that warrants alterations in the detail and sense of the text (Dunn 1970, 315–16). Paul's kinship with this process of exegesis is obvious, but perhaps he is closest, at least in passages like 2 Corinthians 3, to the third type.

Midrash as *parable* seeks the deeper meaning of the words. Scripture is read in terms that are other than those used by the writer on the ground that things are not as they seem. The interpreter speaks about anything other than what the words of the text seem to be saying. Yet the exegete believes that however fanciful his reading may be, he is expressing the original meaning of the text, that is, God's meaning (Neusner 1987, 1–2, 8, 11, 44, 48). It should be noted that Neusner makes no principled distinction between what he calls "parable" and "allegory" (2, 8).

Although the parable type of interpretation was most characteristic of the rabbinic compilations that were put together in the period A.D. 200–600, Neusner notes their similarity to Paul's way of dealing with Scripture (1987, 2). Given the lateness of these compilations, on what grounds might we hold that the kind of exegesis most typical of them could actually have been a historical influence on Paul? First, Neusner has noted that the antecedents of later exegesis are already found in the Hebrew Scriptures (17–18). Second, it is more likely that Paul was influenced by early rabbis than that later rabbis borrowed Christian methods. Third, similar patterns may be seen in Philo, who also belonged to the first century A.D. (Stegner 1984, 38). Fourth, Alan Segal has made the point that it makes more sense methodologically to try to interpret first-century Judaism in the light of the New Testament than vice versa (Segal 1991, 3, 15). That is, the New Testament is a more accessible source than are the early rabbis, whose traditions are found only in later compilations. If Paul was doing what later rabbis were doing, that probably means first-century rabbis were already doing it.

Susan Handelman has picked up and developed what Neusner calls "midrash as parable" and thereby sees the rabbis as precursors of certain postmodern literary-critical tendencies. In her view the rabbinic tradition with its principles of multiple meaning and endless interpretability manifests striking affinities with such recent Jewish thinkers as Freud, Jacques Derrida, and Harold Bloom (Handelman 1982, xiv–xv). According to Handelman the rabbis saw Scripture as a world of intertextuality in which texts echo, interact with, and interpenetrate each other. This generates multiple interpretations in which the text continues to develop, and since the interpretations are regarded as uncovering what was latent and concealed in the text, they are considered to be extensions of the text. The rabbis found a biblical basis for their many interpretations in Ps. 62:11 and Jer 23:29. God has spoken once, but the psalmist has heard twice. God's word is like a hammer that breaks the rock into many pieces (Handelman 1982, 39, 47, 49, 67, 75).

Handelman continues to argue that while a word of Scripture may have many meanings in midrash, the literal meaning is never canceled. This is because in rabbinic logic, items are related by contiguity, juxtaposition, and association rather than by substituting one thing for another with the resultant cancellation of one of them. Thus in rabbinic thought two — or more — predicates can exist simultaneously within one subject. There is room for conflict and contradiction between interpretations. Handelman claims in effect that the rabbis understood Scripture itself formally much as they understood interpretation. They saw the Bible, not as a linear, chronological, propositional narrative, but as an elliptical, nonchronological system of contiguous and juxtaposed signs. All units of the text are seen as simultaneously present (Handelman 1982, 55–56, 76–78).

Although Neusner uses the terms "parable" and "allegory" interchangeably for a type of midrashic exegesis, Handelman wants to distinguish midrash from allegory. In midrash, according to her understanding, concepts exist only in particular forms with the result that the conceptual meanings discovered in interpretation never dispense with or take precedence over the plain meaning in the particular form in which it is found. Allegory, on the other hand, says one thing but means something other than the plain sense. There is a substitution that cancels out something. Handelman believes that Paul wanted both Jews and Greeks to perceive that Scripture says something other than what appears to be the case. Paul, therefore, nullifies the literal meaning of the text and shows himself thereby to be actually an allegorical interpreter (Handelman 1982, 75, 84–85, 88). Handelman is right about Paul at least in some cases, such as the 2 Corinthians passage that we have been considering. Paul here cancels the plain sense, but he does not always do that.

Handelman also asserts that while rabbinic exegesis understands that the text generates a continuous process of competing interpretations and thus allows for the deferral of meaning, Paul, on the other hand, believes that Christ resolves all oppositions and stabilizes all meaning. The Christian desire is to escape the deferral of meaning and the mediation of language and to attain the pure unmediated presence of the ultimate referent — Christ. She bases her judgment here on Gal 3:28 — "There is no longer Jew or Greek, there is no longer slave or free, there is no longer male and female; for all of you are one in Christ Jesus" (Handelman 1982, 88–89).

Daniel Boyarin takes Gal 3:23–4:31 to be the hermeneutical key to the whole corpus of Paul's letters. Under the impact of middle Platonism, Paul was motivated by a desire for the One, an ideal of universal human essence beyond difference and hierarchy, a universal spirit that transcends bodily differentiation. Thus the crucial significance of being in Christ is the erasure of cultural and gender difference (Gal 3:26–29) in favor of a universal human essence that is beyond and outside the body (Boyarin 1994, 7, 14, 22, 24, 28).

Handelman is wrong in saying that Paul wants to escape the mediation of language. True he is concerned to attain a relationship with Christ, but for Paul the saving event occurs precisely by means of language (Rom 1:16; 1 Cor 1:18, 21), and Christ encounters people precisely *as* the word of preaching (Rom 10:6–10, 14–17). Paul may have preferred the preached to the written word, but he regarded the latter as a satisfactory substitute.

Nor does the oneness in Christ that Paul speaks of in Gal 3:28 — and elsewhere — cancel out particularity and differentiation. As we shall see from the discussion of 2 Cor 4:7–12, the "in Christ" — or "with Christ" — factor is not something mystical, not a middle-Platonic universal human essence, but rather something metaphorical. As a close reading of Paul's own text (2 Cor 4:7–12) will show, what believers have in common, what they are one in with Christ, is the form of the *metaphorical story* of Christ's ministry — death and resurrection. But with each individual believer the content that is informed by the story-form comes from the differentiated life of that person, from the particularity of his or her fleshly existence (Gal 2:19–20).

William Scott Green disagrees with the view of Handelman and others that rabbinic exegesis saw the text of Scripture as undecidable in meaning and therefore as generating a multiplicity of competing interpretations and that in virtue of this character midrash was a precursor of deconstruction and left-wing reader-response criticism (1987, 147–51). In Green's judgment the rabbis attributed to Scripture a given and fixed status and interpreted it so as to control its meaning. Rabbinic interpretation guaranteed that Scripture would always refer to and validate the rabbis' own religious ideology. From this Green draws two consequences. First, rather than allowing Scripture to have endless, multiple meanings, rabbinic interpretation limited possible meanings and intended to reject erroneous understandings. Or put another way, instead of promoting multiple meanings it allowed multiple variations on a single meaning. The rabbis had little toleration for the ambiguous, the uncertain, and the equivocal. Second, although rabbinic exegesis did not advance a multiplicity of meanings, it did allow the cancellation of the literal or plain sense (Green 1987, 160–65).

For the moment I have three responses to Green. First, if he is right about the rabbis' rigid control of exegesis from the standpoint of their own ideology, then the rabbis worked, not just within the hermeneutical circle as do all interpreters, but within a vicious hermeneutical circle. It is not possible for the text to challenge the preunderstanding they bring to the text from their ideology. Second, while Green may be right about the rabbis' imposing limits on the multiplicity of interpretations, he has tacitly acknowledged that the rabbis gave an interpretation that is *other* than the plain sense, namely, according to their own ideology. Third, I do not find convincing Green's evidence that the rabbis allowed the cancellation of the literal sense. What his example shows is that the plain sense can be slanted, modified, and stretched, but it does not show that the plain sense has been abandoned. Scholars as different in their orientations as Davies (1993, 20) and Handelman (1982, 55, 75) deny that midrash cancels the literal sense.

From this discussion of midrash I draw three conclusions: (1) The rabbis did privilege the hidden sense of Scripture, a meaning other than the plain sense. (2) They probably did not completely annul the literal meaning. (3) It would be difficult to determine what they would have said in theoretical terms about the limits upon multiple interpretations.

Allegorical interpretation also prefers the hidden meaning of a text. This has already been mentioned in passing and for my purposes warrants only slightly more comment. Allegorizing apparently began in the sixth or fifth century B.C. in Greece and/or Italy and, according to the customary interpretation, with the intention of bringing Homer and other poets into harmony with Greek science and philosophy. Over the next centuries it was used by many writers of various philosophical schools. With the Stoics, for example, God was not anthropomorphic; therefore, anthropomorphic descriptions of the gods in Homer had to be given a meaning other than the literal one. Thus the plain sense was annulled (Grant 1957, 4–7).

Allegorical interpretation did not go unquestioned in the Hellenistic world. Various critics accused the allegorical interpreters of falsely reading their own subjective and fanciful ideas into the ancient poets. But the allegorizers themselves would have denied this and claimed that they were discovering the true, hidden meaning of the text. For example, a certain Stoic of the first century A.D. named Heraclitus states that the "divine" Homer himself used the method of *allegoria*, that is "speaking one thing and signifying something other than what is said" (Grant 1957, 9–10).

David Dawson's recent work has modified somewhat the customary understanding of the originating intention of allegorical interpretation. He begins by affirming that ancient allegory is best understood, not only as a way of reading texts but also as a way of using that reading to challenge older and contemporary interpretations and to promote alternative ways of being in the world. Allegorical interpretation is characteristically challenging because an allegorical meaning obtains its identity from its contrast with the customary or expected "literal" meaning. Yet allegory is not inherently revisionary, for it may be used to bring shocking ancient texts into line with present cultural expectations (Dawson 1992, 1, 7–8, 10).

Dawson argues that Philo, Valentinus, and Clement shared one overriding goal: to convince readers that their allegorical interpretations tap directly into the original source of all meaning and truth and thus surpass all competing readings. But each of the three had a distinctive view of the original and authoritative locus of meaning. For Philo it was the sacred text of the Pentateuch. He read Hellenistic meanings previously unconnected to the books of Moses into the latter. He thus gave Scripture other meanings so that the other meanings might become scriptural. As a result Moses became the true author of the Greek classics, the original philosopher from whom Plato and the other Greeks derived their ideas. Philo learned that Moses' writing could thus become the basis for a revisionary stance toward the dominant Hellenistic culture. More briefly, for Valentinus the locus of meaning was his own mystical vision, and for Clement it was the speech of the divine logos, a transtextual hermeneutical voice (Dawson 1992, 11, 18–19, 73).

At the end of Dawson's book his language relativizes the textual element in allegory still more. Although the Alexandrian readers of Scripture sought to convince their audiences that they were interpreting Scripture itself, they were actually trying to revise their culture through their allegorical readings. Allegory is not so much about the meaning or lack thereof in texts as it is a way of using texts and their meanings to situate oneself with respect to society and culture (Dawson 1992, 235–36).

Boyarin negates still further the idea that allegorical interpretation arose to give currently acceptable meanings to ancient texts. In his opinion allegorical reading originated *not* from the need to apply problematic ancient texts *but* from a profound yearning for univocity, a univocity guaranteed by positing meaning as a disembodied spiritual substance existing, dualistically, prior to its embodiment in language. Allegorical interpretation sought this single spiritual meaning, while midrash rejected both univocity and the dualistic separation of inner and outer, meaning and language (Boyarin 1994, 8, 14–16, 28).

I have two critical questions to pose to Boyarin. If allegorical interpreters were not impelled by the need somehow to retain the authority of ancient texts, why did they not just take the simple path of setting forth their position in a direct way rather than the cumbersome and convoluted road of reading "other" meanings onto texts that seemed not to bear them? If oneness of meaning is essential to allegorical interpretation, how is it that patristic and medieval Christian allegorical interpretation regularly had multiple levels of meaning, sometimes seven meanings but more normally four? In the fourfold scheme (literal or historical, allegorical, anagogical, and tropological) only one of the nonhistorical meanings was specifically called allegorical (Grant 1954, 100–102), but all three of them were allegorical in the sense of nonliteral or other.

I now move from the ancient world to the twentieth century for three brief citations. In *An Introduction to Metaphysics* Heidegger set forth a simple but very useful three-stage approach to interpreting a text. The first two stages seem to propose in effect the identification of the central inner meaning of the whole and the grasping of the unfolding of this in the sequence of the parts. The third stage, the most important, has the goal of judging what humankind is by using violence on the direct meaning of the text to show what does not stand in the words but is nevertheless said (Heidegger 1961, 125, 128–29, 135–36) — the concealed meaning.

David C. Hoy (1982, 35, 38–40) comes to a position similar to Heidegger's in the process of criticizing the view that the meaning of a text is to be found in the consciousness or intention of the author rather than in the language of the text. According to Hoy it makes sense to speak of the intention of the *text*, especially a literary text. This intention is not something other than the poem, something that accompanies it. It is the poem itself, but what the poem *shows*, not just what it says. People often look for the author's intention because they have not yet seen what the text shows — its latent meaning.

My third (post)modern example is one motif from Stephen Moore's deconstructive reading of the Gospel of Mark. Moore is bolder and more explicit than Heidegger or Hoy about how to do violence to the text. It is essentially by reading it in the light of wholly unexpected connections. In Moore's own terms he has attempted to write inventively by combining dissimilar materials to produce surprising coincidences and bizarre overlappings (1992, xvii).

Moore's treatment of the consistent way in which Jesus is misunderstood in Mark derives from the Derridean view that writing is destined to be misunderstood. Jesus is misunderstood as if he were writing rather than speaking. His being misunderstood makes him a man of letters, a writer. Like Jesus who drifts from misunderstanding to misunderstanding across Mark's pages, writing has always been a wandering outcast drifting from (mis)reading to (mis)reading. Just as the Gospel of Mark is a stand-in for the absent Jesus and the only resurrection body Jesus has, so for Derrida the absence of a referent constructs the mark of writing. A brief exchange of letters (mark, Mark) is all that is necessary for a meaningful encounter between the texts of Derrida and Mark (Moore 1992, 15, 17, 19–20, 48).

Here Moore has found a meaning in the Gospel of Mark that is — shall we say — not self-evident. He is clearheaded about what he is doing, but does the transparency of his moves warrant the flimsiness of his justifications for making them? The similarity of mark to Mark for Moore justifies treating Jesus' speaking as writing. This raises again my question, unanswered but still pursued, How much of the reader's reading is too much?

I have taken a selective look at a hermeneutical assumption — the superiority of the hidden meaning — in which Paul participated and which has stretched in numerous variations from ancient to postmodern times. It is altogether probable, when we consider Paul's location in both spheres of influence, that Jewish midrash and Greek allegorizing both affected his interpretive principles and practice. Like his forebears Paul assumed the privilege of the concealed meaning. Yet his clearly and specifically Christian hermeneutical lens and his conclusions about the meaning of the Old Testament give him a particularity and distinction of his own.

I conclude my discussion of Paul as an interpreter of the Old Testament by entering into a conversation with Richard Hays's important and rightly acclaimed *Echoes of Scripture in the Letters of Paul*. Hays affirms two positions that I have difficulty trying to reconcile.

First, early in the book Hays states that the criterion of legitimacy for his own exegetical work is that it should be disciplined by a critical understanding of the rhetorical form and historical context of the Pauline material that he is interpreting. There should be an "authentic analogy" — though not a simple identity — between what Paul's text meant and what he (Hays) takes it to mean (1989, 27–28).

Second, later on in the book Hays argues that even though Paul regarded true interpretation as based on the promptings of the Spirit about the meaning of Scripture and not on historical or literary criticism (1989, 156), Paul's interpretations of Scripture are normative for Christian theology, and his interpretive methods are paradigmatic for Christian hermeneutics (183). Our constraints on the free reading of Scripture should be, like Paul's, theological and not methodological. Our exegesis should be in accord with (1) God's faithfulness to the promises to Israel, (2) Jesus' death and resurrection as the decisive manifestation of God's righteousness, and (3) the shaping of the community of readers by the love of God revealed in Christ (190–91). In a more recent work in which Hays responds to some critiques of *Echoes*, he reiterates his theological constraints on interpretation (1993, 85) but does not reassert the historical- and literary-critical criteria as he did in *Echoes*. It should be observed that Hays nuances his position by stating in a note that Paul's example should be paradigmatic for us, not in a rigidly prescriptive, but in an informative way (1989, 228).

Now my question: If — as Hays states and I agree — our interpretations of Scripture should be critically (methodologically) disciplined while Paul's were not, how can Paul's approach be in any strong sense paradigmatic or normative for us? In my judgment the strains that 2 Corinthians 3–4 puts on the Moses story in Exodus 34 are too great to justify our attribution of the adjective (fully) "authentic" to whatever analogy may exist between Exodus 34 and Paul's interpretation of it. Paul does create some kind of analogy between the situation of the Israelites in Exodus 34 and that of Jews and Christians in his own time, but he does so by giving both the inner meaning of the Exodus story and key words in it meanings that they do not have in Exodus. (I will return to the issue of analogy momentarily.)

The conclusion that I have just drawn about the gap between Paul's text, on the one hand, and his interpretation, on the other, does not mean, however, as Hays claims (1989, 182), that we cannot accept Paul's message if we reject his way of interpreting or certain particular interpretations. One could argue that Paul establishes broad analogies between parts of the Old Testament and his own interpretations while over-Christianizing and thus misinterpreting certain specific texts. I argued in an earlier work that Paul established a legitimate connection between Deuteronomy as a whole and his own theology but that in Rom 10:6–9 he misinterprets Deut 30:11–14 by giving to the term "word" a meaning that it cannot have in its own context (Via 1975, 57–63). Paul has it mean "the kerygma of righteousness by faith" when it means "commandment" in its own context.

We could go further and argue that while Paul's interpretive method in Rom 10:6–10 is arbitrary and his interpretation of Deut 30:11–14 is a misinterpretation of the Old Testament text, the meaning that he attributes to Deut 30:11–14 — the point he makes by using it — is, nevertheless, true. The understanding of the righteousness of faith and the power of the word found in Rom 10:6–10, 17 is true on its own terms. Or it is true if we take Paul as a whole to be true because it is congruent with his overall position. In a similar way Paul's misinterpretation of Exod 34:29–35 in 2 Cor 3:7–4:6 may be a true statement of theological anthropology.

It would be fruitless to fault Paul for not being a historical or literary critic in a self-conscious way, for that would obviously have been impossible in his time. But we can continue to pursue the issue of whether Paul's method of interpretation should be paradigmatic for us in a strong sense by inquiring further into the nature of the analogy that Paul creates between Exod 34:29–35 and his interpretation of it. Paul can make authentic analogies. I judge that the set of meanings he generates in 2 Cor 3:2–6 on the basis of the key terms "Spirit/spirit," "heart," and "new covenant" has a strong continuity with Jer 31:31–34; Ezek 11:19; 36:26–27, which Paul is echoing. In such cases not only Paul's meaning but his means can be taken as normative. But can the method be taken as paradigmatic in such cases as 2 Cor 3:7–4:6?

Whether Paul establishes an authentic analogy between the veil of Exodus 34 and the veil of 2 Corinthians 3–4 is a matter of an interpretive judgment based in significant part on a theoretical decision. "Authentic" is the slippery word here, and different people will judge differently about whether the analogy is legitimate. One important consideration that factors into the decision is a theoretical question that will be answered prior to the decision about whether Paul's analogy is authentic, and Scripture itself neither raises the question nor gives a clear direction about the answer. The question is, Are the Exodus text and Paul's text to be viewed exclusively in a synchronic or vertical way, as if they were simply two items existing simultaneously in the same meaning system? Or are Exodus and Paul to be seen dialectically as both synchronically or vertically related, on the one hand, and also diachronically — historically — or horizontally related, on the other hand?

If the relationship is taken to be undialectically and exclusively synchronic, then the analogy can be viewed as authentic. All we would really need is some connection of diction, and we have that — the word "veil" (and other verbal parallels) in both places. In both passages there is a sense of concealedness, but it is a different sense. However, if the relationship between the Exodus and 2 Corinthians texts is taken to be both synchronic and historical, there must be more than phonetic and verbal similarity and more than a very loose connection between the contextual horizon of the Exodus passage and Paul's contextual horizon in order for the analogy between the two to be regarded as authentic. There must be a *substantial* connection between the inner meanings of the two texts and between the contextual meanings of the key terms in the respective passages. I judge that my comparison of the Exodus passage with Paul's interpretation of it has shown that the connection is not substantial.

Stockhausen has claimed that when Paul interprets Old Testament narrative texts, he pays consistent attention to the context of the cited passages (1993, 145). However, what she shows with regard to Paul's attention to context is that when Paul comments on a certain narrative text, he is likely to view it in light of a larger narrative context (151–54). Or she shows that Paul's use of a theological motif (2 Cor 3:6) from a prophet (Ezekiel) has in view a *complex* of prophetic texts (161–63). She does not show that Paul's appropriation of words or images from a given narrative text interprets these elements in light of a semantic context provided by the text interpreted. And obviously in 2 Corinthians 3–4 Paul's interpretation of the veil has virtually no semantic connection to the veil of Exodus 34.

Since I regard the proper way to connect Exodus and Paul as requiring both the synchronic and the historical, my judgment about whether the analogy that Paul creates is legitimate turns out to be divided. Since the synchronic is a part of the relationship between Paul and the Old Testament, the analogy is partially authentic. It is synchronically legitimate. It succeeds pragmatically and rhetorically. The reader is moved by the persuasive power of the verbal connection to participate in the meaning of the Exodus–2 Corinthians intertext. But from the standpoint of the historical contextual meaning, the veil that Paul says is the same as the one Moses wore is actually so far from being the same veil that the analogy between the two veils is not authentic. And while the reader is rhetorically moved, the reader as critical reader should not, in my judgment, take Paul's way of establishing the analogy between text and interpretation as a proper or normative way of interpreting the Bible, even if the critical reader is also a believing reader. It may be (as Hays has suggested to me) that Paul is not so much exegeting Exodus 34 as making poetic/homiletical use of it. But that means all the more that Paul's methods of interpretation should not be regarded as strongly paradigmatic for Christian hermeneutics, for Christian hermeneutics must include exegesis as well as preaching.

To return to my unanswered hermeneutical question about how much of the reader's reading is too much, I offer this tentative answer. If an interpreter — Paul or we — treats the relationship between texts or between text and interpretation only in a synchronic or metaphorical way and not also in a diachronic or historical way, the result will be a reading in which there is too much reader.

What have I implied about the relationship of historical, literary, and other modes of critical reading to the constitution of revelation? The New Testament, of course, does not explicitly take up this issue. But if God continues to engage in self-revelation, and if the New Testament is to be taken as normative for how this continuing revelation is to be understood, then what the New Testament implies for us needs to be stated. For us, too, the revelation situation is composed of — now — the whole biblical tradition, the Spirit of God, our present historical situation, and human reception. Critical thinking may be a strand in the human reception that responds to the Spirit's testimony about the meaning of Scripture in our time. Criticism is not in the total scheme of things a *necessary* constituent of revelation, for if that were the case, only the learned could receive revelation. But by the same token, it must be affirmed that for those for whom critical thinking has become natural, criticism may be a quite legitimate constitutive element in the actualization of revelation, a way of receiving. With regard to historical criticism in particular, it is finally theologically justified in that it is a way of being reflective about the particularity of meaning, which results from the fact that revelation is actualized in a specific historical situation.

In discussing Paul I have talked analytically about the four factors that comprise the revelation situation. In experience, however, these are not really separable, and that can be seen here in Paul's treatment of the Exodus text. The more an interpretation departs from what might be regarded as a plain reading of a text held to be word of God, the stronger the natural human element. What I — or anyone — regard as a plain reading is, of course, conditioned by my social location, and I do not mean to imply any theological distinction in principle between the plain meaning of the scriptural text and Paul's natural, or even idiosyncratic, imaginative human interpretation. One of my primary claims is that the natural human categories by which the word of God is received are *constitutive* of the revelation — provided the Holy Spirit decides to empower the word-as-received. Paul in 2 Corinthians 3–4 regards the Exodus text as word of God, but he idiosyncratically extends the meaning beyond what anyone could regard as a meaning justified by the authoritative text itself. The idiosyncrasy is *Paul's own* doing. He does it in order to make the Old Testament text natural to himself and his readers. But the inseparability of the divine and the human is seen in that the content and means of this naturalization are the word of God as it occurred in the specifically Christian revelation. It is the knowledge of God coming in the face of Jesus Christ (2 Cor 4:6) that leads Paul to his *own* idiosyncratically stretched and unanticipatable reading of the word of God in the Old Testament. The knowledge of God in the face of Christ provided the motivation and perspective for Paul's interpretation of Exodus 34, but Paul's own natural imaginative talents as an interpreter provided the details.

Paul's Life as a Narrative Metaphor of the Gospel: 2 Corinthians 4:7–15

The final paragraph to be considered (2 Cor 4:7–15) returns to the theme of the paragraph with which I began — the *manifestation* of knowledge (2:14), and now of life (4:10–11) — but with a shift of emphasis regarding the vehicle of the manifestation. In 2:14–17 the emphasis is on the word as the medium of revelation, but there is a suggestion that Paul's life is also a medium. Here in 4:7–15 the emphasis is on his life as the vehicle, but speaking also comes into the picture. He speaks the faith that is enacted in his life — the hope of resurrection for himself and the Corinthians. It is his portrayal of his life that will receive the attention here.

In 2 Cor 2:14–17 God uses Paul's preaching, imaged as an aroma or fragrance, to make knowledge of God's self an actual reality. In 4:7 the content of the effective revelation of God in Christ (4:6) is spoken of as a treasure that Paul carries in an earthen vessel, his bodily existence. In 4:8–12 the revelation takes on the specific content of the death and resurrection of Jesus, and the medium of revelation is no longer Paul's preaching but his temporal existence. Recall that Paul is asserting his suffering and hardships as the expression of true apostleship.

Paul begins in 4:8–9 to describe the pattern of his everyday existence in what appears to be a nontheological way: "We are afflicted..., but not crushed; perplexed, but not driven to despair; persecuted, but not forsaken; struck down, but not destroyed." Here we see four affirmations of loss countered in each case by a denial of defeat. Each antithesis is structured upon a pair of participles, the first affirming hurt, the second denying destruction — afflicted but *not* crushed, for example. The negative is expressed in Greek by *ou* or *ouk* rather than by the expected *mē*. Victor Furnish suggests that this might be because a single idea is being negated (1984, 254). Or the *ouk* could have the effect of strengthening the denial of defeat. We could hardly have a clearer representation of what Langer called the essential comic pattern — the rhythm of upset and recovery (1965, 123–24). Paul, however, does not remain nontheological, for he interprets the affliction that does not end in destruction as a carrying in his body of the death and resurrection-life of Jesus (4:10–11).

Paul's reflections here about his own life and that of other Christians — he uses the first-person plural "we" throughout — take the form of two interlocking metaphors (on metaphor see pp. 129, 184). The first metaphor occurs in the thesis statement of 4:7 — we have this treasure in earthen vessels, or clay jars. The idea of treasure in clay jars might be regarded as a kind of secondary paradox. It is not in itself a *radical paradox* — a logical contradiction nevertheless thought to be necessary because of an underlying depth of meaning that is not self-evident. But the idea of a treasure in a clay jar is a paradox in the lesser sense of the incongruous or what is contrary to opinion. The incongruity is underscored by the fact that a clay jar, in contrast with glass or metal, is fragile, cheap, and of any value at all only when intact. It has no enduring value (Furnish 1984, 278). The secondary paradox of an ordinary (material) treasure in a fragile clay jar perhaps does become radical when it is taken into account that contextually the treasure is not gold or jewels but the light of the knowledge of God in the face of Christ. The metaphor is then constructed by predicating this paradoxical clay vessel of Paul's life.

Paul's life is implied in the subject and verb "we have" in the sentence "we have this treasure in clay jars" (4:7). Paul's life is the subject of the metaphor, and Paul's life, as self-understood and as explicitly portrayed in 4:8–9; 11:16–12:10; Gal 1:13–2:14, is a historical phenomenon, something extended in time. The qualifier of the metaphor is the jar holding the treasure. Semantic tension is created by predicating this spatial-physical object of a temporal pattern. Paul's historical life lived out in time is an inanimate, fragile jar, although a paradoxical one. The purpose of *God* in creating this living metaphor in Paul's life, the metaphor *Paul* has constructed with his own language, is that it might be made clear that the power is God's and not ours. The desire to interpret his own life under the impact of his experience of the gospel is what prompted Paul to create the metaphor.

The metaphor of his life as a clay jar holding a treasure is then expansively elaborated in other terms in 2 Cor 4:8–11. In this second of the interlocking metaphors Paul's life as a physical-spatial fragile jar becomes his story of upset and recovery. And the treasure — the revelation of God's glory in Christ — is the interpretation that he sees his story *as*, Jesus' death and resurrection. The subject of the second metaphor is Paul's story in the form of four variations on the comic — or tragicomic — plot: down but not out. The events of Paul's story are realistic and concrete occurrences in this world, and semantic tension is generated by seeing these downs and ups — this subject — *as* the metaphoric qualifier, that is, as the eschatological death and resurrection of Jesus. Paul's experiences of upset and recovery are the bearing in his mortal fleshly existence of the death and resurrection of Jesus.

That *Paul's* story is seen as a manifestation of *Jesus'* death and life would be a very particular claim and, for many, a surprising claim because the alternation of down and up might simply be seen as the quirks of fate — bad and good luck. Or the reader familiar with the apparently similar hardship lists in the philosophical and ethical literature of the time might have thought that Paul was expressing determination to remain invincible in the face of adversity (Furnish 1984, 280–82). But Paul is neither thanking his lucky stars nor claiming Stoic fortitude. The redemptive pattern of his life is grounded in his particular situation's being seen as — interpreted as — a variation on the Jesus story.

Paul participates in Christ in consequence of this interpretation. He participates as he does because he interprets as he does. Thus the participation in Christ is not a mystical experience but a metaphorical or hermeneutical experience. It is a matter of seeing, understanding, interpreting, one thing in terms of another. It is seeing *as*. Paul is not talking about a direct access of his spirit to the unmediated, exalted Christ nor about an inward experience of his soul (Bultmann 1985, 117). He is rather talking about the experience of a new power in the downs and ups of his concrete, historical existence. This power is mediated by his interpreting his life as an enactment in his fleshly existence of Jesus' story. Paul's life so understood is a lived metaphor: his life *as* a bearing of Jesus' death and resurrection. The life he thereby experiences is the power that holds him up when he is at the bottom and that, as we shall see in 4:12, is extended to the Corinthian community. It is not that the believer's existence does not have negative depths. It is that one is sustained at the bottom.

Bultmann (1985, 111, 113, 120) has stressed that Paul's discussion in 4:10–12 highlights the equivocal and paradoxical nature of the life that is manifested in Paul's body. Paul declares that life is present in him but then in 4:12 speaks as if only death is at work there. Thus the life revealed in Paul is not a condition perceptible in him but is found only in an event, his activity of preaching.

Bultmann is correct that in 4:12 Paul states that death is at work in him but life in the Corinthians. And in 4:13 he declares that in accordance with Scripture he speaks what he believes. But it seems to me reductionistic to claim that in this text life is manifested only in the event of preaching. Paul has very explicitly affirmed that life is manifested in his body, in his mortal flesh — as least as a possibility (4:10–11). True, there would be no meaningful communication apart from the interpretive speaking, but the language would not be exactly what it is apart from the reality of Paul's life to which it refers and which shapes it. The life that Paul speaks about in his body may not be perceptible to others in itself but rather becomes perceptible only through the interpretation of his life that he gives in preaching. But what the preaching manifests is the life present in a specific way in Paul himself.

How *exactly* should we take Paul's statement in 4:12 that death is at work in him but life, in the Corinthians? We should probably interpret it as irony (on irony see pp. 185–89). When Paul praises the Corinthians who have "arrived" spiritually and contrasts himself unfavorably with them in 1 Cor 4:8–10, he is clearly being ironic, even sarcastic, for he tells us as much. Would that you had in fact become spiritual kings (1 Cor 4:8)! What the Corinthians take as genuine spiritual elevation on their own part Paul sees as unfounded arrogance. In Paul's view the faith process for all people involves having the old life broken by the word of the cross so that life might be refounded on a new basis (1 Cor 1:20–21, 28–31). There is no life, apart from participation in the death of Jesus. When Paul then in 2 Cor 4:12 attributes only death to himself and only life to the Corinthians, he is being ironic. The Corinthians will find the resurrection-life of Jesus — if they find it — in the same way that he found it: by being sustained in the midst of earthly life's death-dealing ways, and not as elevation above the latter.

The unexpected semantic tension of a metaphor — Paul's concrete downs and ups *as* an instance of Christ's eschatological story — has power to move people into the new reality described by the metaphor. Paul seems to presuppose that. He experiences his life as a participation in the death and resurrection of Jesus precisely in that he interprets it that way. His metaphor redescribes reality, and the life-*in-death*, present invisibly in Paul and hidden to others but manifested in his speaking, extends itself as life into the lives of the Corinthians (4:12) — as long as they assimilate the irony. They may experience the new reality constructed by his lived metaphor. And the constructing of the metaphor is an expression of Paul's own natural ability to receive the tradition about Jesus and thereby to participate in the constitution of revelation.

Chapter 4

MARK

The Historical Situation

In this section I want to discuss specifically the question of the historical setting of the Gospel of Mark and also to deal in principle with the historical setting as a constituent of actualized revelation for all four Gospels because the theological significance of the historical situation is similar — or identical — for all four. Whenever I use one of the traditional names of the Gospels — Mark, Matthew, Luke, or John — it will mean, as the context may indicate, either the implied author or the Gospel text itself. The historical situation is the event of revelation when it is merged with the other constituent factors, that is, when it is seen in the light of the Jesus tradition as a receiver — the Gospel writer — assimilates the tradition to the exigencies of the situation that he shares with others. This naturalization of the tradition he accomplishes by the use of his own imagination and reflection. For revelation to be actualized it is also necessary that the power of the Spirit imprint the resultant meaning on the hearts of the receiver and his readers or auditors. In what historical settings did the Jesus tradition become revelation for the four Evangelists and — in varying ways and degrees — for their audiences? I mean for the term "historical" to include religious, cultural, and social factors.

Setting and Original Purpose

What then is the setting in which Mark's Gospel emerged? I want to pursue the question of the historical situation and original purpose by looking very selectively and briefly at several scholarly opinions. I will deal more with the conclusions than with the arguments of these scholars and for the most part will not debate them. My purpose is not to achieve a definitive position on the issues but to indicate something of the range of possibilities and to illustrate the variety of opinions.

Martin Hengel, in traditional critical fashion, concludes that Mark was written for Gentiles in Rome in A.D. 69 during a time of severe affliction after the persecution of Christians by Nero in

A.D. 64 (1985, 13, 30). The composition must have been before A.D. 70 because Mark does not refer to the fall of Jerusalem as a past event in chapter 13 but does reflect the pluralism of the religious and political life of Palestinian Judaism that was brought to an end by the Roman conquest of Jerusalem in A.D. 70. More specifically Mark 13:8–9 corresponds to the year of terror in A.D. 69, before Vespasian had mastered the chaotic situations throughout the empire, which he accomplished in the autumn of A.D. 70 (10, 16, 22).

Hengel rejects the more recent view that Mark was composed in Galilee or Syria on the ground that the author is ignorant of the situation in Judea between 66 and 69. Moreover, Hengel claims that the term "Syrophoenician" (*Syrophoinikissa;* Mark 7:26) would have been unintelligible in the East but was used in Rome to distinguish the Phoenicians of Syria from the *Libyphoinikes* of Carthage (1985, 28–29). The hatred of Christians in Mark 13:13 refers to the Neronian persecution of 64, and that is the specific historical situation for the development of the theology of suffering and the cross that is so central in Mark (23).

According to Gerd Theissen, Mark was written in rural southern Syria, near Palestine, shortly after the Jerusalem temple was destroyed in A.D. 70. All three synoptic Gospels were written in reaction to the crisis created by the Jewish War (A.D. 66–74), but Mark was written in the very midst of the war while Matthew and Luke reflect an increasing distance from it (Theissen 1991, 238, 240, 249, 258, 262, 291). Theissen argues that Mark suggests a Syrian connection in a number of ways: for example, the reference to the villages around Caesarea-Philippi (8:27–29) and the influence of Pauline traditions probably gathered in Syria (cf. 1 Cor 11:23–26; Mark 14:22–25). Mark's geographical oddities — misplacing Gerasa on the Lake of Galilee (5:1–2) and the strange route attributed to Jesus in 7:31 — may be ways of connecting the Gospel to the communities that it served (238–39, 242–45). The identification of the Syrophoenician woman (7:26) has the same purpose. Contra Hengel the term "Syrophoenician" did not originate in the West to distinguish Phoenicians from Carthagenians but in Syria itself to distinguish southern from northern Syrians (245–47). At the same time Mark's apocalyptic discourse (chap. 13) and passion narrative (chaps. 14–16) point to Jerusalem. Syria is the most likely locale for this overlapping of Syrian and Jerusalem traditions (240).

In opposition to Hengel Theissen believes that Mark 13:1–2

does presuppose the destruction of the temple (1991, 259), and Theissen assigns to the emperor Vespasian an important place in the Markan context. This emperor had led the empire out of a severe crisis and was understandably revered as a savior sent from God. Josephus prophesied world rule for him and probably transferred messianic expectations to him. In Egypt Vespasian was acclaimed as a god. In this situation the warnings against false messiahs in Mark 13:21–22 could have been formulated against the background of a propaganda campaign for Vespasian, the victorious new emperor. Mark then can be understood as a countergospel over against the good news about the emperor. Mark is the good news about the crucified one who is to be ruler of the world (267–68, 271).

For Theissen the combination of apocalypse (Mark 13) and passion (Mark 14–16) reveals the intention of the Gospel. In his passion Jesus is the model of behavior for the Markan community (cf. 13:9 with 14:55–65; 13:12 with 14:43–50; Theissen 1991, 281). The internal function of the messianic secret is to define discipleship as following Jesus in suffering (8:34–38; 10:32; 15:41; Theissen 1991, 286).

Helmut Koester believes that the Gospel of Mark underwent a series of redactions that produced a total of five versions. Luke used the original; Matthew used the first expanded version; the version that was received into the canon was the fourth one, which was an abbreviation of the Secret Gospel of Mark attested by Clement of Alexandria (Koester 1992, 284–86, 289, 293–302). The original author was not a Palestinian Jewish Christian but rather wrote in the primarily Gentile Christian environment of Syria, in Antioch or another city and after the Jewish War. A city would be the most likely site for the convergence of different traditions that we see in Mark, and one of Mark's purposes was the unifying of these conflicting traditions (Koester 1983, 167, 171; 1992, 289–90).

The original author was primarily a collector who left most of his source materials fairly intact. He was also, however, an author who created an overriding narrative framework to interpret his diverse traditions. The framework is biographical and owes something to the genre of the Hellenistic biography. It enabled Mark to relate everything to Jesus' passion and to put Jesus' death as a saving sacrifice at the thematic center (Koester 1983, 169; 1992, 289). For Koester (1992, 290–92) Mark's concern is essentially christological, and his purpose is to subordinate the christological claims of Jesus as miracle worker to the central christological significance of Jesus' suffering and death. The messianic secret is that God's revelation occurs not in the demonstration of miraculous power but in the crucifixion of the divine human being.

According to Werner Kelber, Mark was written after the fall of Jerusalem to speak for an open, law-free Galilean Christianity and to speak to (and against) a southern, Jerusalem Christianity that was so Jewish in Mark's eyes as to be indistinguishable from the position of the scribes and Pharisees (Kelber 1974, 1, 21–22, 51–53, 59, 62, 64–65, 129–32). In Kelber's view the Jerusalem group, on the one hand, seems to be without hope or fulfillment because it had tied its hope for the coming of the kingdom to the fall of the temple. The temple fell, but the kingdom did not arrive. On the other hand, the Jerusalem group, or its leaders, is guilty of a prematurely realized eschatology. The false messiahs of Mark 13:6, 21–22 are not references to Vespasian, as held by Theissen. Rather they refer to the claim of Mark's theological opponents in Jerusalem that Messiah Jesus is making his eschatological appearance in them (1, 14, 113, 115–16, 138–39).

Howard Clark Kee argues that Mark was written before the fall of Jerusalem, possibly in Galilee but more probably in rural Syria. The picture of the disciples in the Gospel reveals a community summoned to abandon family and business in order to follow Jesus. This produces a transformation in the social and economic structures so that the natural family is replaced by a new community devoted to the will of God (Kee 1977, 87–90, 101–5). Like Jewish apocalyptic communities Mark's church was an alienated group activated by a charismatic prophetic figure to hope for the ultimate political and social transformation of the world (78–81, 83, 86, 93–34, 100).

Burton Mack has given perhaps the most radical interpretation of Mark in recent years. The Gospel was written in some city of southern Syria (not Antioch) in the aftermath of two events that created a critical situation for the author: (1) the destruction of the Jerusalem temple; (2) the failure of the synagogue reform movement (Mack 1988, 166, 316, 318). The synagogue reform movement was one segment of the early Jesus movement, and while the people in this movement thought of themselves as fundamentally Jewish, they had a relatively law-free message to which they hoped to win the synagogues to which they belonged. They failed in this effort and were rejected by the synagogue. This group, which thought of itself as Israelite, found itself unacceptable to the synagogue and thus was painfully uncertain about its purpose and in desperate need of a rationale for its independent existence. The author of Mark was a scribe of the synagogue reform movement and wrote to respond to their crisis (94–96, 318–21, 355).

The Evangelist had access to the conflict stories nurtured by his own group as well as sayings of Jesus, miracle stories, and traditions of the Christ cult of northern Syria. The latter understood Jesus as a divine being and focused on his death and resurrection. Mark used all of these materials in constructing a narrative on the model of the Hellenistic biography (Mack 1988, 98–100, 204–5). The Jesus whom Mark portrayed is a figure of tremendous authority, but despite his authority — and innocence — he is plotted against and killed, an innocent victim in the hands of tyrants. Mark developed the resurrection of Jesus, not as a medium of his spiritual presence, but as the assurance of his eschatological vindication with power (205, 308–9, 355–56).

Mack's very negative evaluation of the Markan theological project (see 1988, 368–76) can be seen concretely in his analysis of the conflict stories. According to Mack these stories do not really record debates between Jesus and the Pharisees or between the synagogue reform movement and the Pharisees. They rather display the way these Jesus people wanted to imagine these conflicts in retrospect. The logic of the dialogues is inauthentic, for it simply assumes and asserts Jesus' authority without giving any rationale for it. The Markan fiction that Jesus won the debates with his opponents compensates for the fact that the synagogue reform movement actually lost them (203–4). The Markan community is enabled by the narrative to see itself in what befell Jesus. If Jesus' own fate was rejection and violence, what else could his followers expect? Jesus' death for the many was understood as effective for the community, and his vindication would also be theirs (167, 321, 355).

The last scholarly analysis to be mentioned is that of Mary Ann Tolbert. She is less specific than the others in her judgments about factual probabilities and also has a different theoretical position regarding the relationship of the Markan narrative to its historical context. Early in her book she opines that Mark was written during a time of war and persecution but that one can hardly be more specific than to say that the author was writing during the second half of the first century to a Greek-speaking, predominantly Gentile audience (Tolbert 1989, 36). Toward the end of her work she concludes that on the basis of the story alone the Gospel could have been written in almost any city of the Mediterranean world. However, Mark's lack of geographical knowledge points away from Palestine. Cautiously she seems to lean toward Rome as the place of writing because Rome opposed public religious gatherings and periodically persecuted Christian preachers. This situation might point to the need for a written tract (305).

Tolbert's approach is literary-critical, and in consequence she pursues the question of Mark's genre. While Mark has its own distinctive qualities, the genre to which it has the most striking affinities is the ancient popular novel (Tolbert 1989, 20, 60, 62, 65, 70–78). What unites the extant examples of these popular novels is the myth of the isolated individual in a dangerous world (64). And one important formal link between Mark and the ancient novels is the combination of the historiographic form with epic and dramatic substance (74).

In Tolbert's view narrative in principle is not well suited for carrying on theological polemic (1989, 303). She suggests that Mark was not written in response to the problems of a particular community but was intended for a wide readership. It was not aimed at groups but was composed for individuals belonging to two categories: (1) Christians experiencing persecution and in need of encouragement; (2) individuals interested in Christianity but not yet fully committed (304).

We have seen some variety among scholarly judgments about the time and place of the Markan composition, and we have observed very considerable variety among opinions regarding the character of the specific religious-social-political situation that may have prompted the original purpose of the Gospel. These proposed purposes express concerns to which Mark may have wanted to naturalize or accommodate the Jesus tradition.

Theological Significance of the Historical Situation

The variety of critical conclusions that we have surveyed shows that it is very difficult to be exact about the historical setting of Mark, and the same thing is true with regard to the other Gospels. The reason why it is inherently difficult to achieve strong probability is that there is very little *clear* and *exact* evidence from sources outside of the Gospels to compare with the suggestions that the texts themselves make about the situations that occasioned them. Moreover, elements that are apparently generated by the surrounding societies or by the dynamics of the Evangelists' communities and that appear in the Gospel texts take on meaning from the literary context or horizon provided by the narrative texts themselves. These internal textual relationships — created by plot, parallelism, metaphorical connections, irony, et cetera — obscure reference to the outside world and make it ambiguous but do not destroy it (Jacobson 1972, 90, 93, 95–96, 112).

The internalizing power of the whole story's horizon means that the social world depicted in a Gospel is most immediately a fictitious narrative world. For example, the critique that Mark has Jesus give of the scribes and Pharisees' view of the law might point to a real historical conflict between Mark's community and the synagogue. But it could also — and to some extent undoubtedly does — derive from the Gospel's programmatic position that the coming of the kingdom in Jesus has greatly marginalized the law and from Mark's composition of stories, or modification of stories, to dramatize that theological claim. We can determine the degree to which a Gospel's narrative world approximates the real world in which the Gospel was written only if we have clear and definite evidence from that real world with which to compare the narrative world. We do not, however, have contemporary external evidence that *tightly* connects the Gospels with a specific situation that closely resembles the world of the Gospel narratives. If we did, we would not see such differences in critical judgments. Nor do the Gospel narratives point definitely enough to their situations of origin for us to identify those situations with high probability.

What are we to conclude from this critical quandary? If we cannot determine the exact situations in which the Gospels were written, we can demonstrate that the Gospels reflect in a broad way various forms of Jewish and Graeco-Roman thought and institutions. It seems not amiss, then, to conclude that the Gospels refer to historical and cultural phenomena with which the readers were somewhat familiar and in which they could feel in some way at home. Clearly the Gospels depict concrete and dramatic life situations as they unfold their narrative worlds. These life situations intertwine tradition, free creative composition, and indirect reference to a real historical world. The last is what makes the (partly fictitious) life situations familiar. It is also the case that a part of what would be familiar to early readers (and hearers) of the Gospels would be the Jesus tradition itself, which they would have heard. At the same time that tradition is now made unfamiliar by the Evangelists' creative composition.

Thus we can affirm that the life situations depicted in the Gospels were not *radically* strange to the readers and hearers and that the Evangelists were seeking by means of the life situations to naturalize the Jesus tradition to the real historical situations of the readers/hearers. That is, given the nature of the life situations as depicted in the previous paragraph, we can conclude that the Evangelists were assimilating the Jesus tradition to a real historical world that was familiar and natural while at the same time stretching and defamiliarizing both the Jesus tradition and the familiar world. This needs to be spelled out somewhat for its theological significance.

The indirect reference to the real historical situation gives the narratives a familiarity and naturalness, a pertinence for the readers without which they would not have a sufficient point of contact with the story. The point of contact with historical reality is necessary if the narrative is to make sense to the readers. The Spirit can imprint on the heart only a meaning that makes sense in the real situation of the recipient of revelation. The theological significance of the real historical element in the Gospel narratives, then, is that it affords an intelligible meaning that the Spirit can use. At the same time the factor of imaginative composition makes the familiar world and tradition also unfamiliar, that is, disclosed in a new light. Without this there would be no unveiling of what was previously hidden.

This all adds up to saying that we can describe in very general terms something of the character of the real historical situations in which the Gospels were written. From such congruence as there is between the narrative worlds of the Gospels and our general knowledge of Jewish and Graeco-Roman life, we can say broadly speaking what — or what kind of — historical situations the Gospels were addressing. The early readers/hearers experienced the Gospels as referring to life situations that were generally analogous to the real situations in which they lived. For modern readers these biblical life situations become part of the linguistic tradition that the modern readers must then naturalize to their real situations — as they also allow their life situations to be transformed. This first section of the chapter has dealt primarily with the kind of historical exigencies that might have prompted the original purposes of the Gospel of Mark. The remainder of the chapter represents my attempt to interpret Mark in the light of my (corrigible) social location while at the same time maintaining a relationship with the horizon of the Gospel that both engages the Gospel's content and reads it questioningly. While my interpretations do not always directly engage the historical situations of the Gospels, I intend that those historical situations should provide parameters for meaning that are not unduly stretched.

The Word as Content and Power

As I move into a more explicit discussion of Mark, I should say that I will not be treating the Gospels as sources or as redactions of sources but as whole stories in which tradition and redaction are both integral parts of content. At times it may sound as if I am contrasting a redactional point (say in Matthew) with its source (Mark). But what I will actually be doing is comparing a point or theme in one whole story with its parallel or absence or transformation in another whole story.

In Mark Jesus' word, as well as the word about him, is an instrument of power. The people are astonished at the authority of his teaching (Mark 1:22), and interestingly this authoritative teaching includes his powerful words that expel the demons (1:27). Teaching and exorcism are joined. His teaching is a power that expels the demonic, a miracle. The miracle is a teaching — an understanding — about the new reality that has emerged in the world. This authoritative word is able to effect healing, forgiveness, and life itself (1:41–42; 2:5, 10–11; 5:8, 13, 41–42; 7:34–35; 9:25–26). This word provides the continuity between the time of Jesus and the church because Jesus' words will not pass away (13:31). His word has as its content the kingdom of God (1:14–15, 38), the cross (8:31–32), and Jesus' ethical demand (7:12–13).

Mark uses the word *logos* (word), a characteristic New Testament term for Christian preaching (1 Cor 1:18), not only of Jesus' speech but also for the word about him. In its first appearance in Mark (1:45) the *logos* is the story of Jesus' healing of the leper that the leper preached (*kērussein* — the characteristic verb for the act of preaching in the New Testament). The result of this "preaching" by the leper and others is that people thronged to Jesus (1:28, 45; 3:7–12). Both the woman with the hemorrhage and blind Bartimaeus heard these stories and, as a result, came to him (5:27) or sought him (10:47). This seeking is interpreted as faith (5:34; 10:52). Thus Jesus' word has the power to bring people to faith.

The Problem of Effective Revelation: The Messianic Secret

In Mark the word as power becomes more ambiguous when it confronts the human condition. How really effective is the power? The word that Jesus preaches and that preaches him is puzzling and mysterious. It makes a disclosure, but the disclosure is concealed at the source. That is what has long been called Mark's "messianic secret."

I argue that Mark's messianic secret is composed of two related paradoxes between which Mark makes no explicit connection. The first I will call the "outsider motif." The revelation given to outsiders (nondisciples), although *given*, is nevertheless concealed. The demons, who know who Jesus is (Mark 1:24), are ordered not to disclose this (1:25, 34; 3:12). Silence about Jesus' performance is ordered by him in connection with three healings (1:40–45; 5:21–24, 35–43; 7:31–37). Outsiders are prevented from understanding Jesus' parabolic word (4:10–12). The disciples are not to tell anyone that Jesus is Messiah (8:30). We could say that this motif has a threefold structure: (1) the revelation is given; (2) it is concealed at the source by Jesus; (3) as a result the people do not grasp his identity or the meaning of his teaching. As a matter of fact, the forbidden word is sometimes spread (1:45; 7:36), but Jesus' intention that he should not be known, that the disclosure should be concealed revelation, cannot be thwarted. The people who hear Jesus identified by the unclean spirit as the Holy One of God obviously do not get it (1:27). Although in 2:10 Jesus uses his primary self-designation — Son of man — there is no uptake of this by those who hear him (2:12). When we reach the midpoint of the story, there are a lot of opinions already in the land about who Jesus is (8:28), but none of them is right. And even after he has in some way accepted the confession that he is Messiah and reinterpreted this to the disciples as suffering Son of man, and has announced to all the officials assembled around the high priest that he is the apocalyptic Son of man, at the end of the story the people refuse to consider that he is their king and call for his crucifixion (15:9–15). And yet some of those from the outside come to faith: the Gerasene demoniac, the woman with the hemorrhage, and the Roman centurion, for example.

The second messianic secret paradox I will call the "insider motif." Jesus *plainly* discloses his true identity to his disciples: he is the suffering-dying-rising Son of man (Mark 8:31; 9:31; 10:32–

34), but they do not understand it (8:32–33; 9:32–34; 10:35–41). That is, when revelation is openly given, human beings resist the existential entailments of what they know intellectually. At the discursive level Peter understands the point quite well enough to reject it (8:32–33). The misunderstanding of the disciples is an unwillingness to accept suffering as the pattern of their own existence.

The insider motif has a twofold structure: (1) the revelation is given; (2) it is misunderstood. The disciple motif lacks the middle item of the outsider motif: that the revelation is concealed by the revealer. One possible elusive exception to this is the strange statement in the story of the walking on the water: He (Jesus) meant to pass them by (Mark 6:48). This suggests that Jesus somehow intends to conceal himself also from his disciples, which brings the insider motif closer to the outsider one and raises the question of the interrelationship of the two motifs. Mark makes no explicit effort to connect them, but the reader-response critic, as least in the Iserian mode, has the right, if not the responsibility, to turn the text into a work by creating cohesion where it was lacking in the text.

The insider motif needs the outsider motif to explain why the disciples, who receive a plain word, do not understand it. They misunderstand in part because they will not to assimilate an understanding of discipleship that involves suffering. But there is more. Jesus gives revelation, but he also veils it. However, he veils it, as we have seen, from outsiders, not insiders. Why then do the insiders not understand? On what ground can the interpreter assert that the concealment from the outsiders applies also to the insiders? It can be asserted on the ground that the insider/outsider categories in Mark are unstable. The two groups exchange places. What is said of the outsiders in Mark 4:11–12 is said of the disciples in 8:17–18. The insider-disciples then are also outsiders so that they, too, do not get it because Jesus conceals it from them. That is, he conceals it from outsiders — which the insiders ironically are.

Why does Mark need to say that revelation fails because the revealer veils what he discloses? The interpreter again, not Mark, supplies the answer to this question. Mark needs the concealment motif in order to connect his Christology to the failure of both crowd and disciples to grasp the revelation. Jesus is Son of God (1:1, 11; 9:7; 15:39) and eschatological Son of man (2:10, 28; 8:38; 13:26–27; 14:62). His word has the power of miracle to bring people to faith (1:25–28; 2:10–12; 10:47, 52). How could a presence and word of this magnitude — the eschatological magnitude — fail if it were not concealed by the revealer himself?

I would like to draw out my understanding of the messianic secret by responding critically to one aspect of Tolbert's interpretation of it in her excellent book on Mark. In her view the messianic secret serves two functions. (1) It shows that Jesus does not seek renown and glory. (2) It buys time, postpones the denouement till the seed of the gospel has been sown in all the soils. Then in Mark 14:62 Jesus publicly affirms that he is the Christ and Son of God, resoundingly smashing any remnants of secrecy (Tolbert 1989, 217, 227–29, 295).

I believe that Tolbert's interpretation misunderstands the nature of the secret in Mark. In saying that the secret is smashed by Jesus' public pronouncement of himself as Messiah and Son of man before the Jewish officials (Mark 14:61–62), she assumes that the secret is a matter of concealing information about Jesus. The very fact, however, that we have secrecy along with the many public disclosures — and she is right about the disclosures — should alert us to the possibility that the secret does not essentially have to do with information. What we see is (1) that information is disclosed, (2) but there is still a secret (as we shall see momentarily); (3) therefore, what is lacking is not information. That it is not information is made abundantly clear in 4:11–12; 6:1–6; 8:17–18. What constitutes the secret is not a withholding of information but a withholding/failure of understanding, existential understanding. The essence of the secret is that people do indeed see and hear but do not understand. Thus the many disclosures along the way, including the climactic one before the high priest, do not in any way dispel the secret. The high priest still does not know who Jesus is. People continue to see and hear without understanding. The Nazareth scene is a good example. Jesus' fellow townspeople acknowledge his miracles and wisdom but finally reject him because they cannot accept the presence of the extraordinary in the familiar. It is too great a strain on their preconceptions.

Secrecy, then, is not a postponement of disclosure until a certain point in the story, but rather enigma qualifies the very nature of the revelation that Jesus brings. It is not a strategy to buy time. And the unfolding of the narrative discourse demonstrates that the secrecy does not terminate. Revelation is still concealed at the very end. The resurrection of Jesus was supposed to clear things up (Mark 9:9). But that hope is made ironical by the fact that no resurrection appearance is narrated, and the message that Jesus is risen is compromised by the fact that the women fail to proclaim it (16:8). Furthermore, the disclosure continues to be concealed beyond the resurrection and into the life of the church since what the disciples so consistently fail to understand — the suffering, death, and resurrection of the Son of man — is the postresurrection kerygma of the church. Thus the concealedness of revelation is Mark's fundamental conviction about the nature of revelation *per se*, although the event of the resurrection slightly shifts the emphasis in the opposition concealed/revealed off of concealed and onto revealed (Via 1985, 54–57). That is, prior to Jesus' resurrection the meaning of his teaching and action is both revealed and concealed, but the stress is on concealment. After his resurrection the meaning of his mission is still both revealed and concealed, but now the stress is on disclosure. There are hints that the disciples have now got the point (Mark 10:39; 13:3–5, 9–11, 13) — in part.

These conclusions lead me to disagree strongly with the contention of Robert Fowler that there is no messianic secret for the reader of Mark because who Jesus is is made clear from the first verse: he is Christ and Son of God (Fowler 1981, 158). But against this it should be observed that the reader is in the same situation as the disciples in Mark 8–10 who misunderstand the post-Easter proclamation of the church. For the reader, as for the characters in the story, the mystery is not dispelled by the dispensing of information but by the achievement of understanding.

Mark 4:11–12 is probably the harshest expression of the messianic secret and, therefore, deserves special attention. Jesus speaks in parables — enigmas — in order that or for the purpose that the outsiders who see and hear might not understand (*hina* introduces purpose clauses). But the mystery of the kingdom has been given to the disciples. Fowler in his more recent book has argued that 4:11–12 should be taken ironically (1) because if it is not, it is contrary to 1:14–15, where Jesus proclaims the kingdom in a clear and straightforward way, and (2) because 4:13 shows that the disciples do not understand any more than the outsiders do about the parable (1991, 101–2, 169–70). Let it be granted to Fowler that the narrative does render ironical the implied understanding of the disciples in 4:11a and also makes ironical the explanations of the parables given to the disciples that are referred to in 4:14–20, 34b. Mark 6:52 and 8:17–21 show that the explanations did not really explain, and the obdurate lack of comprehension on the part of the disciples following Mark 8:31–32 demonstrates that the "open" teaching of those verses was not really open.

But the intention to prevent the outsiders from understanding expressed in Mark 4:11b–12 should be taken at face value and not ironically. Even if the straightforward meaning were contrary to 1:14–15, that would not be a definitive reason for taking it as ironic, for Mark might have deconstructed himself. But the face value meaning is not necessarily contrary to 1:14–15. Mark 1:14–15 states *that* the kingdom was proclaimed but makes no prescription about *how* it was proclaimed or the nature of its reception. Thus it does not preclude the *how* affirmed in 4:11b–12 — that is, that it was proclaimed enigmatically, in order to keep outsiders out. The continued failures of both insiders and outsiders to understand show that Jesus' purpose was in fact to conceal. And the irony that insiders and outsiders change places does not mean that the stated intention to conceal is ironical. That exchange of places rather shows that the intention to conceal affects *all* hearers. Something is said about the nature of revelation: it is veiled at the source.

But the parabolic word of Jesus in Mark not only intends to conceal (4:11–12); it also intends to reveal. Mark 4:21–22 contains four purpose clauses that tell us the intention of the word, imaged as light (a lamp, *lychnos*), is to be seen. Nothing is hidden except for the purpose of being brought to visibility. The word is revealed in order to be concealed (4:11–12) and concealed in order to be revealed (4:21–22). Its ultimate purpose is revelation — making manifest. But concealment is also an inherent part of revelation as Mark understands it. That the concealment is necessary is a fundamental conviction of Mark, and possibly a part of the necessity for the concealment is that it defines Mark's understanding of faith. Revelation and faith mutually define each other. A particular understanding of each is necessary for the understanding of the other. This is the way existence before God presents itself to Mark. It cannot be understood otherwise.

What mediates between — leads from — the word's being revealed in order to conceal and its being concealed in order to be made manifest? It is the word itself. Despite its many and varied failures (Mark 4:14–19), it finally produces a fruitful hearing and acceptance (4:20). In the context of 4:20–22, where hearing is not *contrasted* with understanding as it is in 4:11–12, hearing means hearing-with-understanding. And that for Mark is virtually indistinguishable from faith. The word as concealing-and-revealing and faith interacting with each other mediate between revealed-to-conceal and concealed-to-reveal.

Faith (*pistis*) would be the opposite of the unfaith (*apistia*) that is manifested by the people of Nazareth (Mark 6:6). They in fact sense the authority of Jesus' words and deeds (6:2) but resent the fact that this appears in an ordinary and familiar person whom they know (6:2–3), an artisan and family member. They reject him because the possibility of the eschatological within the ordinary puts too great a strain on their preconceptions. The revealing word for Mark has to be concealing because the eschatological one who is revealed appears only in the everyday. And this defines *faith* as the capacity to see through the ordinary — or even through what appears to be the crazy or possessed (3:21–30) — to Jesus' true identity. The word produces hearing as faith, and hearing as faith enables the concealing word to be a revealing word. The word generates faith, and faith, as the capacity to penetrate the veil of the everyday, sees through the concealing word and the appearance of mere ordinariness to the true identity hidden in this familiar, socially located human being.

But Mark is still more subtly penetrating. He distinguishes faith from preunderstanding, and it is preunderstanding that mediates between word and faith. That is, Mark distinguishes between the measure one brings to hearing the word and the measure one receives from hearing (4:24). And the measure one brings (preunderstanding) defines the measure one receives (faith). Hearing with understanding, or faith (4:24a), is given to those who already have it (4:25a), but those who do not have it will have even what they have (not) taken away from them (4:25b). In sum, the word interacts with preunderstanding to produce faith so that word and faith working together lead from revealed-in-order-to-conceal to concealed-in-order-to-reveal and to salvation.

I shall conclude this section by briefly relating Mark's understanding of the word to two of his other leading themes — the coming of the kingdom of God (1:14–15; 9:1; 10:14–15, 23–24; 12:34; 14:25) and the redemptive suffering and death of the Son of man (8:31; 9:31; 10:33–34, 45; 14:21). Put very succinctly, the kingdom of God is likened to the sowing of seed (4:26), and the sown seed is allegorically interpreted by Mark as the word (4:3, 14). Therefore, the occurrence of the kingdom is the working of the word (4:14–20), the power of the word to produce fruit (4:20).

Mark's most illuminating interpretation of the redemption accomplished by the death of the Son of man is the juxtaposing of the saying that the Son of man gives his life as a ransom for the many (10:45) to the story of the restoration of sight to blind Bartimaeus

(10:46–52). The linking of these two units suggests that the death of the Son of man saves by giving sight. In Mark seeing is an image of understanding (4:12; 8:17–18), and understanding is what Jesus has been trying to lead his disciples to (4:13; 8:21; 9:32), not theoretical understanding, but that which comes from participation in his ministry of suffering self-giving (8:34–38; 9:35–37; 10:35–45). That is the kind of understanding that Bartimaeus has gained, for he demonstrates his sight by following Jesus on his way to Jerusalem and death (10:52). So then Jesus' death as Son of man saves by giving understanding, and the word also saves by giving the understanding that resides in faith (4:13–20, 21–25). This implies that for Mark Jesus' death saves by being manifested in and through the narrative word about his total mission, which has the power to bring people to faith (1:28, 45; 3:7–8; 5:26–27, 34; 10:47, 52; 13:31).

The Contribution of Human Reception to Revelation

Mark, as we shall see, has a more optimistic appraisal of the *strictly human* potential for understanding than does Matthew. This is a little surprising in view of Mark's dark picture of the disciples' lack of understanding and his emphasis on hardness of heart. Hardness of heart is a peculiarly Markan motif that appears four times in the Gospel (3:5; 6:52; 8:17; 10:5). Luke lacks three of these pericopes and lacks the reference to hardness of heart in the one that it contains (Luke 6:6–11). Matthew contains all four of the Markan pericopes but lacks the reference to hardness of heart except in the divorce pericope (Matt 19:1–12).

The heart in Mark (7:19, 21, 23), as in the Bible generally, is the hidden inner core of a person, so hardness of heart is the deformation of that inner core, the seat of will and understanding. Mark 3:5 attributes hardness of heart to Jesus' opponents, in whom it takes the form of a hostility to Jesus that puts ritual correctness above a concern for life. Mark 6:52 and 8:17 ascribe it to the disciples, in whom it expresses itself as a culpable failure to understand the kingdom. In 10:5 hardness of heart is the ground for conduct inappropriate to God's dealing with the world and is attributed to Israel generally and by implication to all people. Hardness of heart is the disfiguration of the wellspring of understanding, faith, and moral resolve and is ingenerate in human beings universally. That being the case, salvation is impossible from the standpoint of human resources but is still possible because all things are possible with God (10:26–27). God contributes everything, and human reception contributes nothing.

Mark's strong emphasis on the universality of epidemic hardness of heart and on the disciples' failure to understand makes it easy to miss the opposing, more optimistic strand in Mark. That is the case with Stephen Moore's book on Mark and Luke, which stresses the failure of the disciples (1992, 13, 22) and concludes that if there is any hope for understanding, it is in the power of the word (26). Yet recall that Mark's Jesus, after speaking about the intention of the word to bring the hidden to light (4:21–22), calls on the audience to hear (4:23). If anyone has ears to hear, he or she is to hear. This is a first-class conditional sentence with the condition in the indicative. It is *not* undetermined *whether but* is assumed *that* people do have ears to hear. And the very fact of putting people under the imperative to hear shows that something can be expected of them. In Mark the measure of understanding that one brings to the hearing of the word has a positive effect on the faith-understanding that is received (4:24–25). Mark, of course, also has in view the opposite possibility. One can have the kind of preunderstanding that prevents understanding (4:25b).

But Mark attributes to human reception universally the actual possibility of positive, generative power. The imperative to hear is addressed in a very general way to "anyone" (Mark 4:23). And while the parable discourse in which this imperative appears is addressed to the disciples and some parts of it to them alone (4:10), the crowd was a part of the audience at the beginning (4:1) and at some point has come back in before the end (4:33–34). Clearly for Mark there are recipients of the word who receive it unproductively — the path (4:15), the rocky ground (4:16), and the thorny soil (4:18). If we look at the whole of Mark 4:10–19, the intertwined reasons for the failure of the word to achieve understanding are complex: the enigmatic character of the revealing word itself, the hostile intervention of Satan, difficult external circumstances, faith's subjective lack of staying power, and a desire for wealth.

But there are also those — imaged as the good earth (gē) — who hear the word with understanding (Mark 4:20). The earth image is then picked up in the parable of the earth producing of itself (4:26–29). Here again the sown seed represents the preached word, and the earth stands for the hearer. The earth produces "of itself" (automatically, *automatē*; 4:28). Something comes from the hearer's own self — the measure of understanding that generates more understanding (4:24–25). This is owed to the created goodness of humankind, which is even more basic than hardness of heart (Mark 10:5–6) although it is never unaffected by hardness of heart.

Fowler has stressed the large role that Mark leaves for the reader in creating the meaning of the Gospel text. The reader has the task of filling in gaps, mediating tensions, answering unanswered questions, and taking up for consideration elements that are ignored by characters (Fowler 1991, 17–18, 36, 57, 74–77, 89, 96–97, 116, 122, 132–33, 135–36, 143, 161, 163, 199). This extends the Markan theme that we have been considering. Since the reader has a part in creating the meaning of the text and since the text conceives of itself as a communication from God — good news about God's Son — the reader's reception has a role in constituting the content of revelation.

In summary, for Mark human beings as such — and not just human beings after they have been illumined by the gospel — are endowed with a capacity for understanding that contributes to the content of revelation. They have a light that merges with the light of the word. As earth they have a power "in themselves" that helps the seed-word to be productive. The initiative in revelation is from God. There is a word from God to be heard (Mark 4:14, 20, 23); there is light to bring things to visibility (4:21–22); there is seed to which the earth responds (4:26–29). At the same time the responsive seeing, hearing, and understanding of human beings makes a constitutive contribution to the content of revelation (4:24–25).

From the standpoint of the implied author the magnitude of the human role can be abundantly seen. We need to keep in mind that all forms carry implicit meaning. Mark employs such short forms as parable, proverb, miracle story, and conflict story and such versatile constructions as metaphor and irony. The narrative as a whole has suggested kinship with tragicomedy (Via 1975), ancient biography (Koester 1983), and the ancient popular novel (Tolbert 1989). All of the aforementioned categories are cross-cultural and not peculiarly biblical; therefore, they demonstrate the continuity between the Gospel and nonbiblical interpretations of reality.

How does this "natural" human contribution relate to Mark's affirmation that salvation is impossible from the human standpoint but possible with God? Mark is making two claims that seem to form a clear contradiction: (1) everything comes from God; (2) something comes from the human side. The Gospel makes no effort to solve the conflict, nor does it give any evidence of being aware of it. Yet in a brief, passing remark it inserts something that moderates the opposition. Even the sower of the seed, that is, Jesus the preacher of the word, the revealer, does not know how the seed sprouts (Mark 4:27–28). The contradictory claims (everything from the word of God but something from human beings) do not confront each other head-on because a mystery is inserted between them. No one knows exactly how revealing word and human reception interact with each other.

We have now seen that the four elements that constitute the revelation situation are present in Mark and are given a particular twist by the presiding horizon of the messianic secret. It is evident that I, in dealing with the four constituents of revelation, have not always taken the same posture toward the text. When treating the content and power of the word, I have sometimes been a reader, placing myself in the story and simply observing the relationships between Jesus and/or his word and other characters. Jesus teaches and casts out a demon by his word, and the people comment on the newness and authority of his teaching (Mark 1:21–28). The word about what Jesus has been doing spreads, and people come to him (1:28, 45; 3:8: 5:27; 10:47). He teaches his disciples about the death and resurrection of the Son of man, but they fail to understand (9:31–32). At other points, however, I have taken a more critical step back from the text. In discussing the relationship between the two messianic secret motifs, I make a claim that is only potentially supported in the discourse of the implied author and is not observed or commented on by characters. Even less explicit in the text — but nevertheless supportable — is my contention that Jesus' own concealment of revelation is necessary in order to connect the failure of people to understand with Mark's Christology. (See the discussion in chap. 3 of the latent meaning of texts.) My treatment of human reception has similarly sought to keep in dialogue the text and my own hermeneutical standpoint. That is also true of my discussion of the historical situation, while in that connection I have also taken into account a number of assessments of the possible relationship between the Markan text and its cultural context.

These different postures are justified because understanding a text requires attention to a multiplicity of factors: author, text, historical context, readers, interpreter (with his or her unique subjectivity), social location of interpreter, etc. It is appropriate to focus on different factors at different times and for different purposes. They cannot all be foregrounded at the same time.

Chapter 5

MATTHEW

The Historical Situation

I shall look very selectively at Matthean scholarship regarding the historical setting and purpose of the Gospel. While differences of opinion are probably not as diverse as is the case with Mark, there is still considerable variety. Matthew's explicit mention of the word "church" (*ekklēsia;* 16:18; 18:17) naturally influences judgment about the nature and purpose of the Gospel and probably exercises some control over the variety of critical opinions. There are also other important factors that give to Matthew a certain definiteness and probably limit its multiple interpretability in comparison with Mark.

The Gospel of Matthew had connections with both Jewish and Gentile Christianity. The strong Jewish flavor can be seen in the affirmation of the authority of the law (Matt 5:17–20; 23:1–2), although Matthew's legal strand is moderated by grace themes and is less unambiguous than it may appear to be (see Via 1990, 83–89, 134–37). Nevertheless works of obedience are a condition for salvation in Matthew (5:20; 6:15; 7:21–27; 16:27; 18:34–35), and the Gospel is replete with elaborate demonstrations that Jesus fulfills the eschatological hopes of Israel. On the other hand, Matthew gives his unqualified support to the Gentile mission of the church in his climactic conclusion (28:18–20) and acknowledges the mixed nature of the church (13:24–30, 36–43, 47–50; 22:8–10, 11–14). Scholars differ in their assessments of both the Jewish and Gentile elements as well as in their interpretations of the interrelationships of those two dimensions.

There is fairly general agreement among scholars that Matthew was written between A.D. 80 and 100 and that its community was located somewhere in Syria or nearby (e.g., Kilpatrick 1946, 140; Davies and Allison 1988, 130, 138; Koester 1983, 171; Meier 1979, 13–15). There is considerable difference of opinion, however, about exactly where in the Syrian region to place it, about the particular religious-historical-cultural situation to which the author was responding, and about the precise purpose of the response.

That is, there are divergent views about the situation to which Matthew was seeking to naturalize the Jesus tradition as he also reinterpreted the tradition and defamiliarized the cultural world.

In this section I am presenting the historical conclusions of the scholars discussed and am for the most part not debating with them. In the first part of chapter 4 I gave my own assessment of the diversity of scholarly opinion and of the complicated relationship between narrative world and real historical world as that pertains to the Gospels. It should be pointed out, however, that the scholars surveyed here hardly glance, as they draw their historical conclusions, at the fact that a narrative world is interposed between the text and the real world and between the reader-critic and the real world. Nor does one notice a lot of literary-critical close reading of the subtle nuances of Matthew's understanding of the law.

I begin with those who emphasize Matthew's Jewish connections by briefly noting G. D. Kilpatrick's judgment that Matthew wrote — probably with the approval and authority of his community — in close contact with and in opposition to Pharisaism and probably in a Phoenician port city. In Kilpatrick's view the evangelist's purpose was to compose a comprehensive and suitable gospel book for the liturgy and exposition of the church (1946, 140).

In the opinion of W. D. Davies and Dale C. Allison, Matthew's Jewish atmosphere, along with its support of the mission to the Gentiles, points probably to a Jewish Christian author writing in Syrian Antioch, since Antioch was a major Gentile city with a large Jewish population (Davies and Allison 1988, 58, 137, 144). While Matthew neither polemicizes against Jewish Christianity nor abandons the Jewish mission, he does manifest an animus against the leaders of Judaism (134, 137–38). This hostility is understandable against the background of the efforts of the Pharisees at Jamnia to consolidate Judaism and to make it more homogeneous in the years following the destruction of the temple in A.D. 70. Two important initiatives of this Pharisaic movement were (1) the curse against Christians, which was added circa A.D. 85 to the twelfth benediction of the synagogue prayer known as the Eighteen Benedictions, and (2) the beginning of the codification of the oral law that culminated in the Mishnah circa A.D. 220. Davies believes that Matthew, and especially the Sermon on the Mount, is to be understood as a Christian mishnaic counterpart to the activity of the Pharisees at Jamnia (1964, 256, 265–66, 275–76, 315).

With regard to Matthew's response to his Christian context

Davies holds that the Gospel is seeking to validate Jesus' words for the life of the church by moderating the radicalness of Q's understanding of Jesus' teachings. It does this by making the teachings regulatory. In Matthew we see a neolegalistic society emerging (Davies 1964, 401). However, despite this acknowledgment Davies is reluctant to say that Matthew had modified Jesus' own intention in any really distorting way (433, 435).

One of the reasons for locating Matthew in Antioch is that Ignatius of Antioch in the early second century apparently made use of the Gospel. But that reasoning is not unproblematical, and William R. Schoedel takes up the question of how Ignatius can be indebted to gospel material of a Matthean kind and yet exhibit a type of Christianity so different from that of Matthew's Jewish Christianity. The Antioch of Ignatius can hardly have been the context for the writing of Matthew, and yet the gospel materials of a Matthean type used by Ignatius point to the Antioch region as the provenance of Matthew (Schoedel 1991, 144, 151). Schoedel considers various possible solutions to this puzzle and seems to favor the view that Matthew was written in the general area of Antioch and then was brought to and received by the church there (151, 176).

With regard to Matthew's provenance Alan Segal manifests a certain tendency to favor Galilee (1991, 16, 27) but seems actually to prefer the less-specific alternative of the geographical arc between Galilee and Antioch (19, 26–27, 29). The locale must have been a place where Greek was spoken and where there was a significant number of both Jews and Gentiles (29). Matthew's community was a part of Jewish Christianity (8), and these Matthean Christians were distinguished from ordinary Jews by their worship of Jesus as Lord (9, 15). This Christian confession, however, had not separated them from the synagogue, of which they were still a part (5, 34).

In Segal's opinion Matthew's position on the law was a more mature and evolved version of Peter's moderating attitude, and it attempts a compromise between a stricter Jewish Christianity and Gentile Christianity (1991, 11, 18, 20). Matthew promotes retention of the law and loyalty to it, although the law is completed by Jesus' interpretation of it. The entire body of the law is still in effect for Matthew's community, but it is to be evaluated through the principle of love. The Christian confession of Matthew's community notwithstanding, these Christians are still within the spectrum of Jewish law observance (21–22, 31). Matthew is fighting against both a charismatic lawlessness, which might have Paul in mind, and a Pharisaic literal overinterpretation of the law (21–22).

In the same collection of essays in which Segal's piece appears Robert Gundry argues for a very different position. Matthew's community has made a clean break with Judaism and regarded itself as a separate entity. It was on the way to becoming the church of Ignatius's time (Gundry 1991, 63). The kingdom has been taken from Israel and given to a people producing its fruit (Matt 21:43), Jesus' people (1:21; Gundry 1991, 63–64).

Some decades earlier than Segal Gerhard Barth had developed a position quite similar to Segal's on the point of intracommunity dynamics but somewhat different on the issue of the law. For Barth Matthew no longer belongs to the strict Jewish Christian wing of the church that demanded that Gentile Christians adopt the food laws of Judaism, but evidently it does belong to a more moderate Jewish Christianity (1963, 163). The law of Moses is definitely for Matthew the law of God, and Jesus' teaching is not a new law but a new understanding of the law of Moses (158–59). Actually Matthew is engaging opponents on two fronts. Against a group of Hellenistic antinomians or libertines who believed that Jesus had abolished the law, Matthew defends the abiding validity of the whole Old Testament law (94–95, 162–64). Against the rabbinic view of the law, he argues the right interpretation of the law, an interpretation oriented to Christology and the love commandment. This leads him at some points to contradict individual Old Testament commandments (94–95, 105).

Andrew Overman acknowledges that the Matthean community had a mission to the Gentiles but concludes that the community's struggle with "formative Judaism" (Jacob Neusner's term) was the dominant, if not sole, factor that determined the shape of the Gospel (Overman 1990, 121, 145–46). The term "formative Judaism" stands for the synthesizing and constructive process that was going on in Palestinian Judaism after A.D. 70 until it developed in A.D. 135 into rabbinic Judaism, which consolidated its position after A.D. 200 (Overman 1990, 35, 154).

Overman's position seems to be that Matthew's community has broken institutionally with the synagogue (1990, 56–57); however, the community is strongly Jewish theologically while at the same time being an arch rival and opponent of formative Judaism. On the one hand, Matthew takes his stand squarely within contemporary Judaism, for he and his community claim the same tradition and history as their opponents in formative Judaism. Unlike Mark, Matthew does not give the "Jewish issues" over to the Jewish leaders (148, 157). On the other hand, formative Judaism and Matthew's community are locked in strong opposition to and competition with each other, for they have extremely divergent interpretations and understandings of Israel's law and traditions. Matthew seeks to vindicate his community in the face of formative Judaism, claims to have the true interpretation of the law, and believes that his community is the true and only faithful Israel. Anyone considering membership in the two groups would recognize that their rival claims were irreconcilable and that a choice would have to be made between them. Matthew's community and formative Judaism are two competing forms of late first-century Judaism (147–49, 153, 155, 157, 159).

Many of the social developments within the Matthean community can be understood as responses to the conflict and competition that it was experiencing. The harsh language directed at the Jewish leaders shows that formative Judaism was gaining the upper hand while Matthew's group was the underdog. The community must have been primarily Jewish in composition, for the slurs against the Gentiles (5:47; 6:7; 18:17) would not have been sympathetically received in a community with many, or any, Gentiles. Matthew's church was interested primarily in internal community formation but was beginning to look outward to the Gentile world (Overman 1990, 73, 154, 157–58).

For Overman the community of Matthew was probably located in Palestine, for that is the provenance of its competitor. Matthew's strong interest in Galilee points more specifically to that part of Palestine. Some of Matthew's imagery suggests a city, possibly Sepphoris or Tiberias. Both were domiciles of the Jewish Sanhedrin during the late first century; either was big enough to accommodate the competition between formative Judaism and Matthew's church; and either was sophisticated enough to produce a Gospel like Matthew (Overman 1990, 158–59).

Gerd Theissen vacillates slightly between saying that Matthew was written in eastern or northeastern Palestine (1991, 249–50) and that it was written somewhere in Syria — possibly Damascus or the Decapolis — but not in Antioch. Antioch apparently advocated the mission to the Gentiles from the beginning (Acts 15:1; Gal. 2:1–14) while Matthew shows traces of a struggle with it (10:6; 15:24; Theissen 1991, 251, 258). This Jewish tendency in Matthew is seen also in his redaction of the great banquet (22:1–14). The king's invitation to the feast succeeds only after the destruction of the city, which Theissen takes as an allusion to the fall of Jerusalem in A.D. 70. The bringing into the banquet of all kinds of people after the fall of the city, which resulted in a mixed community (22:11–14), suggests that Matthew's church began to extend its mission to the Gentiles only after A.D. 70 (271–72).

Because Matthew and his community are more distant from the Jewish War and its aftermath than Mark was, Matthew can turn his attention from the external problems of the war to issues internal to the church. The Evangelist is concerned about Christians' hatred of one another (Matt 24:10) and about the lawlessness caused by false prophets (7:21–23). The end of the world for Matthew is not so much a rescue from a desperate situation as a motivation for ethical action. The major task of the community now is to conduct its life in "normal times" according to Jesus' teachings (Theissen 1991, 271, 274–75).

Helmut Koester is willing not to specify the location of Matthew's community any more closely than in Syria (1983, 172) but may imply the probability of Antioch (147, 161, 167, 172). This setting is indicated by Matthew's continuation of the Petrine traditions and his use of Mark and Q (Koester 1983, 147, 161, 172). While Matthew bases his biography of Jesus on the Markan narrative with its stress on Jesus' passion, Matthew's focalizing of the discourses shows that for him the foundation of the church is not Jesus' miracles or death but his teachings (1992, 329–31).

Matthew, of course, accepts the Gentile mission, but the strong Jewish influence is seen in his presentation of Jesus' life as the fulfillment of God's promises to Israel (Koester 1992, 331) and in his claiming of the Old Testament wholly for Christianity, while also radicalizing it (1983, 175). Matthew's historical purpose was not so much to enter into polemics with opposing theological positions as to combine the conflicting traditions of different "sides" in Syrian Christianity in order to provide a canon for a unified and universal catholic church (1983, 171).

For Amy-Jill Levine, Matthew has superordinated a social axis, such as elite versus marginal, above the religious and ethnic distinction between Jew and Gentile. Leaders of both Jews and Gentiles who prevent others from participating are criticized while "marginal" is associated with "faithful" and includes both Jews and Gentiles (Levine 1988, 4, 6).

Matthew's restriction of Jesus' historical mission to the lost sheep of the house of Israel (10:5–6; 15:24) is not contrary to his universalism but serves the purpose of enacting the fulfillment of Scripture's promises to Israel. Moreover, the lost sheep of Israel do not refer to all of Israel but to those marginalized Jews who have been betrayed by and distanced from their leaders. With the Great Commission (28:19–20) this exclusivity is abrogated, although the mission to Israel is never terminated, and the privilege of Israel is extended to the Gentiles. Thus for Matthew the church contains both Jews and Gentiles, but these terms are not really functional for him, but rather both groups stand outside the church. The church contains Jews and Gentiles, but the church is neither Jewish nor Gentile. It is not the new or true Israel. It is a new kind of body introduced by Jesus' resurrection, which is simply church — *ekklēsia* (Levine 1988, 10, 14, 43, 56, 108, 166, 168, 242–43).

I find a certain problematic tension in Levine's claim that Matthew's church is not Jewish when she at the same time maintains that Matthew does not abrogate Israel's law (1988, 180–84). Were it not for this latter claim — strange in view of her overall interpretation — Levine would stand rather neatly between those who hold that Matthew understood his community as primarily Jewish Christian and those who maintain that he understand it as primarily Gentile Christian. I turn now to a much briefer look at the latter position.

In a 1947 article Kenneth Clark held that the Gentile bias of Matthew can be seen in the virgin birth concept, the heightening of miracle, the rejection of Israel (21:43), the denunciation of Pharisees (chap. 23) and Sadducees (16:6), and the Great Commission (28:19–20). Neither an interest in genealogy nor a concentration on teaching material can be attributed to Judaism in a peculiar way. Moreover, all kinds of Christians made use of the Old Testament and Jewish eschatological motifs, and the Jewish particularism of Matt 10:5–6 and 15:24 is overshadowed by the Gentile mission in the Great Commission (Clark 1947, 165).

In Clark's opinion none of the arguments for Jewish authorship rules out a Gentile author, but it is very difficult to attribute some elements of the Gentile bias to a Jewish author (1947, 165–66). Even a Hellenized Jewish Christian would hardly have taught the final rejection of Israel. Paul did not (Rom 11). Clark finds the rejection of Israel not just in Matt 21:43 but also in the parables of the two sons (21:28–32), the wedding feast (22:1–14), the ten virgins (25:1–13), the talents (25:14–30), and the sheep and the goats (25:31–46; Clark 1947, 166–67). The author of Matthew was a Gentile Christian who was persuaded that the Jews had rejected the gospel, so God had turned from them to Gentile Christianity as God's chosen people (172).

Georg Strecker has argued at length that the Jewish elements in Matthew derive primarily from the pre-Matthean church tradition used by the author of the Gospel and are not characteristic of the author himself (1971, 17–18, 28). On the other hand, the author's own (redactional) literalistic misunderstanding of the Hebrew parallelism from Zech 9:9 (cf. Matt 21:5–7) is to be explained by Hellenistic, not Jewish, thinking. Similarly the suggestion of the Matthean Jesus to the Pharisees (12:9, 11, 14) that even they would lift an animal out of a pit on the sabbath actually contravenes the rabbinic prohibition of such an act (Strecker 1971, 18–19). Matthew distinguishes the Jewish scribes as "their" scribes (7:29) from Christian scribes (13:52; 23:34) and the Jewish synagogues as "their" (4:23; 9:35) or "your" synagogues from the Christian community (Strecker 1971, 30).

On the issue of the Jewish law (which Clark hardly discusses) Strecker acknowledges that Matthew has Jesus assert its imperishability (5:17–20) but stresses that for Matthew, Jesus fulfills the law. This means that Jesus' teaching reinterprets the law in such a way that the ceremonial law is canceled and the ethical law is radicalized. The result of the reinterpretation is that certain parts of the law of Moses are abrogated (Strecker 1971, 144–47).

From such arguments Strecker concludes that the author — "redactor" for Strecker — and his church are to be located in Gentile Christianity. One might argue, he suggests, that Matthew represents a Hellenistic universalistic Jewish Christianity, but there is no way to distinguish that from Gentile Christianity. This does not mean for Strecker that there are no Jewish Christians in Matthew's church and is not meant to deny that there are traces of Jewish thought in Matthew's traditional material. Strecker does not believe that there is polemic going on in the Matthean community. Rather the Jewish element is to be understood as representing an older stage in the development of the church's life, which will still have some influence on the future but has been incorporated into the Gentile Christian position (Strecker 1971, 29, 34–35). (Strecker's programmatic distinction between tradition and redaction, it might be observed, is more useful for trying to determine Matthew's historical situation than it is for interpreting Matthew's Gospel as a whole story.)

I bring this survey to an end by noting that on the basis of evidence similar to that already mentioned John Meier concludes that Matthew's church had a foot in both the Jewish and Gentile camp, probably starting out as strongly Jewish Christian but becoming more Gentile (1979, 14). Furthermore it is probable that this Christian community was an independent institution separate from the synagogue (16) and that the author was a Gentile (18–21).

Having discussed at some length in the preceding chapter the theological significance of the historical setting of the Gospels in general, I repeat here very summarily only what would seem to be the two most important conclusions as they pertain to Matthew. First, the imaginative narrative world of the Gospel of Matthew would have been close enough to the real historical world of the readers for the latter to have had a meaningful point of contact with the narrative world. The narrative world would contain both familiar and defamiliarizing elements. Second, the Holy Spirit could use the meaningful point of contact to turn the story into revelation by imprinting it on the hearts of the readers. As I shall try to show, for Matthew the word has power to re-form the heart (13:19, 23). The familiar point of contact enables the story to make sense. The defamiliarizing elements disclose something new. The Spirit gives the disclosure power.

The Word as Content and Power

Matthew affirms in a programmatic way that the eschatological revelation, the salvation promised by Isaiah, has now occurred and has occurred as light shining upon those sitting in the darkness (4:12–16). Immediately after that Matthew tells us that Jesus began to preach and gives us a summary of the preaching: repent for the kingdom of heaven has drawn near. Jesus has recently received the Spirit and the divine approval at his baptism (3:16–17) and has just defeated the devil's efforts to tempt him (4:11). Therefore, he is empowered so that his word (4:17) can be the vehicle for the divine light (4:15–16).

Jesus' word in Matthew is powerful. It can heal (Matt 8:8, 13; 9:2, 6b–7), control nature (8:26), and shape human commitments (9:9). His ethical teaching strikes the crowds as having an authority that distinguishes it from the teaching of the scribes (7:28–29). And the word about Jesus, the stories of his miracles, is also a word of power. As a result of the spread of this word people come to Jesus (8:5) with the request for healing (8:5–6; 9:18; 15:22), and this coming with expectation is interpreted as faith (8:13;

9:29; 15:28). Thus the circulating word about Jesus brings people to faith.

In Matthew's interpretation of the parable of the sower, the seed, on the one hand, is — surprisingly — people who are sown into the ground. It is the hearers of the word who are sown into different kinds of soil (Matt 13:20, 22–23). This is enforced in 13:37–38, where the good seed sown by the Son of man is people. But it is also the case that the seed is the word sown into the hearers (13:19). The Son of man sows the hearer as seed into the world (13:37–38) and also sows the word as seed into the hearer, the word being the means of placing the hearer in a certain historical situation with an understanding of that situation (13:23). Thus Matthew has a word-event theology. Grace occurs as the working of the word.

The Problem of Effective Revelation: The Messianic Secret

The messianic secret is less extensive and less dominating in Matthew than it is in Mark. Matthew's portrayal of the first messianic secret paradox — the outsider motif in which revelation is given but concealed at the source — is attenuated in comparison with its occurrence in Mark but is nonetheless present. We have seen that in Matthew stories of Jesus' miracle-working power circulate among the people and bring some to faith. Moreover, his miracles have been worked in public and should have been attended to (Matt 11:20–24). Yet knowledge about Jesus' miracles (8:4; 9:30; 12:15–16) and about his identity (16:20; 17:9) is withheld both by Jesus (8:4; 9:30; 12:15–16; 16:20; 17:9) and by God (11:25). Thus Matthew like Mark has the paradox of hidden revelation, revelation hidden at the source at which it is given. Jesus charges the blind men whose sight he has restored to see that no one knows about this (9:30–31). They report it anyway, but the apparent violation of his command to silence is rendered ironical by the fact that his command intended to prevent knowledge wins out. What Jesus does and says is in fact not apprehended by the crowd (11:20–24; 27:22–26). And in Matthew, as in Mark, the secret is not a matter of a lack of information but of existential understanding. The priests and Pharisees do understand the intellectual content of the parables of the two sons and the wicked tenants and even perceive that the parables apply to them (21:45–46). But their perception does not shape their conduct. They want to arrest Jesus, and in the end the leaders persuade the people to call for his crucifixion (27:15–26). As in Mark, Jesus' confession to the authorities that he is Christ, Son of God, and Son of man only enrages them (26:63–67).

With regard to the second paradox—the insider motif in which revelation is clearly given but misunderstood—disclosure to the disciples is more effective than it is in Mark; nevertheless, the situation of the disciples is not unambiguous. The secrets that are disclosed to the disciples are not immediately perceived (Matt 16:9), for the disciples like others have to see through the veil of Jesus' everyday ordinariness (13:53–58) in order to see him as Son of God (14:33). Their faith then is never complete. They are often accused of little faith (6:30; 8:26; 14:31; 16:8), and even after the resurrection they—or some of them—doubted (28:17). Nevertheless, as we shall see, Matthew's view of the disciples is decidedly more optimistic than Mark's.

On the issue of the intentionally enigmatic character of Jesus' parabolic speech it is usually thought that Matthew softens Mark's harsh position (Beare 1981, 293–94; Donahue 1988, 64–65; Kingsbury 1969, 49). Where Mark has an "in order that" (hina) Matthew has a "because" (hoti). The assumption of commentators is frequently that Matthew says Jesus speaks in parables because the people cannot understand—in the hope that the parables will help them. Matthew pulls back from Mark's view that Jesus was intentionally enigmatic. There is, however, no substantive difference between Mark and Matthew on this point. The motif of hearing dominates Matt 13:13–15, and the connection of 13:15 to 13:13 needs to be noted. Jesus' speech sounds like riddles to the crowd because they cannot understand what they hear (13:13). And they cannot understand what they hear because (gar) God has hardened their hearts: note the divine passive here (13:15a). Paradoxically the people also have shut their own eyes (13:15c)—also intentionally, in order that (mēpote) they should not see (Via 1990, 99–106). This adds something to the condition of total darkness, which appears in 6:22–23. Human beings intend the blindness— and so does God.

Matthew's parable discourse does not go on, as Mark's does, to say that what is concealed is so concealed for the purpose of being made manifest. The import of that difference we must still pursue.

The Contribution of Human Reception
to Revelation

I begin with a discussion of Matt 6:22–23 and will seek to show that for this text the human vantage point for understanding, which should give light, is actually total darkness. Human beings under the actual conditions of existence have no light of their own to merge with the light of God's self-disclosure, no role in constituting the content of revelation. Elsewhere I have argued this case at somewhat more length (Via 1994a).

Matt 6:22–23, which in form-critical terms is a wisdom saying expressing a general truth about humankind, has a threefold structure (a modification of the outline found in Betz 1985, 73–74). I begin with what could be called a grammatical-philosophical approach. (1) There is a thesis or theme sentence that states a possibility: "The eye is the lamp of the body." (2) Then follows a commentary on this thesis, formed as a balanced antithetical parallelism: "if your eye is healthy . . . if your eye is evil" (my translation). (3) A conclusion is drawn about which of these possibilities is actualized: "the light in you is darkness."

Let me give a bit more substance to this structure. The *thesis* that the eye is the lamp of the body states an ontological possibility or possibility in principle that may or may not be a possibility in fact. But the statement is a declarative sentence in the indicative mood. Why then do I say that it does not state a fact but only a possibility, and a possibility in principle at that?

The *commentary* turns what appears to be a fact into an uncertain possibility: "If your eye be sound, your whole body will be illuminated. But if your eye be evil, your whole body will be in the dark" (my translation). These are, grammatically speaking, third-class conditional sentences. They state two ways in which the eye may function qualitatively, and they state these in a very contingent fashion. The conditions are expressed in the subjunctive mood and thus state conditions that are undetermined or uncertain. They may or may not be fulfilled. The eye is the lamp of the body, but it is undetermined how it will function. It may be sound and produce light. But it may be evil and produce darkness. Since the eye is a lamp that may produce darkness, the eye is not a lamp in fact but only a lamp as a possibility in principle.

The *conclusion* is actually a further commentary on the original thesis, a conclusion about which of the eye's two possible ways of functioning is actually realized. Here we have a first-class condition in the indicative mood, a condition determined as true: "If your eye — or the light in you — is darkness (and it is), then how great is the darkness" (my translation). So we learn in the conclusion that the negative possibility in principle is the actual state of affairs. The body in principle has an eye, a lamp, a source of light, but in actuality the light is darkness — an oxymoron, the combination of opposites.

I argue that the eye as the lamp of the body in Matt 6:22 is in significant part the same as the light in you in 6:23b. It also needs to be pointed out, however, that the eye is not absolutely identical with the light in you in every way, and that is true because of certain metaphorical connections in the text. My contention that the eye as the lamp of the body is the same as the light in you is supported by the obvious inherent similarity of the lamp (*lychnos*) and light (*phōs*) images. Both phenomena radiate. Moreover, Matthew uses the same two terms together and synonymously in 5:14–15. Another argument in favor of identifying the eye as a lamp and the light is that in the text both lamp and light are attached to the person, the personal self. The light is explicitly the light *in you*. And the lamp is the lamp *of the body*. The personal pronoun "you" represents the person or self, and so does the body. Thus both lamp and light signify the self's capacity to see, and for Matthew seeing is a symbol for understanding (13:14–15).

I turn now to my claim that in this text the body is the self. In biblical thinking the term "body" can refer to one's physical presence in the world, one's physical body, or it can be a metaphor for the whole self (Via 1990, 68–70). I argue that in our text it is a metaphor for the self. One argument for this is that it is parallel to the personal pronoun "you." Beyond that the adjectives that are predicated of the body suggest the cognitive-subjective rather than the physical. The body will be illuminated, that is, in the light (*phōteinon*), or in the dark (*skoteinon*). The connotation of the physical that attaches to the body inevitably plays upon the words used here. The physical is in fact what creates the semantic tension from which the metaphor results. To speak of the physical body as illuminated or enlightened or, on the other hand, as in the dark is puzzling because it is literally pointless. Thus the relationship between the noun and the adjectives predicated of it is tensive and thereby suggests a nonliteral level of meaning. The knowing self and not the physical body is in view.

The self sees or fails to see, but it sees with the eye, which as part both belongs to the whole self and is distinguished from it. What is the seeing of the eye that is both the whole self's seeing and not the whole self's seeing? In what perspective would it make sense to say that one's vision or understanding, which is only a partial understanding, can give either total clarity or total obscurity? That claim would make sense if the partial or limited understanding — the eye as lamp — were understood as the angle or vantage point from which one sees, one's presuppositional starting point. As the point from which one sees, one's presupposition or preunderstanding, the light of the eye is not the totality of what one understands. But as the vantage point the eye as lamp-light is fused with the total vision and shapes it to some degree. Thus the sound and evil eye are two kinds of preunderstanding. In principle either is possible. But in actuality the human condition is that the angle of vision is so deformed — so much in the darkness — that nothing whatsoever is seen; only darkness obtains.

I have been interpreting this text at the level of ontological-epistemological-hermeneutical discourse. I take it that the text refers to how one comes to understanding or how one fails to understand. Is that correct? Or is that even one legitimate level of interpretation among others? If Ulrich Luz is right, I have been on the wrong track, for he states that the text is not concerned with the nature of human beings but with their action (1989, 397–98).

John Elliott also asserts that Matt 6:22–23 has an exclusively ethical meaning (1994, 74, 78). He has set our passage in the context of the evil-eye belief in the Mediterranean world generally. The essence of the belief was that certain individuals, animals, demons, or gods have the power to cast a spell or produce a malignant effect upon every object on which their eye or glance might fall. The power of the evil eye can destroy life and health. This belief was especially fostered in societies that perceived goods to be in short supply and life to be essentially competitive and conflictive. The evil eye is an oppressive weapon in this conflictive world (Elliott 1988, 46, 52; 1994, 51–64), a means of acquisition at the expense of others.

With regard to our text Elliott believes that the larger cultural context as well as the immediate literary context (Matt 6:19–21, 24) confers the moral sense of acquisitiveness on the evil eye in Matt 6:22–23 (1988, 61). Elliott in fact maintains that the conventional Mediterranean ideas about the evil eye "govern" Matthew's meaning and that the resultant moral message can be completely stated simply in these terms: show no envy but rather liberally share your substance with others (1994, 74, 78). At the same time the contrast with "sound" (*haplous*) eye in 6:22 and the theological element in 6:24, 25–34 give the added sense of disloyalty to God (1988, 61).

I think that Luz and Elliott are right in what they affirm and wrong in what they deny. The adjective "sound" (*haplous*), which modifies eye, can mean "healthy," especially in light of its association with the Hebrew root *tam* (Luz 1989, 396). Thus when modifying "the eye" understood metaphorically, as in our text, it can mean "illuminating." The adjective "sound" can also, however, have an ethical connotation (Prov 11:25; 2 Cor 8:2; Jas 1:5; Guelich 1985, 329–30), suggesting uprightness, sincerity, and generosity. Especially does the moral connotation of generous attach to the adjective *haplous* from its contrast with the envy associated with the evil eye (Elliott 1994, 71, 73, 75). In like manner the adjective "evil" (*ponēros*) can mean "unhealthy" (Luz 1989, 396; Guelich 1985, 331). Thus when modifying "the eye" understood metaphorically, *ponēros* can mean "obscuring." But obviously "evil" also has an ethical meaning (Guelich 1985, 330). Many scholars have interpreted the sound eye and evil eye in terms of generosity and liberality versus stinginess and acquisitiveness (Davies and Allison 1988, 640; Gundry 1982, 113; Beare 1981, 182; Hill 1972, 142; Betz 1985, 85).

To insist that the ethical meaning alone is at work here is a reductionistic imposition of a conventional cultural code on Matthew's text that disallows the free play of Matthew's ideas and images that may break with convention. And it ignores the capacity of close reading to discern unexpected nuances. I have no doubt that the ethical dimension of meaning belongs to this text. Yet the text displays a discernible shift of focus from the general Mediterranean idea of the evil eye as a negative power by which people inflict injury on others to the evil eye as a condition through which one injures oneself, although the latter meaning can also be found outside of the Bible. That points us back to the ontological-hermeneutical level of meaning.

The hermeneutical and ethical levels of meaning complement and, in fact, interpenetrate each other. The saying itself may be more strongly hermeneutical, but the ethical is not absent, and the context is distinctly ethical. The ethical dimension materially affects the hermeneutical claims, the claims about how one comes to understanding or its opposite. The most immediate context (Matt 6:19–21, 24) suggests that the sound eye is the recognition of the untrustworthiness of earthly treasure or money. The heart directed toward material wealth, on the other hand, will have a distorted picture of reality.

I want to turn my attention now to two metaphorical relationships in the text that have not yet been discussed. I understand metaphor to be not mere ornamentation but a redescription of reality. Moreover, metaphor is not primarily a transfer of meaning from one noun to another. Rather metaphor is an utterance in which meaning is transferred from one semantic field to another semantic field that had hitherto been separated from the first. A meaning is wrenched from its normal context and placed in another. A meaning is predicated of something to which it seems not to belong. In view of the factors of identification and predication, the logical, if not the syntactic, model for a metaphor is the sentence. Metaphor then is tensive language, is primarily an affair of semantic tension. The tension is not between the new meaning (created by seeing something as something else) and some alleged original or primitive meaning. It is rather a tension between the new meaning and meaning that is established by ordinary usage and found in the dictionary. The metaphorical meaning puts a strain on conventional wisdom (Ricoeur 1976, 37, 47, 49–50, 68; 1984, 14–15, 20, 44, 48, 98, 229–31, 290–92, 299; Soskice 1985, 19, 21–23; Wheelwright 1954, 25–26; 1962, 42–44, 46–50, 53–55, 70–74, 78–80, 86).

The thesis of our text is "The eye is the lamp of the body." Is this sentence a metaphor? In order to answer that question we must first consider more carefully what the sentence actually seems to say. The eye is a lamp, and for Matthew a lamp shines, radiates, emits light onto objects (5:15). Thus in 6:22 light goes out from the eye. This seems to bring the thought of the sentence into line with the understanding of vision that is found in the Mediterranean world generally (Elliott 1994, 66–67) and in particular in the Hebrew Bible and Jewish sources. According to Davies and Allison (1988, 635–36) premodern people, including the Jews, believed that the eye contains a light or fire that makes sight possible (Prov 15:30; Lam 5:17; Dan 10:6; Sir 23:19; T. Job 18:3). The *Testament of Job* reference is particularly revealing: *hoi emoi ophthalmoi tous lychnous poiountes eblepon,* "My eyes acting like lamps were seeing (or searching out)" (Kraft 1974 on *T. Job* 18:3). A lamp is its own source of light, not a channel for light from elsewhere. Davies and Allison state that only since about 1500 in the West has the intromission theory of vision been universally adopted. The ancients held an extramission theory. Thus it is anachronistic for modern commentators to interpret our text as if the eye were a window through which light entered the body from outside rather than the source of its own light (Davies and Allison 1988, 635–36). In the understanding of Jewish culture, the movement of vision is from inside to outside.

What about Hellenistic culture? I will consider both the Platonic and Aristotelian traditions. Evidently Plato's position is that the light from within, which defines the eye's faculty or sight, having coalesced with the daylight, collides with external objects and then reverses itself and carries the motions of objects back to the soul (*Republic* 507B–E; *Timaeus* 45B–46A). But does Plato imply that something comes from the initiative of objects as well? He does speak of the fire of vision coalescing with the fire of reflected faces (*Timaeus* 46B). Apparently the object is not purely passive. Something like this seems to be the interpretation of Plato in Theophrastus (371–287 B.C.), who is our most important source for earlier Greek physiological psychology according to G. M. Stratton (1917, 15). In Theophrastus's assessment Plato's view is midway between those who say that vision falls upon objects (proceeds from the eye) and those who hold that something is borne from the visible object to the organ of sight (Stratton 1917, 69, 71). This interpretation shows that Theophrastus was aware of two different theories of sight current in his time. For some, vision occurs as an outgoing process from the eye, and for others, it occurs as an incoming process. Theophrastus seems to side with what he takes to be the majority of the scientists of his time, those who hold that the organ of vision is itself a phenomenon of fire, for he rejects the idea that vision is generated by the object's imprinting the air and the air, in turn, the eye (Stratton 1917, 99, 111, 113).

How would the reader who read from a popular Mediterranean, Jewish, or Platonic position read Matthew's thesis sentence, "The eye is the lamp of the body"? He would not read it as a metaphor. She would not read it as a semantic tension that effects a redescription of reality. This reader would experience a succinct statement of conventional wisdom, one that accorded in a straightforward way with current theory of vision. The eye *in fact is* a lamp.

The reading experience would have been different for an Aristotelian. According to Aristotle, a sense is affected by the thing perceived — color, flavor, or sound (*On the Soul* 2.12). How does this work? Aristotle rejected as nonsensical Plato's belief that the eye is of the nature of fire and that sight occurs because light issues from the eye as from a lantern. If that were the case, the light from the eye would not go out in the dark, and vision at night would be possible. The eye consists in fact of water, not fire, and the power of vision resides in the water's transparency, a quality it shares with the air (*On Sense* 2). It is unreasonable, Aristotle continues, to suppose that vision occurs because light is emitted from the eye and coalesces with the daylight or with an object. Vision is impossible without light, but vision is generated because the object perceived causes the sense to operate. The sensible object sets in motion the medium of sensation — whether that medium be light or air — and the motion, received by the eye, is what produces vision (*On Sense* 2).

The Aristotelian reader, assuming that vision proceeds from the object through the watery transparency of the eye, would read Matthew's thesis sentence as a metaphor. She would experience considerable semantic tension in the claim that the eye is a radiating light and would be prompted to look for a nonliteral meaning. That effort would be encouraged by the metaphorical expressions in the first commentary — the body in the light or in the dark. The modern reader would have much the same experience as the Aristotelian.

I turn now to a briefer discussion of the relationship between the lamp of the body and the light in you. I argued earlier that the lamp of the body and the light in you are equivalents of each other. If the eye then *is* the lamp of the body (Matt 6:22a), it is also the light in you. That conclusion obviously means that we can also say that the light in you is the eye. The text supports that reading. The light in you is exactly the same thing as the eye. My discussion will proceed on the metaphorical level of the text's understanding of the eye and vision — the eye as the presuppositional vantage point for understanding.

Again, within the text the light in you is the eye, but when we consider the intertext composed of Matthew and certain elements in the Greek and Jewish traditions, the picture becomes more complex. For Plato the eye is not identical with the light but is the opening through which the light flows from within. The light is more than the eye. The Jewish tradition offers similarities, and I choose here to consider two such texts from the LXX that provide an intertext with Matt 6:22–23. The first of these (Deut 15:9) expands the meaning of the eye, and the second Prov (20:27) enlarges upon the meaning of the light.

In Deut 15:9 (LXX) the hidden, lawless word in the heart is

made parallel to and synonymous with the eye's being evil or stingy (*ponēreuomai*) to the brother. Since in biblical thinking the heart is the center of the whole person, the hidden core and the seat of understanding and will, the synonymous parallelism of eye and heart metaphorically, but not literally, identifies eye and heart, part and whole, external and internal. Thus intertextually the eye in the thesis statement "the eye is the lamp of the body" means more than the literal eye and more than the eye as preunderstanding. The eye is not just a part of the self but is rather the self's organizing center. This has been established by the intertext of Deut 15:9 and the thesis stated in Matt 6:22a before we move to the commentaries on the thesis found in 6:22b—23.

In Prov 20:27 (LXX) the light (*phōs*) is identified with the spirit of humankind that searches out the person's private inner parts. The noun translated "spirit" (*pnoē*) ordinarily means "breath" or "wind," but it can shade off into the sense of "spirit" (*pneuma*), which is surely demanded by the context here. Since the light in humankind in Prov 20:27 is the spirit that has access to the inner-most recesses of the self, it is more than the eye of Matt 6:22a–23a, even when the eye is understood metaphorically as understanding, for the eye in Matthew 6 is understanding as a limited vantage point from which to comprehend. The intertextual connection between Prov 20:27 and Matt 6:23b draws the light of the latter into the semantic field of the former — light as spirit that searches out the inner person. The light, then, expanded intertextually as the spirit that searches out the human depths is *more* than the eye as the (intratextually) limited preunderstanding. However, the expanded intertextual meaning of light is very nearly the equivalent of the expanded intertextual meaning of eye — the eye as a synonym for heart, the self's organizing center.

There is a complication in Prov 20:27 that should be noted. The searching spirit is not just light but is specifically the light of the *Lord*. Does that mean — contrary to normal Jewish thinking — that the human spirit is metaphysically identical with the divine light? Or does it mean — as the broader Jewish context would suggest — that the human spirit is guided by the divine light?

My conclusion from the foregoing is that the light in you in Matt 6:23b can shade off into meaning the human spirit in its innermost depth. Therefore, it is not unambiguously identical with the eye of 6:22–23a. The relationship between the eye as lamp and the light in you is tensive and therefore metaphorical. That is to say, that is the case when the eye as lamp is understood as the limited presuppositional vantage point for understanding and the light in you is understood as the searching human spirit that knows the deepest secrets. *Intratextually* the light in you is straightforwardly the eye as lamp. Both mean the same thing: preunderstanding. But *intertextually* the partial vision of preunderstanding (eye) is tensively identified with the much more penetrating vision of the spirit (light in you). *Intratextually* the light in you is the part (the eye). *Intertextually* the light in you is something approaching the whole (the penetration of the spirit). I am taking the far-reaching knowledge of the spirit to be the substantial equivalent of the illumination of the whole self (Matt 6:22b).

What is the import of this metaphorical connection? The part (eye as lamp) is the whole (light in you). We have already observed that in Matt 6:22b–23a the angle of the eye *affects* the whole understanding of the self. The metaphorical identification of these two elements intensifies that relationship and suggests its reciprocity: not only does the limited angle of vision guide to some significant degree the total understanding of a person but an enlargement in one's total understanding can reform the vantage point from which one sees. The partial understanding of preunderstanding becomes less and less partial.

It must be remembered, however, that in our text the actual case for humankind generally is that the light in you is darkness (Matt 6:23b). People are blind (7:3; 11:20–24; 23:16, 17, 24, 26). And given the double meaning of "the light in you," the angle of vision is too deformed to give true understanding, and whatever understanding one has is too darkened to correct the point from which one understands.

Matt 6:22–23 is a wisdom saying, but it can be plausibly argued that it is an implicit manifestation of an underlying narrative structure. The structure that I propose is one in which the (1) beginning is a moment of possibility that gives way in the (2) middle to some actualization of possibility in a process that in turn leads in the (3) ending to a consequence (Bremond 1970, 247–52; 1978, 33).

When this narrative logic is applied to Matt 6:22–23, the three parts of the implicit plot do not correspond to the three parts of the wisdom saying. Yet I do not believe that the narrative structure has been forced on the text. Rather the diction of the latter and the structure fit each other. The implicit plot that emerges from segmenting the text according to the narrative structure unfolds as follows.

The beginning of the plot is comprised of Matt 6:22a–23a. That is because in this stretch of text we remain in the realm of possibility, a possibility with two alternatives. We are still in the mode of "you might do this" or "you might do that." No fate-determining decision has been made. The middle of the plot is composed of 6:23b. Even though "if the light in you is darkness" is a conditional clause, the indicative mood suggests an actual decision. The possibility of having an evil eye has been realized as the darkening of the source of light. The ending of the implied plot is composed of the second clause of the final conditional sentence (6:23c) — "how great is the darkness!"

The story, relatively speaking, is long on beginning and short on middle and ending. It wants the reader to be impressed with the possibilities offered — even if the positive possibility turns out not to be actually available. The "how great" shows that the decision to turn the potential light into actual darkness results in a fate from which there is no human escape, a darkness unimaginably great. The narrative level of the text dramatically underscores the magnitude of the final darkness.

It is paradoxical that Matthew uses the contrast of the good and evil eye to deny that people in the process of fallen history, who stand outside of Christian faith, have any light of their own to see the truth of reality. For Matthew this assertion about the darkened mind of those who stand outside of the light of the gospel is a truth claim. But in order to make this claim he employs a conceptual construct — the whole eye versus the evil eye — that had wide cross-cultural currency and was not the peculiar property of the biblical tradition. Matthew's articulation of the revealed gospel word, evidently for the Evangelist the only source of light, makes use here of a cultural category that presumably for Matthew derives from the darkened mind of unredeemed humankind.

My hermeneutical-epistemological level of interpretation is supported by the fact that the meaning that I have proposed for Matt 6:22–23 displays its influence in the negative answer that Matthew gives in other contexts to the question whether the natural person can know the truth or contribute to revelation. I want now to enlarge on Matthew's position by showing that Matthew is more pessimistic than Mark on the question of what human reception *as human* has to contribute to the constitution of the divine self-disclosure. Matthew diminishes the capacity of natural human beings to understand the gospel. His treatment of Markan elements that offer a positive appraisal of the understanding of natural human beings attenuates the actual possibility of human reception's making a constitutive contribution to revelation. Mark's forceful paragraph about the illuminating intention of the word and the positive, receiving measure of human understanding (Mark 4:21-25) is missing as such from Matthew, although some fragments from it appear in other Matthean contexts.

Mark's statement about the intention of a lamp to shine (4:21) is found in a different version in Matt 5:15, where the note of intentionality has been removed and the light is no longer an image for the revealing word of Jesus but for the disciples (5:14) and their works (5:16). Mark's statement about the intention of the hidden to become manifest (4:22) appears also in a different version in Matt 10:26 with the purpose element missing. This saying is made to apply to the preaching of the church (Matt 10:27).

Mark's summons to "anyone" to hear with understanding is missing from Matthew, as is Mark's claim that the measure of understanding that one brings to hearing defines the measure one receives. And as for the statement that to the one who has, more will be given, Matthew uses it in two places. He attaches it to the parable of the talents (Matt 25:29), and he uses it in his parable chapter (chap. 13), but he removes it from the Markan position, where it can apply to both the disciples and the crowds, and puts it before the interpretation of the sower, where it can refer only to the disciples (Matt 13:12). The mysteries of the kingdom are given to the disciples but not to outsiders because these mysteries are given to those who already have. Thus it is the disciples alone who are identified as those who have and thus receive more. The disciples already have a call (4:18-22; 8:18-27), ethical instruction (chaps. 5-7), and authority for a mission (10:1-8); therefore, they can be given to know the mysteries of the kingdom. The crowd has nothing and thus will lose even the nothing it has. The Markan seed parable about the earth's producing of *itself*, which thereby attributes considerable initiative to the human subject as human, is missing altogether from Matthew.

Matthew modifies thoroughly Mark's tendency to ascribe constitutive reception to human beings as human. He treats the elements involved in such a way as to bring them into line with the position of Matt 6:22-23. The light of human understanding that might have merged with the light of the gospel to generate a true understanding of reality is in actuality darkness. Thus revelation occurs as the overwhelming of human darkness. Matthew is more pessimistic than Mark on the issue of human beings as human.

The darkness/bad eye/false knowledge of human beings as such in Matthew has a substantive content. Those who are blind and in the shadowy darkness of death (Matt 4:16; 6:22–23; 7:3; 11:20–24; 23:16–17, 19, 24, 26) are those who value the praise of others (6:2, 6, 16; 23:5) and the wide gate and easy way (7:13). People refuse to see the truth about themselves (7:3; 23:26–28) and about God's dealings (11:20–25; 13:15), and in self-deception they believe the comfortable, self-serving lie that they tell themselves (Via 1990, 92–98). They believe that the broad, easy way rather than the narrow, hard way is the road to salvation (7:13–14). They will not be able to see God as the only source of well-being, for God works in secret (6:4, 6, 18). Nor will they have grasped the radical demand for love and mercy (5:7; 9:13; 12:7; 23:23) that claims both action and heart in concord (5:20–22, 27–30; 7:16–20; 23:25–28). They are blind to the fact that they even have an inner depth of being (23:25–28) upon which God places a radical demand as well as to the fact that there must be correspondence between outer act and inner disposition. They think that the act is all that God requires and ignore the claim upon the heart (5:20–48).

True understanding comes solely through the gospel since human beings have no light to contribute. In the face of the darkness the word effects both understanding (Matt 13:11a, 16) and moral enablement (13:23; 18:27, 33). What the revelation in the gospel gives is an understanding of what the kingdom of heaven is accomplishing (13:11, 15–17, 19, 23, 51–52), who Jesus is (14:33; 16:13–20), and what the ethical will of God really requires (5:20; 7:21; 12:50). The light of the word also enables the union of act and heart (7:15–20; 12:33–37) and the appropriation of the Son of man's death and resurrection as the shape of one's own existence (16:21–26; Via 1990, 99, 109–23).

Since in Matthew Jesus' word is in some sense a new law and both his word and life constitute the event of grace, the relationship between law and grace calls for more attention. Matthew places a certain emphasis on the will of God (6:10; 7:21; 12:50; 18:14; 26:42), and the law of Moses may express the will of God. The written law does in 5:17, 21, 27; 19:17b–19, and so does the oral law in 23:2–3, 23.

But the law may also be opposed to the will of God. We may note two instances in Matthew 5 where the written law is seen as opposed to the will of God as reinterpreted by Jesus. The law of Moses forbade breaking an oath (Lev 19:12; Deut 23:21) and required that oaths be taken in certain circumstances (Exod 22:10–11). Therefore, the prohibition of all oaths in Matt 5:34

contradicts the written law. The law of equal retaliation is stated several times in the Old Testament (Exod 21:24; Lev 24:20; Deut 19:21). Not only is the *lex talionis* a fundamental element of Israelite law but legal systems generally rest on the basic insight that social order requires the punishment to be commensurate with the offense. Thus when Matthew's Jesus forbids all retaliation (5:38–39), he not only contravenes specific Mosaic laws but undermines a foundational legal principle. In Matt 15:20 the oral law regulating hand washing is rejected. One may then conclude that the law, written and oral, is for Matthew a possible clue to the will of God, a trace left on Israel's religious culture by the will of God (on the trace idea see Via 1985, 96–97, 135–36). But the law is not a formal authority. It does not in and of itself say adequately and unequivocally what one must do to fulfill the will of God.

Matthew understands Jesus' teachings, which reinterpret the law, as "commandments" (5:17–19; Via 1990, 83–84). That is consistent with the fact that there is a sense in which Matthew takes Jesus' imperatives as law. Matthew in my judgment is not an ethical legalist, for he does not think that the believer's moral responsibility can be formulated finally in rules. But he is to a significant degree a theological legalist. That is, obedience to Jesus' commandments is a condition for salvation (6:15; 7:24–27; 16:27; 18:34–35). What one does is all important. This becomes problematic when it is recognized that for Matthew the action — *praxis* (16:27) — that is the condition for salvation (5:20) includes not just deeds of love but a pure and forgiving heart (5:8; 18:35), an inner self free from anger and lust (5:22, 28). Law generically belongs to the public arena, and its requirements must be within human capacities (Ogletree 1983, 111). The Old Testament legal tradition is aware of those conditions (Deut 29:29; 30:11–14), and Matthew also seems to regard Jesus' commands as possible — doable (7:24–27; 11:28–30; 19:17–22; 23:23) — however much we may question this.

It appears to me that Matthew has two schemes for relating grace, the performance of Jesus' commandments and eschatological salvation. According to the first one grace is the power (Matt 13:20, 23, 37–38) that enables the inner disposition and action (7:16–20; 12:33–37; 13:23) necessary for salvation (7:24–25; 16:27). Salvation is achieved in human beings by God. The paradox in this scheme is that human beings must achieve the same salvation by their own effort (5:20; 6:14–15; 16:27; 18:35). Grace as power and theological legalism can go hand in hand. What people must do seems to be calculable: they stand or fall on the basis of their actions (7:24–25; 16:27). And yet this calculability in Matthew's theological legalism is challenged by his nonlegalistic ethic: If what one must do ethically cannot be calculated in rules or laws that constitute a formal authority that specifies definitive requirements, then it cannot be easily calculated how much is necessary for salvation and whether or not one has done enough.

The second scheme is based on grace as forgiveness, and this has a paradoxical relation to the first scheme. Action grounded in a renewed heart and produced both by God and by human beings is necessary for salvation, but if that necessary righteousness fails, God still saves by forgiving, canceling the debt (Matt 1:21; 9:1–8; 18:27; 20:9–15, 28; 26:28). Jesus' death ransoms 20:28) by giving the insight that enables following (20:29–34). But the ransom saying is also connected to the eucharistic saying in 26:28 because both interpret Jesus' death redemptively. Given this connection and seeing that 26:28 understands Jesus' death as conferring forgiveness, we must understand the ransom as forgiveness as well as enablement.

The relationship between grace and law in Matthew is complex, tensive, and subtle. Therefore, when it is simply stated that Matthew has subverted Jesus' subversive wisdom by turning it into the conventional wisdom that one's relationship with God is based on requirements and rewards (as is stated by Borg 1994, 173), Matthew has not been read with care or penetration.

We have looked at Matthew's pessimistic view of the understanding of the natural person and have briefly considered the content of the revelation that may overwhelm human darkness. What about Matthew's portrayal of the disciples? Disciples are defined in significant part in Matthew as those who understand the gospel — and do it. In 13:11 Jesus reminds his disciples that he has given them the secrets of the kingdom and pronounces them blessed because they have seen and heard what the prophets and righteous longed to see and hear but did not (13:16–17). Not only have the disciples seen and heard it but they have understood it (13:51). The light of revelation has turned them into light so that they can be light for the world (5:14–16).

Gerhard Barth has argued that while Matthew includes some of the functions of faith in understanding, he really brings the intellectual element in understanding to the fore. Thus understanding is the presupposition for faith, and faith is trust and volition, from which the intellectual element has been excluded and transferred to understanding (Barth 1963, 107, 110-14). Luz takes essentially the same position (1989, 103-4, 107).

I have argued elsewhere (1990, 112-14) that while the two terms "faith" and "understanding" suggest different emphases, they significantly overlap and interpenetrate, and Matthew makes no programmatic distinction between them. Faith has its intellectual component: the conviction that Jesus can work miracles is a cognitive element. On the other hand, understanding comprehends the whole person. I cite one theme.

The position that seems to be normative for Matthew is that understanding is the initial response to the word of the kingdom, which should take root in the heart (13:19, 23), for the heart is the seat of understanding (13:15). When it does take root, it produces ethical fruit (13:23), which means that it is understanding that has constituted the very being of the disciple — the tree that produces good fruit (7:17-18). That is to say, since proper understanding produces ethical fruit and the good person (tree or heart) produces ethical fruit, understanding virtually is, or at least constitutes, the person. Thus understanding embraces the life of discipleship from beginning to end and cannot be called the intellectual presupposition of faith.

Now on the question of the faith and understanding of those who have in fact made the decision to accept the overpowering word of God, who have become followers, Matthew is more optimistic than Mark. Disciples in Matthew are those who understand (13:16-17, 51-52; 14:33; 16:12; 17:10-13), while the disciples in Mark characteristically fail to understand. Stephen Moore interprets the misunderstanding of Jesus in Mark in light of the deconstructionist motif that writing, cut off from a speaker, is in principle a wandering outcast, drifting from (mis)reading to (mis)reading. Thus the Markan Jesus is modeled on the written word, is misunderstood as if he were writing rather than speaking (Moore 1992, 11, 15-17). However that may be, Matthew's enhancement of the disciples' understanding can be quickly and dramatically illustrated from two stories.

In Mark at the end of the feeding of the five thousand and the walking on the water, the narrator tells us that the disciples were astounded because they did not understand about the loaves but rather had a hardened heart (Mark 6:52). This scene is enlarged in Matthew by the addition of Peter's walking on the water, and the disciples' reaction to these events is postponed until Jesus and Peter's return to the boat. Then in place of Mark's reference to the disciples' lack of understanding and hardness of heart, we read that they worshiped Jesus and confessed him as Son of God (Matt 14:33).

In Mark when the disciples are perplexed about the meaning of the leaven of the Pharisees and the leaven of Herod, they are harshly criticized by Jesus as hard-hearted and put in the category of outsiders (Mark 8:17–18; cf. 4:11–12). The story ends with the question put by Jesus to the disciples: "Do you not yet understand?" (Mark 8:21). There is no indication that they do. In Matthew, on the other hand, the criticism of the disciples is much milder (Matt 16:8), and the story ends with the assertion "Then they understood" (16:12).

How does this claim of effective revelation bringing disciples to faith and understanding relate to the dismal picture in Matt 6:22–23? The light-giving possibility of the sound eye has been turned into darkness. That is said about human beings generally and thus includes the disciples. That same inclusiveness is found in 4:15–16. The light has come to the *people* who sit in darkness. The disciples have been moved from darkness to light. But in view of 6:22–23 and 4:16 they have no light to merge with the light of God's self-disclosure in Jesus. Human reception has no role whatsoever in constituting the content of revelation. The disciples have been brought into the light because God's light has simply overcome their unrelieved darkness.

Revelation and Eschatology in Matthew and Mark

How are we to understand the phenomenon that Mark is relatively optimistic about the constitutive role of reception or preunderstanding in human beings in general but is relatively pessimistic about the ongoing understanding of those who have actually become disciples, while Matthew is relatively pessimistic about the light of understanding in human beings as such but optimistic about the faith and understanding of disciples, those who have made a commitment? Perhaps there is the hint of an answer in questioning what assumptions Mark and Matthew might be making about the relative weight of realized and futuristic eschatology. Or to approach it from the other side, what Mark and Matthew say about the reception of revelation tells us things about their eschatology that the explicitly eschatological passages themselves do not tell us.

Mark has both realized (1:15) and futuristic eschatology (8:38–9:1; 13:24–37; 14:62). It is difficult to say which one is dominant. Futuristic eschatology may seem to be more prominent, but then the whole story is told under the aegis of realized eschatology (1:15). When one considers, however, the strong emphasis on the failure of the disciples and others to understand the coming of the Messiah, the force of realized eschatology is relativized. Revelation is minimally effective, though not totally ineffective. Mark draws dark and almost tragic conclusions from the fact that full revelation is projected into the eschatological future. Thus it is future eschatology that is stressed.

The paucity of understanding in Mark's narrative world derives from the complementary ways in which he defines the divine and human sides of revelation. (1) God has chosen to give full self-disclosure only in the eschatological future; therefore, when God's Son appears in history to ransom humankind, his identity is veiled and his speech is enigmatic. Moreover, the pattern of human existence that is revealed is shockingly difficult — finding life through death. (2) Human beings as human have a positive measure of understanding to bring to the hearing of the word, a measure that can receive the word, merge with it, in such a way as to generate greater understanding. But this measure has been so afflicted by hardness of heart that the actual possibility of receiving revelation has been greatly reduced, though not eliminated. When understanding fails, is it primarily because revelation has been concealed and projected into the future or because hardness of heart has deformed human receptivity? Exactly how human reception — positive or negative (Mark 4:25) — and divine word intermingle, Mark leaves in the realm of mystery (4:27b).

Matthew also has both realized (11:12; 12:28, 40–42; 13:16–17) and futuristic (5:22; 7:19, 24–27; 16:27–28; 24:1–25:46) eschatology, and one might hazard the judgment that, considering only texts that bear directly on eschatology, futuristic eschatology gets the emphasis. When, however, one observes the enhanced picture of the disciples' capacity to understand the gospel, that factor tacitly brings the eschatological presence of God's rule into the foreground, and futuristic eschatology is relativized. Its force turns out to be less than it appears to be, and final revelation is more present than projected into the future. However much Matthew appears to look to the future, and even though the light *in* human beings as human has become darkness, the light of the gospel has in fact overcome that darkness in the case of disciples.

Is the Light in You Total Darkness?

We have considered at some length that Matthew in an overt way denies to human reception a constitutive role in defining the content of God's revelation. But is there in Matthew a less explicit countervailing or deconstructive tendency? Is there any indication that "the light in you" that has become darkness nevertheless contains some light?

For Matthew understanding is an exercise of the imagination in the sense of being able to comprehend the meaning of symbols. The disciples understand when they see that the leaven of the Pharisees and Herodians has nothing to do literally with bread (Matt 16:8, 11–12). The disciple, moreover, is to exercise his or her imagination very much in the sense defined by Samuel Taylor Coleridge; that is, imagination is the magical power that balances and reconciles discordant qualities: sameness with difference, general with concrete, new with old (Coleridge 1854, 363–64, 372–74). When the disciples in Matthew reply unequivocally to Jesus that they *have* indeed understood all the parables and interpretations of chapter 13, the one who understands is then described as a scholar who has been made a disciple of the kingdom (13:52). This scholar of the kingdom is like a householder who brings out of his treasure things both new and old. Matt 12:34–35 identifies the treasure metaphorically with the heart and sees the heart as the source of language. To understand then is to be able to combine in language the new and old that issue from the heart. It is to think imaginatively.

What are the old and the new in Matthew's view of the matter? Thus far we have been talking in this section about disciples. But one becomes a disciple at some point, and before the call to discipleship (Matt 4:18–22; 9:9–13) one was not a disciple. Thus in the context of the call to discipleship, the old is the natural human condition, which is evil (7:11) — the darkness (4:16) that needs to be repented of (4:17). The new is the gospel and the call itself. But 13:52 suggests that the old is not to be totally discarded, and that could be because the natural person, though being evil, can still make valid judgments about what is good (7:11).

Valid discernment about the morally good is rooted in the heart, for the heart is the source both of moral action (Matt 7:17–20; 13:19, 23; 23:26) and of understanding (13:15). The location of understanding in the heart obviously implies that arriving at understanding through interpretation originates in the heart (13:18–19,

23), and Matthew expects disciples to be able to interpret Jesus' teaching (13:51), his and their historical situation (16:6, 9, 11–12), and his identity (16:13–16). Since both moral judgment and interpretation are grounded in the understanding of the heart and since valid moral judgments are ascribed to human beings as human — in fact as sinful — then by implication Matthew also attributes valid interpretive understanding to human beings as human, understanding that could merge with the light of revelation. Thus the reception of revelation contains a definitively human element and is not something wholly accomplished in the interpreter by the word of Jesus that simply overcomes an unrelieved human darkness.

This line of thought can be extended by a look at Matt 12:33–37. This passage focuses on the significance of language for human destiny. One's language comes from one's heart, and one is finally justified or not on the basis of one's words. In 12:33 Matthew's Jesus places the hearer under the imperative to bring tree and fruit, heart and word, into harmony. We need to recognize that for Matthew salvation resides in wholeness, the accord of tree and fruit, heart and action, inside and outside, the understanding of the heart and expression in words (5:21–22, 27–30; 7:15–20; 12:33–35; 23:26). Putting the hearer under the imperative to achieve this accord assumes that it does not actually exist. The person addressed is unredeemed. He is like the Pharisees addressed in 23:27–28, who are whitewashed or righteous on the outside but corrupt and rebellious within. But the imperative mood itself assumes that the person to whom the command is directed has some capacity to carry it out. Matthew implies, then, that the unredeemed person in whom heart and word are in discord can bring them into accord. She can achieve proper understanding (tree or heart; 12:33–34) and express it in appropriate language (12:35–37) and appropriate action (7:15–20). The human being as human is not totally incapable of redemptive understanding.

The foregoing point requires further amplification. Matthew puts the reader under the imperative to cleanse the inside of the person in order that the outside — action — might become clean (23:26–28). However, he also requires the doing of the right thing so that vision-understanding might be cleared up (7:5; 13:15). This is a human responsibility. But how can the requirement be achieved when human beings in the actuality of historical existence live enshrouded in darkness (4:16; 6:22–23) and overcome by self-deception: the wolf in sheep's clothing (7:15) yet unaware of the contradiction (7:3–4; 23:23–28). This wolf-sheep is absorbed in Matthew's inclusive concept of the self-deceived hypocrite (see Via 1990, 89–90, 92–93, 96, 128) that becomes Matthew's image for human being universally apart from the gospel. Only the enabling power of the word of the kingdom and cross can create faith, renew the understanding of the heart, and generate appropriate action (4:17; 7:28; 8:5–6, 13; 9:26, 29–31; 13:11a, 16–17, 19; 16:21; 20:28–34). But despite this enablement from God the righteousness achieved by human beings is still really their own (5:20; 6:14–15; 7:24–26; 16:27; 18:35).

Recall again (1) the necessity of enabling grace and (2) the self-contradiction (sheep-wolf) of human beings under the conditions of historical existence. But however much both of these things are true for Matthew, human beings in principle (latently/ontologically) are whole beings at one with themselves. It is *not possible* for a bad tree to bear good fruit or a good tree, bad fruit (Matt 7:18). It is *not possible* for a person to act against what she or he is. Since for Matthew people obviously do act contrary to their nature (7:15; 23:23–28), when he says that this is not possible, we should take the implied wholeness to belong to the ontological and not to the ontic, or actual, dimension of existence (see Via 1990, 78–80). Thus the wholeness achieved by both the grace of the gospel and human will is the actualization of what human being is "naturally" from the beginning. The gulf between human beings as human and believing disciples is less radical than it appeared to be. The very parallelism between human being as human and human being as formed by the gospel shows that there was something there in the naturally human that corresponded and responded to the proclamation of the gospel.

Let us pursue this theme by recalling that the statement "to her who *has* will more be given" (my translation) in Matt 13:12 is applied to disciples in a context in which a key issue is how to interpret Jesus' parables (13:18, 36, 51–52). What the disciples *have* on the basis of their prior experience is some degree of interpretation, and the more that they will be given is better interpretation. They are to be interpreters (24:32), for they are to follow a teacher, one of whose roles is to give interpretations (13:3–9, 18–23, 24–30, 35–43, 47–50).

The same saying — to the one who has will more be given — is also attached to the parable of the talents (Matt 25:29), which defines a fundamentally human situation. The one-talent man understands the world as threatening and himself as a victim. Thus he hides his money and refuses to risk it in the market, hoping to hold on to what he has. But when called to account, he must forfeit even the one talent he has. Not to risk is to lose. The one who risks nothing loses everything; therefore, the kind of having that gets more having is the kind that risks its possession and accepts the unknown.

If we bring together the two Matthean texts that employ this saying — to the one who has will more be given — then the disciples' making of interpretations becomes one instance of an essentially human pattern: risking in the hope of gaining. The disciple risks the interpretation of the human reality in relation to God that he or she already has in light of the new interpretation that is given in Jesus' parabolic preaching. The old interpretation is risked in that it is allowed to fuse with Jesus' new parabolic interpretation and thus to become something different. The fusion of old and new is the "more" that will be given.

We see that in Matthew's text old and new are not completely stable categories, for they are tensively merged as they are brought forth from the heart in the interpretation of the disciple-interpreter. This interpretation is both old and new. The old is the human understanding of reality that is encountered by Jesus' new parabolic preaching, the gospel of the kingdom (Matt 4:23; 9:35). And even disciples still retain an element of the naturally human darkness (4:16). Disciples are in the group (5:1–2) that is informed about the darkening of the human light (6:22–23) and is addressed by the words "if you then being evil" (7:11 — my translation). The light of human understanding has been darkened, but as we have now seen, not totally so. Human understanding is old in relation to the new parabolic word. The former was there before the gospel. But this old element — human receptivity — is also new in that the human perspective that merges with the gospel is not exactly identical with the self-understanding held prior to the encounter with the gospel. Rather it is the hitherto unknown in oneself that is drawn out by the word of the kingdom. This human element is old because it was there in the self prior to hearing the gospel, but it is new because it was not expressly articulated in one's self-understanding until the gospel elicited it. Moving into this previously unknown is the risk that the disciple takes.

For Matthew, then, the light of the gospel is not the only new element in the constitution of revelation. The scholar who has been made a disciple of the kingdom brings forth from his own treasure, her own heart (Matt 12:34–35), her *own* seat of understanding and language, things both old and new (13:52). For example, the explicit interpretations and interpretive contextualizations that Matthew gives to the parables of Jesus in chapter 13 are newer than the parabolic word that generated them. Also the new perspective that Matthew brings to the tradition can be seen, for example, in such smaller constructions as the highly poetic form in which Matthew casts the Beatitudes (Via 1990, 123–27) as well as in the imaginatively constructed narrative world of the Gospel as a whole.

The revelation composed of the merging of Jesus' initiating word with human reception is symbolically represented by the new wine in new wineskins (Matt 9:17). The wine is the revealed word, while the skins are human reception. In order for the wine to be available at all there must be wineskins. The new skins are, so to speak, called forth by the new wine and shaped by it. The old skins could not have contained it and have made it accessible. At the same time the skins have an integrity of their own that cannot be reduced to the wine.

We see that there is in Matthew an implicit tendency to attribute a constitutive role in revelation to human reception. How do divine word and human reception interact? Matthew does not give us an explicit clue and does not contain Mark's (4:27b) statement that the nature of the interaction is a mystery even to the revealer. Matthew does, however, point elusively in that same direction. As we have noted, Matthew's Jesus says in passing that the human condition is evil (7:11a): "if you then being evil." But there is more: "if you then being evil know how to give good gifts to your children" (my translation). This is a first-class condition in the indicative: if you being evil know how to do the good — and you do. Human beings though evil are credited with valid judgments about the good.

On the other hand, in 12:34 Matthew's Jesus in effect denies that people, being evil, are able to speak the good. This, of course, agrees with our conclusions about the eye as the lamp of the body in 6:22–23. Both knowing (13:15) and speaking (12:34–35) are expressive of the heart. Thus Matthew says in effect that the heart of sinful human beings, human beings as human, both is (7:11) and is not (12:34) the seat of good. What human reception contributes to the constitution of revelation remains ambiguous. But it cannot be maintained that Matthew consistently affirms that the light in you is darkness or that he denies that human reception has any light at all to merge with the light of the gospel.

Chapter 6

JOHN

The Historical Situation

As J. Lewis Martyn has suggested (1979, 15–17), we should resist the temptation to think of the Gospel of John as a timeless spiritual document detached from its ancient setting and should seek to interpret it in light of the specific circumstances in which it originated. Following the procedure of the two previous chapters, I shall deal very selectively with conflicting opinions about various aspects of John's historical setting and purpose, giving more attention to conclusions than to arguments.

The History-of-Religions Background

In recent decades Judaism and gnosticism have been the primary candidates for providing the milieu out of which Johannine Christianity emerged, with the search for background focusing increasingly on Judaism (Smith 1989, 276; 1995, 17). As Moody Smith points out, however, it is not necessary to make an either/or decision between Jewish and Hellenistic influence, nor were these two religious complexes mutually exclusive (1989, 276; 1995, 20). The gnostic Nag Hammadi documents may show that even if the hypothesis of a pre-Christian gnostic redeemer proves to be highly improbable, there may have been in the milieu of Johannine Christianity a pre-Christian gnosticism influenced by Judaism (Smith 1989, 278–79). My discussion will pay particular attention to the hypothetical pre-Christian gnostic redeemer myth, the logos concept, and the Jewish Wisdom figure.

I begin my brief survey of scholarship with Rudolph Bultmann. He believes that John represents an oriental Christianity whose background was Judaism, but Judaism of a gnosticizing type (Bultmann 1955c, 10, 13). The strong Hellenistic gnostic element in this Judaism is responsible for John's dualism of light and darkness (1:5; 8:12), heavenly and earthly (3:12, 31), and truth and falsehood (8:44). At the same time John has modified the gnostistic element. He has demythologized the cosmological dualism by regarding the world as God's creation rather than as something evil and by rejecting the idea that the human spirit is a fragment of the divine light held captive in this evil world (1955c, 5–6, 10–11, 13). Bultmann believes that the gnostic background accounts especially for John's presentation of the sending of the Son of God after the pattern of the preexistent redeemer myth, which had already influenced Hellenistic Christianity. In Bultmann's view the name of the preexistent revealer — Logos — also comes from gnostic language (1955c, 6, 12–13).

According to Bultmann's construction the gnostic redeemer is a preexistent figure of light, son and image of the highest God, who has sent him down from the light-world to bring knowledge. On earth the redeemer assumes human form and reawakens those whose spirits are sparks of light to their heavenly origin. He teaches them about the journey back to the heavenly world that they will begin at death. After his earthly work is over, he prepares the way for the redeemed, going before them as he is exalted in victory to heavenly glory (Bultmann 1951, 167, 175).

C. H. Dodd, unlike Bultmann, seems to doubt that there was a developed pre-Christian gnosticism (1953, 97–98), but he acknowledges that there was probably a pre-Christian, syncretistic gnostic tendency, which was quickened into gnostic systems by contact with Christianity (101). John shared with this gnostic tendency an interest in redemption through knowledge (*gnōsis;* 17:3) but differed from it on what constituted this knowledge (114). Dodd also recognizes certain parallels between John and the corpus of Egyptian religious texts known as the Hermetic Literature. These texts focused on the god Hermes, and Dodd refers to their outlook as the higher religion of Hellenism (10–11). They speak of salvation as knowledge of God (14) and attribute agency in creation to the Logos (29). While Dodd affirms a kinship between the Hermetic writings and one side of Johannine thought, he questions whether there was substantial borrowing on either side (53).

In addition to observing such religious parallels, Dodd also traces possible philosophical influences and posits a certain philosophical dimension in John. This comes out especially in his discussion of the Johannine logos concept and the relationship of John to Philo. Philo thought of himself as a loyal Jew but, as is well known, interpreted the Jewish Scriptures in terms of the popular Platonic-Stoic philosophy of the time (Dodd 1953, 54). Dodd holds that the parallelism between Philo and John on the logos concept is "remarkable" (71), although he acknowledges that in Philo the logos is not personal and does not become incarnate (73).

We can approach Dodd's analysis of the history-of-religions background of John's logos concept by listing four affirmations made in the Johannine prologue:

1. The Word (Logos) was with God (*ton theon*; 1:1b).

2. The Word was God (*theos*; 1:1c).

3. All things became through the Word (1:3a).

4. The Word became flesh (1:14a).

In Dodd's judgment items 1 and 3 can be accounted for in significant part against the background of the word of Yahweh in the Hebrew Bible (Ps. 33:6; 119:89; Dodd 1953, 268–69). But these same motifs also have parallels in Jewish Wisdom literature (274–75). And while the affirmation in item 4 that the word became flesh in one person is unique to John, the claim in the Wisdom literature that Wisdom became immanent in human beings and made them friends of God (Wis 7:24, 27; Sir 24:8–12) is remotely similar to the Johannine incarnation doctrine (275). This leaves us to deal with item 2 — the word was God. Stoicism would have agreed with this as well as with item 3 (280). And Dodd maintains that John's thought about the Logos rests on the Stoic distinction between the logos in the mind (thought) and the logos spoken (word). Behind these two senses lies the idea of that which has rational order (263).

Yet Philo remains the real source of John's claim that the word was God. The latter cannot be accounted for from either the Old Testament or Jewish Wisdom literature. But Philo does state that the Logos is God (Dodd 1953, 276, 280). In fact items 1 and 3 from John's prologue also have parallels in Philo (276). And Stoicism is ruled out as the effective influence because Stoicism understood the divine logos as immanent in the universe while for John the Logos is eternally beyond the world, although incarnate in Jesus. Thus John is dependent on Philo, for whom also the logos is transcendent, due to the influence of both the Old Testament and Platonism (280). If Dodd does not say that John borrowed directly from Philo, he does say that the Philonic kinship and reference are both intentional and specific (227, 279–80).

In light of this background Dodd can summarize the meaning of the incarnation in John by saying that it is the concentration in one person of the whole creative and revealing thought of God, which is also the rational meaning, plan, or purpose of the universe (1953, 277, 280, 282). Dodd concludes his discussion of John's logos concept by stating that the prologue of John's Gospel gives in brief outline a philosophy of life, a *Weltanschauung* (285).

Wayne A. Meeks is critical of Dodd's philosophical approach to the Fourth Gospel and affirms the correctness of Bultmann's insight that any attempt to understand the puzzle of the Fourth Gospel must begin with the myth of the preexistent redeemer who descends from the heavenly world above to earth and then makes an ascending return (1972, 44). Meeks is critical, however, of Bultmann's formulation of the pre-Christian gnostic redeemer myth. Bultmann's synthetic myth is an abstraction that obscures the variety of actual myths in extant texts. And Bultmann's myth is too heavily dependent on the Gospel of John, for whose Christology it is supposed to be a source (Meeks 1972, 45).

Meeks observes the common scholarly agreement that the Jewish Wisdom myth in some form lies behind both the Johannine Christology and the gnostic myths of the redeemer and the preexistent divine soul. The question, he says, is whether the Johannine and gnostic myths are independent variants of the Wisdom myth or one has influenced the other (Meeks 1972, 46). Meeks seems to answer the question both ways. On the one hand, Meeks distinguishes John from gnostic myth. The Fourth Gospel has no gnosticlike myth about the preexistent, heavenly origin of the human soul (68, 71). On the other hand, Meeks states that the relationship between the Johannine Christology and gnostic myths was probably reciprocal (72). While critical of Bultmann's formulation, Meeks seems not to reject the hypothesis of a pre-Christian gnostic redeemer.

Other scholars, however, extend less credence to the pre-Christian redeemer myth (Brown 1981a, LV; Smith 1995, 67). Charles Talbert gives these reasons for being skeptical of the pre-Christian myth: (1) The myth is not demonstrably present in pre-Christian sources. (2) Gnosticism could have existed without it. (3) John clearly does have a preexistent descending and ascending redeemer, but that pattern can be found in both Hellenistic and Jewish nongnostic texts prior to and parallel with the origins of Christianity. Graeco-Roman sources speak of the descent of the gods Jupiter and Mercury. Such a myth is reflected in Acts 14:8–18, where Barnabas and Paul are taken for Zeus and Hermes. Two strands in Judaism present descending/ascending redemptive figures. One of these is the Wisdom tradition, and the other is Jewish angelology with its angel of the Lord and archangels. In some Jewish circles these two streams merged with each other and with the logos theology. The titles that figure in this Jewish synthesis — Word, Son of God, Son of man — figure prominently in the Fourth Gospel (Talbert 1977, 53–57, 61, 66, 75–77).

Increasingly in recent years the Wisdom figure has been identified as the primary source behind John's logos concept and his theology more broadly. Yet, as Smith has pointed out, neither the noun *sophia* (wisdom) nor the adjective *sophos* (wise) appears in John. Perhaps John preferred "Logos" to "Wisdom" because he thought that a masculine noun could be more appropriately applied to the person of Jesus (Smith 1995, 17–18). In any case the exchange of terms would have seemed natural since Wis 9:1–2 uses the terms "Logos" and "Wisdom" synonymously as God's agent in creation. Raymond Brown sees not only a conceptual connection between John's Logos and Jewish Wisdom but also holds that the most decisive formal and stylistic influence on John's discourses is the speeches of Wisdom in such books as Proverbs, Sirach, and the Wisdom of Solomon (1981a, LXI).

Norman Petersen, while holding that John appropriated much of the Wisdom theology, also points out that John is critical of certain aspects of it. In John 6:27 the food that perishes is the law as understood by Moses' disciples and Wisdom as the wisdom tradition understood her. In Judaism the law and Wisdom are agents of life in this world, but for John eternal life is not of this world. John derived from the wisdom tradition the notion of the Word's being with God from the beginning. But whereas in John the Word *is* God from the beginning, Wisdom was created by God (Sir 24:9; Petersen 1993, 111, 121–23, 130).

I conclude this subsection with a further reference to Brown. Brown thinks it improbable that early gnosticism was the background of the Fourth Gospel and holds that the similarities that John has with Philo and the Hermetic Literature are not such as to suggest direct borrowing but rather point to a common background. John shares with the Qumran literature an emphasis on love within the community and a modified dualism that is not found in the Old Testament. But again the parallels are not strong enough to suggest direct dependence (Brown 1981a, LVI–LIX, LXII–LXIII). Smith regards the similarities between John and Qumran on dualism and eternal life as "striking" (1995, 16–17).

In contrast to the Hellenistic influences Brown regards the Palestinian Jewish impact on John as strong and maintains that the great currents of Old Testament thought — messiah, servant of Yahweh, king of Israel, prophet — are prominent (1981a, LX–LXII).

The Social-Historical Situation

Very influential has been the argument of Martyn that the story in John 9 — about the man born blind who was restored to sight by Jesus and who was driven from the synagogue because of his faith in Jesus (9:22, 34) — reflects actual experiences of the dramatic interaction between John's church and the synagogue (1979, 37; Brown 1981a, LXXIV–LXXV, LXXXIII–LXXXVI; 1981b, 690–91; Smith 1995, 55, 62). According to Martyn, 9:22 suggests that there has been (1) a formal decision, (2) made by Jewish authorities, (3) to bring against Christian Jews, (4) the dramatic measure of excommunication from the synagogue. Martyn argues that this action had been taken prior to the writing of the Fourth Gospel and affects Jews who had confessed Jesus as Messiah assuming that they could remain members of the synagogue. The Johannine community has been shaken by this action to separate from the synagogue those Jews who wanted to hold dual allegiance both to Moses and to Jesus as Messiah (see also 12:42 and 16:2; Martyn 1979, 38–40, 50, 61).

Martyn observes that the major stabilizing force in Judaism after the fall of Jerusalem was the rabbinic academy assembled in Jamnia under Johanan ben Zakkai. He argues that John 9:22 refers to the reformulation of the twelfth benediction of the Eighteen Benedictions made late in the first century A.D. during the period of Gamaliel II. The prayer placed in the center of Jewish worship a petition that God may cause Christian Jews (and others) to be destroyed and excluded from the Book of Life. The purpose of the benediction — the curse on heretics — was to make Judaism a monolithic structure by expelling those who did not conform to Pharisaic orthodoxy (Martyn 1979, 52–60).

Meeks develops the self-understanding of the Johannine community and the social function of the Gospel in light of the community's self-understanding. Due to the trauma of separation from the synagogue the Johannine community has a negative identity, fears being orphaned, and feels that it no longer belongs to the world (John 14:18; 17:14–15; Meeks 1972, 55, 66). The descent/ascent of the Redeemer speaks to this situation. The man who comes down from heaven is alien from all in the world, but those few who respond to him become progressively more enlightened until they, too, become detached from the world (17:14–15). Being detached from the world has the specific social dimension of breaking with the synagogue and joining the Johannine community (69).

The Gospel defines and vindicates the existence of the community that apparently sees itself as alien from the world, under attack, and misunderstood. Over against this alienation is the church's unity with the ascended Christ and through him with God. A primary function of the Gospel is to reinforce this community's social identity in isolation from the world (70–71).

Petersen has pursued especially the linguistic side of the Johannine community's social alienation. This church has become an outcast society, the sons of light, and they have created an antilanguage in order to legitimate for themselves their identity as an antisociety. The antilanguage is John's special language (Petersen 1993, 5). This language is part of the community's coping response to having been rejected by a society to which it once belonged, the dominant society of which it is now a marginalized minority. But this minority has the new identity of "sons of light" (John 12:36) as opposed to the "sons of the devil" (8:44). John's language response is to accept the polarization of the disciples of Jesus and the disciples of Moses and to invert the terms of the conflict. Those who have been rejected are the sons of light. Those who have been hated by the world are to hate the world (12:25; Petersen 1993, 80–82, 86–87). Petersen's analysis of John's language will be further discussed later in this chapter.

Smith sounds an appropriate warning against characterizing John's view of the world or the human situation as simply a by-product of the Johannine church's struggle with the synagogue (1995, 84; see also Meeks 1972, 71). Craig Koester amplifies Smith's suggestion by opposing the idea that the Johannine community was an introverted one living within a closed system of metaphors. Rather the Fourth Gospel presupposes a spectrum of readers from various backgrounds. Probably Jewish Christians were at the center of the audience, and fear of expulsion from the synagogue was a factor in the social situation. But the Gospel also presupposes that Samaritans (John 4:7, 39–42) and Gentile Christians from a non-Jewish background (7:35; 12:19–23, 32–33; 17:18–21) were a part of the Johannine community (Koester 1995, 18–24). Moreover, John used signs to show that Jesus is the Messiah (20:30–31) in the face of the fact that miracle working was not an important messianic expectation for first-century Judaism (Koester 1995, 75). These considerations suggest that the Johannine community was not a monolithic one totally consumed by the trauma of expulsion from the synagogue.

Author, Date, Place, and Purpose

Most scholars would probably date the composition of the final form of the Gospel of John between 90 and 100 A.D. It is hardly earlier than the reformulation of the twelfth of the Eighteen Benedictions, which occurred about 85 A.D. And the fragment of John 18:31–33, 37–38 in P[52], probably composed early in the second century, rules out a date much later than 100 A.D. (Brown 1981a, LXXXIII–LXXXVI; Smith 1989, 273).

Few scholars would argue for authorship by John the son of Zebedee, one of the Twelve. Raymond Brown, however, leans strongly toward the view that John, the son of Zebedee, is the Beloved Disciple (John 13:23; 19:26–27; 20:2–3; 21:7, 20–24), an eyewitness whose testimony is true (also 19:35). This would make John the disciple the source of the tradition behind the Fourth Gospel (Brown 1981a, LXVIII–CI). C. K. Barrett, on the other hand (1957, 98), while admitting that the Beloved Disciple probably refers to John, holds that there is no evidence that this reference was derived from John or that it rests on good historical tradition. Alan Culpepper observes that the Beloved Disciple has to be introduced to the reader as someone unknown and thus is a largely fictionalized character with no roots in the tradition (1983, 215).

Recent scholarship has shown relatively little interest in John's geographical place of origin (Smith 1989, 273). Brown posits a probable Palestinian origin for the tradition (1981a, LXII) but favors Ephesus as the place of final composition (CIII–CIV). Helmut Koester, on the other hand, in light of the close relationship to syncretized Judaism and ties with Palestinian geography regards Syro-Palestine as the most probable place of origin (1992, 245).

Brown sees as the primary purpose of the Fourth Gospel simply the desire to preserve the tradition and its insights. However, several more specific purposes may be noted: (1) to offer some apologetic against the followers of John the Baptist (John 1:8–9, 20; 3:28, 30; 10:41); (2) to attack the religious position of Judaism; (3) to polemicize against the Christian heresy of Docetism, that is, that Jesus only seemed to be human (1:14; 6:51–58); and (4) especially to move Christians to continue in and deepen their faith in Jesus as Messiah and Son of God (20:31) (Brown 1981a, LXVII–LXXVIII). Dodd, however, maintains that strengthening Christian faith is the secondary purpose of the Gospel (1953, 8–9). The primary purpose is to appeal to non-Christians who are concerned about eternal life and possess some degree of religious awareness.

I summarize here for the Fourth Gospel my conclusions about the theological significance of the historical situation: (1) The imaginative narrative world of the Gospel of John would have been close enough to the real historical world of the readers for them to have had a meaningful point of contact with the narrative world. The narrative world would contain both familiar and defamiliarizing elements. (2) The Holy Spirit could use the meaningful point of contact to turn the story into revelation by imprinting it on the hearts of the readers. The familiar point of contact enables the story to make sense. The defamiliarizing elements disclose something new. The Spirit gives the disclosure power.

The Word as Content

The theme of revelation has a centrality in the Gospel of John that is unique among the New Testament witnesses (Smith 1995, 24, 75). Many decades ago William Wrede (1971, 182) stated that the Johannine Jesus tirelessly presents to individuals and crowds, to friends and opponents, the most exalted secrets about himself, the Father, and their relationship. Perhaps one reason why John stresses revelation is that he is aware that his dualistic view of reality makes it a problem. God is above and Jesus has come from above, while human beings are from below and can only deal with earthly things (John 3:6, 31–32; 6:46; 8:23).

How can the chasm be bridged? John focuses on the issue of revelation because he wants to assure his readers that it has been bridged. And he uses symbolic language to do it. A Johannine symbol is constituted from an image, action, or person that can be perceived by the senses — light, darkness, water, bread, door, vine — and an interpretation that gives it a transcendent significance (Koester 1995, 1–4, 7). Or in different terms a Johannine symbol has a body that enables us to see into its soul, the depth dimension of which it is a manifestation (D'Sa 1987, 36, 44–46). In the light of such a definition Jesus — flesh and divine Logos — is the primary Johannine symbol (D'Sa 1987, 37; Koester 1995, 32–33). John's symbols hold earthly reality and the realm above in indissoluble amalgamation. Thus God's glory is seen, not brilliantly shining through Jesus' flesh nor beside it, but only hidden in it (Bultmann 1971, 63).

This section and the next one will deal in a fairly straightforward way with the Johannine view of the content and power of the word of God. Then we shall begin to look into the configuration of problems that contextualize the fact that a revelation of such transcendent meaning and power should prove to be actually effective for so few.

In distinction from what appears in the synoptic Gospels the word of God as content in John does not begin with the preaching of Jesus nor with the Old Testament word that predicts and prefigures him but with the Word that in the beginning before creation both was God (*theos* with no definite article; John 1:1c) and was *not* (the) God (*ton theon;* that is, with the definite article; 1:1b, 2) — since it was distinguished from God by being with or toward (*pros*) God. The divine Word became flesh in — as — Jesus (1:14). This is the horizon of meaning by which the narrator introduces the reader to the Gospel story. The narrator also tells us in the prologue that this one who comes from God speaks what he learned with God (1:18; cf. also 3:31–32; 6:46). Shortly thereafter Jesus appears on the scene and begins to speak and act. Since Jesus *is* the Word of God become flesh and communicates what he saw and heard with God (1:18; 3:31–32; 6:46), then the word he speaks is also God's (3:34; 17:8). But before I consider Jesus' testimony to himself, and John's further testimony to him in the narrative that flows from the prologue, I want to survey several views of the relationship between the prologue and the succeeding narrative. What is the literary relationship between the preexistent Word and the narrative of the spoken word? Form shapes meaning.

For Edwyn C. Hoskyns the words of Jesus are meaningless apart from their relationship to the word of God. On the other hand, the prologue moves not *to* but *from* Jesus. His coming is assumed throughout the prologue. The latter is not so much a preface to the Gospel as a summary of it (Hoskyns and Davey 1948, 137). Dodd sees the prologue as intending to catch the attention of a Hellenistic audience oriented to the logos idea in order to lead that audience to the historical actuality rooted in the Jewish tradition. That the Word became flesh and we beheld his glory is the substance of what is to be related (1953, 296). Barrett refers to the prologue as an introduction written to give the narrative an absolute theological framework. Yet Barrett's description of the prologue shows that he regards it as a summary as much as an introduction (1957, 125–26). J. A. T. Robinson argues that the prologue is virtually a conclusion that has been placed first. It is not that the prologue controls the narrative in such a way that the historical elements become illustrations of the timeless truths of the prologue. Rather the prologue and epilogue were written after the composition of the body of the Gospel. The historical narrative is primary, and the prologue is a meditative theological inference drawn from the history (Robinson 1965, 65, 67, 71–72).

Ernst Käsemann believes that the prologue is the Evangelist's reworking of a Christian hymn (1969, 152) and denies that it is either a summary or an introduction. Like the Gospel it should be understood as bearing witness to the presence of Christ (165). Since for Käsemann the prologue seems to function more briefly in the same way that the narrative does, I do not see how in his view it is substantively different from a summary. In any case he claims that the Gospel is a commentary on the crucial statement in the prologue: "we *saw* his glory" (John 1:14b, my italics; Käsemann 1969, 163). This affirmation epitomizes Käsemann's difference with Bultmann, who, as we have seen, stresses the *hiddenness* of the glory in Jesus.

For Francis D'Sa the hermeneutical key to the Fourth Gospel is the thematic development that unifies the prologue and the narrative. This theme can be stated as follows: to believe in Jesus is to see him as the symbol that expresses concretely the world's having its being in the Logos. That the language of God dwells and speaks in Jesus helps us to discover that God's word speaks in and through the world (D'Sa 1987, 37–39). The being of the Logos in the beginning (John 1:1) and his sharing in God's glory (1:14; 17:5) is the necessary apriority for the temporal manifestation of glory in Jesus' signs (2:11; D'Sa 1987, 40). Thus for D'Sa the eternal Logos — in an unproblematical way — is the basis for the words and acts of the earthly Jesus.

It is otherwise for Werner Kelber, in whose view John's exaltation of the Logos as divine, preexistent, and of un-derived origin is the quintessential logocentric gesture. The Logos is thus made the foundation of all reality, a transcendental signified beyond the world and time (Kelber 1990, 90). This move decenters or displaces the semiautonomy of the words (plural) of Jesus in favor of the Word (91–92). According to Kelber this foundational status of the Logos brings John into conflict with Jacques Derrida, who denies that there is or can be a transcendental signified (rational meaning) that is independent of all signifiers (sensible media of expression). There can be no God because there can be no ultimate signified, no pure intelligibility, that has not fallen into the play of signifiers in their differences (Derrida 1980, 7, 13–14, 71, 73).

There is no signified that is present in itself, referring only to itself. Rather all signifieds belong to a chain of signifieds, and each takes its meaning not from itself but from its difference from other signifieds (Derrida 1979a, 139–40). Thus signifieds are really signifiers (Derrida 1980, 7, 14, 73).

Kelber observes that although in the Gospel the Word has decentered the words of Jesus, the Word is then decentered or deconstructed by its entry into the human situation. This takes place in the words of the text (Kelber 1990, 92). But this decentering is not complete because the very words and acts that achieve the displacement of the transcendent Logos also assert the transcendent privilege of this same Logos (92–93). Kelber sees John's problem epitomized in the tension expressed in John 1:14. The Word can either become flesh and forgo glory or reflect glory and deny flesh (93) but evidently not both. Revealing glory would correspond to the transcendence of the Word, and becoming flesh would correspond to the Word's being decentered. It appears that Kelber regards John's failure to reconcile the irreconcilable and achieve consistency as a theological flaw. But I would judge that John was not trying to reconcile irreconcilables by reducing one to the other. He was rather staking out a position that required maintaining both the glory and the enfleshment. The revelation of glory is hidden in the flesh of Jesus (again Bultmann 1971, 63). Revelation is both real and hidden. Both need to be affirmed, not because — or not only because — John was fated by the logocentrism of Western metaphysics but because he observed that the revelation of the Word brought some to faith — we saw his glory — but that many more rejected Jesus — the glory is hidden. It is not as if John were trying to decenter the divine Word totally and ran afoul of Derrida despite himself. This is not to say that John does not deconstruct himself at certain points, as we shall see. And his theological position does disclose an existential problem, the problem of faith. How does one believe — receive — a revelation that is so hidden and whose reception is so fraught with obstacles? These are issues yet to be considered.

Stated succinctly, the relationship of the prologue to the Gospel narrative is that the divine Logos who became flesh in Jesus continues to speak himself in Jesus' words. That Jesus continues to speak the word (*logos*, singular) of God (John 15:3; 17:14) suggests that the divine preexistent Logos in some sense sustains what Jesus speaks. That Jesus speaks the words (*hrēmata*, plural) of God (3:34; 15:7; 17:8) suggests that the Logos is displaced by being refracted through the multiplicity of words whose meanings may not always be harmonious. That Jesus speaks both the word and words of God means that however problematical the words may be in their interrelationships it is still the word of God that is coming to expression. The Logos is divine, so it is God who encounters people in these words. But the fact that the Word is refracted in the words means that the Word as it reaches human beings through media of this world is neither transparently clear nor free of tensions.

Throughout the course of the narrative Jesus has a great deal to say about his identity as revealer, about his relationship with God and the import of that for revelation. Many images and motifs are used to express his significance as revealer (see Petersen 1993, 58–59, for a complete tabulation of the Fourth Gospels' identifiers of Jesus). Jesus affirms that he is the Messiah (John 4:25–26), and he is the Son to whom the Father has given the divine function of giving life and judging (5:21–22). He is also the one who gives the living water of eternal life (4:10, 14; 7:37). More than this Jesus claims that he *is* the light of the world (8:12; 9:5; 12:46); the bread of life who has come down from heaven (6:35, 38); the resurrection and the life (11:25); and the way, the truth, and the life (14:6). He is the gateway to life (10:9–10) and the good shepherd who lays down his life for the sheep (10:11, 14–15). His death — his being lifted up on the cross (3:14; 8:28; 12:32) — is also his exaltation. Jesus' death is the hour of his glorification (2:4; 4:21; 5:25, 28; 7:30, 39; 8:20; 12:16, 23; 13:31), the crucial moment of God's revelation (Smith 1995, 119–20).

Jesus affirms his unity with God (John 10:15, 30; 14:10–11, 20; 17:11, 21), the result of which is that to see or receive Jesus is to see or receive God (12:45; 13:20; 14:9). Jesus is who he is as the revelation of God, on the one hand, because he has come from or been sent by God (3:31–32; 5:36; 6:38, 44–46, 51, 57, 62; 7:29; 8:16, 23, 26, 38, 42; 13:3; 15:15; 16:28; 17:8, 16). On the other hand, as a human being he is an apt vehicle of God's intention because he claims no authority and does nothing on his own (5:19, 30; 7:16, 28; 8:28, 50; 12:49–50; 14:10, 24). It is because Jesus makes nothing of himself that he becomes a translucency to God. But he is not a transparency, as the difficulty of apprehending revelation will make clear.

Given this emphasis on Jesus' identity as revealer, we can see a certain plausibility about Bultmann's contention that Jesus communicates no specific truths about what he saw with God or the origin of the world or the fate of human beings but simply calls people to himself as the revealer sent by God (1955c, 41, 62–63). But it is not quite the case that Jesus' words are practically all about himself. He also speaks about God's love for the world (John 3:16) and God's intention to save it (3:17). The words of Jesus also have to do with discipleship to him. Jesus' death and exaltation (12:32) is connected to the necessity of the disciples' losing their lives to find them (12:24–26) by means of the way motif (14:6). Jesus in his death and exaltation is the way in which disciples are to follow (12:26) to enact their own death and new life (12:24–25). *Their* following (12:26) is at the same time their being drawn by Jesus (12:32). And having been loved by God and Jesus, disciples are to manifest love in the community (13:14–15, 34–35; 15:12–13).

For the characters in the Johannine narrative the revelation is Jesus himself speaking and acting. For the reader, on the other hand, Jesus is no longer present, and the revelation is limited to his words and the word about him that the Gospel is. But from the Johannine standpoint this is by no means a serious loss, for Jesus' word is the equivalent of Jesus. What is said about Jesus is also said about his word. Jesus is truth and life (John 5:24; 11:25; 14:6) and so are his words (6:63; 17:17; Bultmann 1955c, 63–64). And since the standpoint of the narrator of the Gospel agrees with the standpoint of Jesus (Smith 1995, 27; Staley 1988, 112), the whole Gospel narrative — words and acts or signs — is the revealing word.

The Word as Power

Jesus' word is power because God has given Jesus the Spirit without measure (John 3:34; Barrett 1957, 189). The Spirit is the source of the word's power, and the word is the instrument of the Spirit. The effect of the word's power is that it gives faith and life. In the miracle stories the healing word restores physical life (4:50–53a; 5:8–9; 11:43–44). Then this healing word with its power becomes the symbol (4:50–53a, 53b) for the capacity of Jesus' word as a whole to generate faith and confer eternal life (4:41; 5:24–26; 6:63, 68). In addition the word cleanses the disciples so that they can bear the fruit of ethical action (15:3–12).

Those who receive the light of revelation are enabled to become children of light (John 12:36). That is, they too become sources of the revealing word. The disciples have the Spirit bestowed upon them by the resurrected Jesus (20:22). The Spirit reminds them of what Jesus taught them (14:16–17, 26; 15:26) and even gives them insights into his word that they were not able to receive during his earthly mission (16:12–15). The word of Jesus thus continues in the church empowered by the Spirit, and like Jesus' own word it is able to bring people to faith (17:20). That the Gospel narrative itself has the purpose of generating faith and conferring eternal life is simply an instance of this (20:29–31).

The Effectiveness of Revelation: Creation, Believers, and Unbelievers

In John revelation is composed not just of words but also of signs — deeds or deeds-and-words. However, since the sign motif is intertwined with John's sense of the ambiguity of revelation and the difficulty of receiving it, it seems well to introduce the latter topic before engaging the sign concept. We have seen that for John the word is powerful, but it is also the case that it is effective for relatively few. In this section I want to indicate briefly what the two responses to revelation are and sketch the theological horizon within which John understands them.

Everything that is came into being through the agency of the Logos (John 1:3). In him was life, and this life was the light of human beings (1:4). Thus it seems that the life that enlightens is implanted in human beings through creation. Therefore, in 1:9 when the text refers to the light that enlightens every person, it could well be speaking of this light given with creation even though the reference to the *light* coming into the *world* in 1:9 is probably an anticipation of the *Word* becoming *flesh* in 1:14. That is, "the true light that enlightens every person" (my translation) in 1:9 both looks back to creation and forward to the incarnation.

Thus the whole human world came into being through the Logos-light. There is nothing that does not exist by means of the light (John 1:3, 10a). The world created by the Logos is his own (1:11). Since 1:10 refers to the world created through the light, "his own" in 1:11 has to mean all people (Käsemann 1969, 144) and not Israel (Dodd 1953, 270; Meeks 1972, 61). But when the light came into the world as the flesh of Jesus (1:9–10, 14, 17), his own (human) world did not know or accept him (1:10–11). Yet some did accept him and believe in his name (1:12). Thus both those who reject him and those who accept him belong to the same human world enlightened by the Logos through creation. Both are his own.

And yet humankind created by the enlightening Logos now belongs, as we have seen, to the world below, which is contrasted with the divine world above. This is the ambiguity — enlightened but separated — of the human situation, an ambiguity that makes revelation problematical. In John 3:12 Jesus asks Nicodemus and others like him (second-person plural pronoun) that if he has spoken to them in earthly terms and they have not believed, how will they believe if he should speak heavenly things. There is an irony, however, in Jesus' reference to earthly things. True, he has spoken of birth (3:3), water (3:5), and wind (3:8), which are earthly things. But it is birth "from above" (3:3), the Spirit goes with water (3:5), and the wind (*pneuma;* 3:8a–b) becomes Spirit (3:8c). So actually Jesus has spoken of earthly things that are more than earthly. John 3:12 suggests that speaking of purely heavenly things would be totally unproductive of belief. Thus the only hope for the human understanding of God is for Jesus to speak in earthly terms that have elusive heavenly meanings. This is the kind of language that Jesus uses throughout the Gospel. And although many miss the elusive heavenly meanings, the equivocal heavenly-in-the-earthly is the only possibility. The Johannine symbols are not unambiguously clear. Therefore, the very possibility of understanding and faith is placed in the realm of the problematical.

Given the hiddenness and ambiguity of the revelation, how does John account for its reception by those who do accept it? Given the reality and power of the revelation, its eschatological impact (John 1:32; 3:17–21; 4:35–36; 5:24; 11:25), how does he account for the repudiation of Jesus by those who reject him, who refuse both the light given in creation by the Logos and the light that comes in the incarnate Logos? How does John explain Jesus' rejection by his own? Both those who receive and those who repudiate are his own. These questions will be taken up after the discussion of signs as a medium of revelation.

Signs

Jesus' signs are formally parallel to his symbolic language. A sign in what I will call John's "normative" sense is composed of a sensible act — changing water to wine or multiplying bread and fish — that is more than physical and has a depth of meaning (John 2:11; 6:26). The meaning is typically developed by Jesus' words. The formal parallelism prompts John to use words and deeds as interchangeable synonyms (14:10–11). And in the end the signs are taken up into the narrative and are a part of the revealing word (20:31–33), as far as the reader is concerned. My procedure will be to draw some general conclusions from several sign passages and then to take a fuller look at chapter 6 — the feeding of the five thousand.

The normative view of signs is seen in John 6:26, which will be discussed later. It is seen in a very compact way in 2:1–11, and especially in 2:11. The changing of water to wine at Cana is a sign that manifests Jesus' glory. Jesus' glory in the Fourth Gospel is God's glory, which Jesus the Son has shared from eternity (1:14; 17:5). And God's glory is God's reality and presence (Smith 1995, 121–22). This revelation of glory evokes the faith of the disciples.

In John Jesus' works (*erga*) are virtually the equivalent of his signs, for signs are "worked," performed, or accomplished (*ergazomai;* 6:30). Jesus' works then testify that he is the one sent by the Father (5:36). Again in 10:32, 37–38 (cf. 14:10–11) his works are from God and show that he and the Father indwell each other. Here there is an implicit criticism of the Jews for not believing.

The normative sign in John either evokes faith or justifies a criticism of unbelief. The sign ought to be believed. Yet there is in John a sense of a different type of sign that ought not to be believed. I will simply call this the "reduced" sign. In John 4:47–48 Jesus complains that the royal official and others like him (plural "you") will not believe unless they see signs and wonders. The term "wonders" here may contribute to the negative connotation of the signs. The official had asked Jesus to heal his son. When Jesus speaks of signs in this sense and attributes the desire for them to others, he is saying that they misunderstand a sign to be a physical marvel rather than a physical reality that manifests a transcendent depth. Or as Petersen puts it, the sign is seen as pointing to or proving something outside of itself, such as Jesus' authority, rather than being itself the manifestation of Jesus' identity as the one from above (1993, 35–36). We see the reduced sign in 2:18 and probably in 6:30.

There are other passages in which the nature of the signs and the resulting faith is ambiguous. In John 7:31 many in the crowd believe in Jesus because of his signs, but it is unclear whether the narrator thinks they believed because of normative signs or reduced signs. The same is even more true for 2:23. In 11:45–48 many Jews believed because they had seen the raising of Lazarus, which is designated as a sign. But what sign did they grasp, that

Jesus is the resurrection and the life (11:25) or just that Lazarus was raised from the dead? We cannot be sure, although the latter is suggested in that the chief priests and Pharisees also refer to Jesus' signs — hardly in the normative sense. That reduced signs are in mind seems probable but not certain in 12:12–13, 17–18. The crowd that came out to hail Jesus as king of Israel did so because they had heard the testimony of the crowd that saw the raising of Lazarus. The latter is here called a sign. We have seen that the ambiguous signs are not equally ambiguous.

Perhaps when signs are portrayed in such a way that they cannot be clearly understood as either normative or reduced, the ambiguity might mean that what distinguishes the two types of signs is not so much a quality inherent in the signs themselves as it is the different responses of the beholders. A normative sign generated faith in the Johannine sense — the apprehension of the divine Word or glory in Jesus. Or a normative sign justifies the narrator, who is a believer, in criticizing the lack of faith. A reduced sign is a sign as sought (John 6:30) by an unbeliever (6:36, 44). So signs themselves are ambiguous and misinterpretable. What a sign is seems to depend on whether faith or unbelief is evoked.

But the case is not quite that neat, for it is not *just* a matter of faith or unbelief. Sometimes when faith is mentioned, the question arises as to what kind of faith is in view. Is it normative faith (a grasp of Jesus' true identity that changes one's existence; 3:13–21) or reduced faith (astonishment or marveling sufficient to overwhelm hostile doubt; 2:18; 6:30)? Uncertainties remain because in some sign contexts it seems impossible to discover definitively the nature of the faith attributed to the beholders. The faith of those Jews who witnessed or heard about the raising of Lazarus (John 11:45–48; 12:12–13, 17–18) is slightly ambiguous but is probably reduced faith. It is not so much an apprehension of Jesus *as* the resurrection and the life as it is being impressed by the raising of Lazarus (11:45; 12:17–18). The narrative strongly suggests that reduced faith finally degenerates into unbelief. The Jewish crowds who believe in Jesus and want to make him king because of his (reduced) signs (6:15; 11:45; 12:12–13, 17–18) finally call for his death (18:39–40; 19:6–7), perhaps persuaded by the high priest's logic at the literal, pragmatic level: it is well to have one person die for the nation (11:48–53). The unbelieving Jews, then, are portrayed as finally willing his death but are by no means prepared to accept the entailments of the theological claim that his death is his exaltation (12:32–34). The outcome of the story ironizes the earlier faith of the Jewish crowd and shows it to have been only apparent.

In other cases the nature of faith in signs is more genuinely ambiguous. In John 7:31 the nature of both signs and faith is undetermined, if for no other reason, because of the statement's brevity. It is a summary statement presenting a contrast to a rejection of Jesus (7:25–30). The ambiguity gains texture in 4:46–54. Jesus rebuffs the official's request for the healing of his son by saying in effect: you only want marvels (4:48). Nevertheless, Jesus promises him that his son will live. Thus when the narrator tells us that the man believed Jesus (4:50), we seem to have only reduced faith — belief in the possibility of miracle. Yet when we are told again shortly thereafter that the man — and his whole household — believed (4:53), we suspect that this is a second act of faith and one of a deeper dimension. There is a slight suggestion of a continuity in which reduced faith at least moves toward normative faith, and not into unbelief. Reduced faith may not be flawed without qualification. That the second act of faith is something more than reduced faith is suggested by the fact that the ending of this story parallels in content the ending of the first sign (2:11), which says that the *disciples* believed in Jesus. Both endings mention the sign and faith. We have seen then that reduced faith can either turn into unbelief or move toward normative faith.

In John 2:23–25 the ambiguity of faith prompted by signs is intense and inescapable. This summary statement tells us that during the Passover many believed in Jesus' name because they saw his signs. But Jesus did not entrust himself to them because he knew what was in humankind. The point is underscored by the double use of the verb *pisteuein*. Many believed (*pisteuein*) in his name, but he did not trust (*pisteuein*) their faith. This means that the faith is portrayed as flawed. It was reduced faith. It is simply baffling that the narrator should place this critique of the crowd's faith in Jesus' mouth since in the brief description of the faith itself the latter is quite normative.

In John the names of Jesus the Son and God the Father represent Jesus (14:13–14, 26; 15:16, 21; 16:23–24, 26) and God (5:43; 12:28; 17:6, 11–12, 26) themselves (Bultmann 1971, 59; Brown 1981a, 11). Therefore, the name of Jesus is a quite proper object of faith (3:18), and faith either *in* (*eis*, into) Jesus or *in* his name is one of several ways in which John expressed normative faith (Bultmann 1955c, 70–71) or the most characteristic way John described this faith (Dodd 1953, 183). In 1:12 faith in the name of Jesus is the same thing as receiving Jesus, and it is the human side of the interaction that actualizes being a child of God. In the Gospel's climatic statement of purpose (20:30–31) signs have the purpose of generating faith, and Jesus' name is the source of eternal life.

John 2:23–25 is a single narrative unit in which the description of faith portrays it as thoroughly normative while the reaction of Jesus to it portrays it as flawed and reduced. The faith of the many is equally both normative and reduced. This uncertainty or undecidability about the nature of faith suggests that there is no firm boundary between the two kinds of faith and hence no stable distinction between the two kinds of people who have it. It may be that John's text intends to make a clear distinction between normative and reduced faith, but the difficulty in making the difference unambiguous undercuts deconstructively that intention.

I turn now to the sign of the feeding of the five thousand because it is one of the richest and most interesting of the signs and because discussing it enables me to include sacrament in the understanding of revelation. There are tensions in the story and the dialogues that follow it, which might result from problematical editing of source materials — or could simply be John's tensive way of telling the story. In any case I shall try to make sense of the text as it stands. One tension is that the word "sign" does not always have the same meaning or is not seen from the same vantage point. Another is that while the people who participate in the feeding respond by hailing Jesus as the prophet who is to come into the world (John 6:14) and by wanting to make him king (6:15), the next day these same people address him merely as "rabbi" (6:25) and imply that he has performed no sign (6:30).

John tells us that after the feeding and the gathering up of the leftovers, when the people saw the sign that Jesus had done, they said, "This is indeed the prophet who is to come into the world" (6:14). Their judgment has reference to the Jewish expectation that God would send a prophet like Moses (Deut 18:15, 18). And since these people credit Moses with having given them the bread from heaven (John 6:31; cf. Exod 16:4, 15; Ps 78:24; Wis 16:20) — or at least that is what Jesus takes them to have meant (6:32) — and since Jesus performed the sign of miraculous food, then Jesus must be the prophet like Moses. But the sign they saw was a reduced sign. They simply saw the satisfying of physical hunger (6:13–14, 26b), as they had seen the sign of healing physical bodies (6:2). They had not, however, *really* seen the sign — in the normative sense.

On the next day some of the five thousand sought Jesus out on the other side of the lake. These people clearly are among those whom Jesus had fed, as John 6:22, 24 show (contra Petersen 1993, 34). There is no indication that they are a different crowd, as is seen especially in the fact that Jesus addresses them as people who had eaten their fill of the loaves (6:26). But their enthusiasm for Jesus has evidently suffered some diminution, for now they only address him as "rabbi" (6:25). Jesus tells them that they are looking for him, not because they saw signs, but because they ate bread and were filled (6:26). Since Jesus *contrasts* seeing signs with the physical benefit of being fed, he means "sign" in the normative sense, a manifestation of his true identity. The narrator and Jesus do not disagree. The former means that the people did see signs in the reduced sense (6:2, 14). Jesus means that they did not see signs in the normative sense (6:26). What they saw they saw with blinded eyes (12:39–40) and so did not really see. Not to see the sign in the full sense is to fail to grasp the superfluity of meaning.

Jesus' point is that if they had really seen the normative sign, they would not have thought of Jesus as the one who can multiply the bread that perishes (John 6:26b, 27a) but would have understood that Jesus is the Son of man who gives the bread that endures for eternal life (6:27). As the dialogue continues, the crowd becomes a bit polemical, and Jesus develops more fully the meaning of the sign. He tells them that the work of God is that they should believe in him (6:29). They reply with a question about what sign he is going to perform that they might see it and believe in him (6:30). Their ancestors ate from the manna — the bread from heaven — that Moses provided (6:31–32). What can this request for a sign mean since they have already seen the miraculous feeding and been much impressed (6:14–15)?

One possible interpretation is that they have decided that Jesus has not really performed a sign, since the feeding does not really compare with Moses' bread from heaven. On the other hand, their implying that they have not seen a sign from him *might not* signify that they had literally not seen a sign in their (reduced) sense of a sign, but rather the implication might have a dramatic and polemical force. They had seen signs in their sense but in the heat of argument were not going to admit it. Jesus' reply is that Moses had not really given the bread from heaven (6:32), but apparently only the bread that perishes (6:27). It is God who gives the true bread from heaven (6:32). The bread of God, the bread of life, is

Jesus himself, who has come down from heaven for the life of the world (6:33, 35, 38).

I conclude the discussion of John 6 with a very summary representation of the dialectical play between physical and spiritual — earthly and heavenly — in the chapter. The physical dominates the story of the actual feeding and continues to be the focus until 6:27, where Jesus distinguishes the food that perishes from the food that endures for eternal life, which the Son of man will give. The eternal or heavenly (6:31–32), having been introduced, now governs the dialogue, and Jesus is no longer merely the one who will *give* the food of eternal life but presents himself as *being* the true bread from heaven whom God gives (6:32–33) and the bread of life who has come down from heaven (6:35, 38). Jesus does not just nourish physical life but is the source of eternal life.

There is a return to the physical with the Jews' complaining criticism of Jesus' claims to be from heaven: he is simply Jesus, the son of Joseph, whose father and mother they know. He belongs to the familiar world. In reply Jesus reiterates his claim that he is the only one who has seen God (6:46) and is the bread of life who has come down from heaven and who confers eternal life (6:48–51b). Then Jesus dramatically recurs to the physical with the startling assertion that the bread that he will give for the life of the world is his flesh (6:51c). Eating the flesh of the Son of man and drinking his blood is the only vehicle of eternal life (6:53–56). Physical and spiritual are joined in the affirmation that this *flesh and blood* — the elements of the Eucharist — are the bread that came down from heaven, which is to be distinguished from the merely physical bread that Moses gave (6:58).

Jesus recognizes that this inseparability of earthly and heavenly might offend some of his disciples (John 6:61); thus, he returns again to the spiritual. The physical elements of flesh and blood are the bread from heaven because Jesus is the Son of man who keeps the connection open between earth and heaven: he descends and ascends (6:62). This connection is the virtual equivalent of the work of the Spirit (6:63a). Such a relationship between the descending/ascending Son of man and the Spirit is also affirmed in the birth-from-above discourse (3:5–6, 8, 13). John is not arguing that any flesh can be the vehicle of the Spirit but that only the flesh/bread with which Jesus is identified can be because Jesus is absolutely unique. He is the only one who has been with God, who has seen God, and who has made known what he has seen (1:18; 6:46).

We were surprised when, after the strong emphasis on Jesus' heavenly origin and his critique of earthly food (John 6:27, 46–51b), Jesus states that the bread he will give for the life of the world is his flesh (6:51c). We are surprised again when, after the declaration that Jesus' flesh is uniquely the vehicle of spiritual reality (6:51c, 53, 56, 58, 62–63a), he tells us that the flesh benefits nothing (6:63b). It is the Spirit that gives life (6:63a), and Jesus' words are spirit and life (6:63c). And then Peter confesses, "You have the words of eternal life" (6:68). John then interprets the Spirit as the power of Jesus' words to give life.

John began this sign at the physical level (the multiplication of loaves and fish) and ended at the spiritual — the Spirit as Jesus' words. Beginning with the physical and ending with the spiritual does not mean that the physical is simply devalued, superseded, and renounced in favor of the spiritual. That would not be compatible with John's belief that it is from the incarnation of the Word in the flesh of Jesus that we have received grace and truth (1:14, 16–17). The flesh by itself is without benefit, but it is the necessary vehicle for the Spirit. The incarnate Word, flesh-and-Spirit, extends itself throughout history, manifesting life, in the mode of the elements of the meal. These elements are made meaningful and effective in that they are contextualized by Jesus' words — and the Gospel narrative — that act as the power of the Spirit.

The Why and How of Believing

Disciples as Believers

The revelation of God's glory in word and sign is received by faith. *Disciples* are those who believe. Jesus has made known to his disciples everything that he heard from the Father (John 15:15; 17:6), and they have believed (2:11; 6:67–69). Discipleship is defined by faith, and to believe is to understand (Smith 1995, 98). Knowledge and normative faith overlap each other. Perhaps it is understanding that in considerable part distinguishes normative faith from reduced faith (Bultmann 1955c, 73–74). Knowledge or understanding is not a further development beyond normative faith, for the two categories can be used synonymously (6:69; 16:30–31; 17:6–8), and both lead to eternal life (3:15–16, 36; 17:3, 6–8).

The Reasons for Believing

What are the reasons for believing? Given the ambiguity of revelation, how does John account for the faith of those who do believe?

According to Meeks the fact that some who belong to the earth respond to the heavenly revealer cries out for a mythological explanation that John does not give. John does not explain faith by saying in mythological terms that the spirits of believers also come from heaven (Meeks 1972, 68, 71). But, we should say, John does give some reasons that stay closer to the situation of historical encounter. I shall discuss these issues with the following questions in mind: (1) Why do people believe; what is the subjective intention on the part of the believer? (2) How are people able to believe? (3) Is it possible — in the light of God's choice — for some not to believe? The discussion will show that questions 1 and 2 penetrate each other and cannot be separated.

In John 1:1–14 there seem to be three moves in the process of actualized revelation: (1) the light comes into the world (1:9) or the Word becomes flesh (1:14); (2) some receive him or believe in his name (1:12a–b); (3) to them he gave power to become children of God (1:12c). Receiving him is distinguishable, if not separable, from the preceding initiative of the Logos/light as well as from being given the power to be a child of God. Being made a child of God is a consequence of receiving the light in Jesus.

Receiving by faith is a human responsive act, but in context it is performed by the light's own who have been created by the light. Thus reception is enabled both by being created by the light and by the appearance of the light in Jesus. The independence of faith is further qualified by John 1:13. Here those who receive the light are said to have been born, not from human desire, but from God. Being born from God (aorist indicative) seems to precede their faith and can hardly be distinguished from becoming children of God (1:12b). Thus being a child of God or being born from God is not just a consequence of faith but also an enablement of faith. Furthermore, being born from God can hardly be distinguished from being born from above (3:3, 7; *gennaō* in both cases). And the latter results from the Spirit (3:5–6), which is given with the descent/ascent of the Son of man (3:13–14).

In John 3:18–21 the subjective content, intentionality, and independence of faith come somewhat more strongly to expression. People believe because they have a purpose in view. Bultmann holds that the purpose clauses in 3:20–21 do not express subjective and conscious intention but rather in gnostic fashion express the tendencies of the two natures — light or dark (1971, 158). I believe that Bultmann's contention should be resisted for three reasons: (1) it is an insufficiently close reading of the details; (2) it imposes gnostic ontology on John; (3) it expresses the bias of most twentieth-century biblical interpretation against psychological meanings.

The person who comes to the light in John 3:21 has to some extent seen the light, been brought to a conscious awareness of something. Otherwise the intention to have the nature of her deeds made manifest, exposed to greater light, makes no sense. The person in 3:20 who hates and rejects the light in order that his deeds might not be exposed as evil is involved in self-deception. The person who deceives himself by repressing an unpleasant truth about himself has to be somewhat conscious of the unwelcome element in order to have a motive for wanting to make it unconscious. And the desire to make the unpleasant, conscious element unconscious is intentional because the person intends to escape the pain caused by the unacceptable truth. The concealed truth, however, is not completely repressed, so that the self-deceived person paradoxically knows and does not know the truth at the same time.

The person who comes to the light in John 3:21 is, then, a self-deceived person coming out of self-deception. She has dimly known that her deeds are accomplished by God and not by herself. This partially revealed and partially concealed truth, she intends to have further illuminated by the light of revelation.

Faith, therefore, is an intentional move in which people act to carry out their own purpose. Faith is defined in relation to the coming of the light, which in John 3:18–21 has the function of exposing what people are and which may be John's most important symbol (Koester 1995, 123; Petersen 1993, 64, 72, 80). Faith, then, is coming to the light for the very purpose (hina; 3:21) of having it shown, made visible, what one's situation really is. And what that situation really is is that one's deeds or works have been accomplished in or by God. Thus while people may act and act intentionally, in the end their deeds are not wholly their own. The work that God requires in John — believing in the Son of man whom God has sent — is God's work, what God accomplishes in them (6:27–29). It is possible for one to come to the light only because God draws one (6:44–45). It seems that to come to Jesus one must have a predisposition to believe, a predisposition given by God (6:65).

Why would people intend to be exposed as not finally being the source of their own ultimate well-being, as not being the ground of their own action? The reason for intending to have one's nonautonomy exposed is suggested by John's reference to the believer as one who does the truth (John 3:21a). In John truth is reality, especially God's reality (Dodd 1953, 175–79; Bultmann 1955c, 18–19). The Evangelist suggests that people in the end want to be in accord with reality. It is worth being exposed as not being the source of one's own deeds in order to be in touch with reality, with God who is the true One (3:33). Truth and life are two sides of the same thing, the way to which is Jesus (14:6). It is worth having one's nonautonomy brought to light in order to rest on reality, a reality one does not command. Faith grasps this disclosure that we are not the ultimate source of the faith on which we stand — this shock to our false autonomy — as an act of God's love (3:16), for the revealing act puts us in touch with the truth (3:21, 33). It is *love* that requires us to embrace reality. To have this kind of faith is to be born from above. Faith understands that it is love that requires us to face painful reality.

I agree with those who hold that there is no contradiction in John between faith as an intentional decision made in freedom and the claim that faith is dependent on God's enablement (Smith 1995, 94–95, 98). God's predisposing act of grace opens up the possibility of free human action. As Bultmann puts it (1955c, 23), God's predisposition occurs not literally prior to the decision of faith but rather occurs within it.

It seems to me, however, that there are at least a couple of texts in John that fall out of the category of enablement and into the category of a divine determination that more or less eliminates free human intentionality. Disciples are disciples because Jesus chose them, not vice versa (John 15:16, 19), and those whom Jesus chose are God's own whom God gave him (17:6, 9). I now cite three passages that seem to express an intensifying divine determination. First, Jesus has lost none of those given to him except the one destined by Scripture to be lost (17:12). Second, Jesus has not lost them because *God wills* that they not be lost (6:39). And third, in fact it is *not possible* that Jesus should lose what God has given him (10:29). There is a distinction and tension in John between not being able to believe without being drawn by God (3:21; 6:44, 65) — the necessity of enablement by God — and, on the other hand, not being able not to believe if God does draw one (6:39; 10:29) — the impossibility of not believing.

The Ambiguity of Disciples' Faith

We have seen that disciples are defined as those who believe, and we have considered John's reflections on the why and how of faith. Yet while disciples are those who believe and understand, somehow — or sometimes — they do not. Thus their faith and knowledge are ambiguous. I am inclined to disagree with the view that in John believing and not believing are sharply distinguished and one is either in or out (Bultmann 1971, 155; Smith 1995, 95). We have observed that the disciples believe and understand now, in the narrative present. But in a number of other passages, their faith or understanding is lacking and will be completed only in the future at Jesus' resurrection or with the giving of the Spirit at his glorification (John 2:22; 7:39; 12:16; 13:7; 14:20; 16:12–13; 20:9). Somewhat more pejoratively in 16:31 Jesus questions whether the disciples do now in fact believe and in 14:9 questions whether Philip knows him. We have noted that the Jewish crowd's earlier (reduced) faith is ironized by their final rejection of Jesus. But the disciples' failures apparently do not ironize their faith, or not very much, for at the end, despite the deficiencies, they are still Jesus' disciples and have a future with him.

John has little to say directly about why the believing disciples at many points in the story have less-than-adequate faith or knowledge. But we may draw some interpretive conclusions about why the disciples can be represented during the narrative as both having and not having normative faith. It is the interpreter and not the narrator who makes the explanatory connection explicit. The most comprehensive reason suggested is the fundamental way that John narrates the story of Jesus, the way he portrays the protagonist. The inconsistency of the disciples' faith corresponds to that portrayal. The Jesus of John's Gospel is portrayed as the earthly Jesus of the past who has not yet been glorified. But this fleshly figure of the past speaks also as the one who has already been resurrected and exalted (John 3:13; 6:62; 17:11) and has already won the victory over the world that will result from his future death (16:33; O'Day 1991, 159–62). Thus John's protagonist is both the Jesus of the past who has not been glorified and has not given full revelation and also the glorified Jesus who has given the Spirit and full revelation and who lives on in the community.

During Jesus' ministry prior to his resurrection and the giving of the Spirit the disciples do not believe properly or understand fully because full revelation has not yet been given. Jesus speaks in figures or dark sayings (*paroimia*), and only in the future will he speak in plainness or openness (*parrēsia;* 16:25). The disciples then claim that they are hearing him *now* in openness (16:29), but that is when Jesus questions whether they really believe (16:31). Yet he then paradoxically affirms that he has already conquered the world (16:33). So why should they not hear plainly? The revelation that confronts them as puzzling dark sayings is not some particularly esoteric strand, but rather Jesus' whole message appears to them as puzzling (Wrede 1971, 192; O'Day 1986, 105).

But then, as we have seen, the Jesus of John's narrative is already the glorified Son who has already given the Spirit (14:17). Therefore, the disciples have full revelation and do believe and understand (2:11; 6:67–69; 17:6–8). The change from dark sayings to plainness or fullness is not as much an increase in the content of revelation as in effective power that comes with the giving of the Spirit.

Since in John the time before Jesus' resurrection and the time after it overlap each other, revelation is both obscure and plain, and faith is both partial and adequate. Since the disciples are paradoxically confronted with both partial and full revelation, their unbelief and misunderstanding are directed in some part to the full or plain revelation. Therefore, the fullest revelation meets with unbelief, not only on the part of those who overtly reject it but also on the part of those who accept it.

The disciples' (modest) failures of faith, then, are connected to the paradoxical overlapping of the times. And they are also connected to the gap that we have observed between the transcendent origin of Jesus and the earthly origin of the disciples (Wrede 1971, 187). Beyond that Jesus does not want to give them more than they can endure (John 16:12). Finally, the disciples' lack of faith and understanding means that they participate to some degree in the situation of unbelievers; therefore, the reasons that John gives for the unbelief of unbelievers apply also to the believing disciples in their unbelief.

The Why of Not Believing

Recall that in John all humans are created by the divine Logos and are his own (1:3, 11). But many of his own did not accept him (1:11). John for the most part reduces the various Jewish groups simply to "the Jews," who can at times also be called "Pharisees." The Jews are the unbelieving opponents but are not the same as

Israel since some Israelites come to believe in Jesus. John, in assigning this role to the Jews, has them represent the world in its opposition to Jesus (Bultmann 1955c, 5; Smith 1995, 30, 49–50, 80–81, 89).

As in the discussion of the reasons for believing, in the consideration of the reasons for not believing the reasons sort themselves out into three categories: (1) the subjective stance and intention of the unbeliever, (2) a multifaceted destiny that makes belief problematical, and (3) a fate that would seem to make faith impossible — as a free act. By *destiny* I mean a set of circumstances in which a person must decide and act, in this context a set that limits the possibilities to be chosen in an adverse way but does not completely cut off freedom to choose. Since destiny makes faith difficult but not impossible, the failure to believe when destiny defines the situation must be assigned to the subjective stance of the person as well as to the extrasubjective factors of destiny. By *fate* I mean a condition in which there is no freedom, or no freedom to do the right thing.

The Subjective Intention of the Unbeliever

As faith is defined in relation to the coming of the light, so is unfaith (John 3:19–20). And unbelief, like belief, is, as we have observed, an intentional act based on human interests. Unbelievers hate the light and love the darkness and do not come to the light in order that (*hina*, expressing purpose) they should not be exposed. Exactly what is it that unbelievers do not want to have exposed? Several nuances are suggested here. Since unbelievers are the opposite of believers, who are willing to have exposed that their deeds have been accomplished by God, the unbelievers must be unwilling to have it disclosed that the faith in which life resides (3:16, 36) is God's work and not theirs. They do not want to face the fact that life is not at their own disposal. They would rather live in the darkness of not knowing and be deprived of life than to face the truth about themselves.

The narrator also says that the unbelievers loved the darkness *because* their deeds were evil. Both the terms *ponēros* and *phaulos* are used for evil, and both have moral connotations (Bultmann 1971, 157). What evil deeds did they not want exposed? For John these worthless deeds might be their lack of love (13:14–15, 34–35; 15:12–13). Evil deeds are also expressions of the volitional posture that seeks finite security and rejects the life that comes from beyond — that attempts to assert autonomy. Belief is inhibited by receiving praise from each other rather than seeking the glory of God (5:44). Again some Jews believed — with a reduced faith — but would not confess it because they feared expulsion from the synagogue. They too loved human praise more than the glory of God. They were loathe to relinquish the security of social solidarity (12:42–43). Will is a factor in understanding. Resolving to do the will of God is a condition for discerning the truth about Jesus' teaching (7:17). The misdirected will is governed by the effort to speak out of one's own resources and to seek one's own glory (7:18).

The Destiny of Unbelief

In the Johannine narrative world there is a tightly woven texture of adverse destiny. In the first place the revelatory event itself is problematical. Jesus' true identity is not obvious but is rather hidden. Sympathetic characters mistake his identity and have to be told by him who he is (John 4:19, 25–26). And unsympathetic characters take him as the merely human son of Joseph (6:41–42). In the latter case explicit revelation (6:35, 38, 40) does not overcome unbelief. In fact the revelation generates resentment (6:41–42). Since there is a strong sense in which Jesus is his word, the obscurity of his identity is enforced by his making important statements in symbols that can be taken in more than one way. The characters who hear him typically take the wrong way (3:3–6, 9; 4:10–13).

On the one hand, the Jews fail to understand Jesus because his words are obscure. He says the same kind of thing to the Jews that he says to his disciples. For example, he tells both that he will be with them a little while longer and then leave them and they will not be able to follow (John 7:32–34; 8:21; 13:33; 16:16), and neither understands him (7:35–36; 8:22; 13:36–38; 16:17–18). If this saying when addressed to the disciples (13:33; 16:16) is a dark saying (*paroimia;* 16:25), is it not when addressed to the Jews (Wrede 1971, 203)? It must be since 10:6 explicitly says that Jesus spoke to the Pharisees in *paroimiai*. On the other hand, Jesus speaks to the Jews clearly, they have seen his works, and still they misunderstand him (15:22, 24; 18:19–21) — apparently because of their recalcitrant will (Wrede 1971, 203).

The Johannine Jesus does not reflect on the relationship between these two motifs: (1) the word of Jesus is obscure; (2) the word is clear and plain but is misunderstood out of ill will. Nor does John state as Mark does — even if parabolically (Mark 4:26–27) — that the relationship between word and hearer is a mystery. But that mystery is tacitly suggested by the fact that both of these motifs are present in the Johannine texture.

The Jews' relationship to their Scriptures gives to their destiny a long-term historical dimension. A destined propensity not to believe is suggested by the theme that they belong to a religious tradition that misinterprets Scripture. They think that they have eternal life in Scripture, but they miss the real import of Scripture — its testimony to Jesus — and are condemned by Moses for their lack of faith (John 5:39–40, 45–47). Also they mistakenly believe that Moses gave their fathers bread from heaven (6:31–33). Traditions about the messiah prevent the Jews from seeing Jesus as Messiah. In fact they use two opposing traditions against him — that none will know where the messiah is from (7:27) and that the messiah will be from Bethlehem (7:41–42). The contradiction in the claims that they make from tradition doubtless points to the perversity of their will. The conviction of the Jews that they already have the truth and that as descendants of Abraham they are free prevents them from recognizing the truth in Jesus and receiving real freedom from him (8:31–40). The Jews' posture is entangled in an adverse historical process.

John's presentation of the role of Scripture in Israel's life displays the interaction of freedom and destiny. Scripture is authoritative (John 10:35) and is a true witness to Jesus (5:39, 45–46), but the Jews refuse to believe in its true meaning (5:47) and do not will to come to Jesus (5:40). Believing in Moses properly seems to be a condition for believing in Jesus' words (5:47). The perverse will of the Jews imposes on Scripture a misinterpretation (6:31–33), and the misinterpretation becomes a power that makes belief in Jesus difficult, for one's wrong choice becomes an enslaving destiny (8:34) that then victimizes one and curtails freedom.

The adverse destiny in the Johannine narrative world also has a natural dimension. Those who do not believe belong to the flesh, the earth, the world, the region below (John 3:6a, 31–32; 8:15, 23), and this location in nature — contrasted with the realm of Spirit and heaven — has a negative impact on how they believe and judge.

The last question to be taken up in this section is whether God or the Johannine Jesus *intentionally* blinds the unbelievers. Wrede believes not (1971, 203). However, in John 9:39 Jesus came into the world for *krima* (judgment or separation) in order that (*hina*, expressing purpose) those not seeing might see and that those seeing might become blind. Perhaps it should be said that while the intentionality of Jesus' concealing action is not as overt in its effect on unbelievers in John as it is in Mark (4:10–12), it is nevertheless present in John. Jesus' purpose is behind the blindness of unbelievers, but that purpose works itself out dialectically within a human dynamic. Jesus came in order that those who see might become blind (9:39), but then we see that those who see are actually those who *think* they see (9:40–41). Because they think they see, they reject the light and thus remain in the darkness of sin (9:40–41). These are the same people who speak out of their own resources (7:18) and prefer the darkness to the truth about themselves (3:20–21).

We also have divine intentionality and causality in John 12:37–40. The failure of the Jews to believe despite Jesus' many signs occurs in order to (*hina*) fulfill Isaiah's question about why the Israel of his time failed to believe his message. Then it is stated that the Jews of John's narrative world were *not able* to believe in Jesus *because* Isaiah said (or because as Isaiah said) God "has blinded their eyes and hardened their heart" (12:40a). In the LXX of Isa 6:9–10 the prophet reports that God told him to tell the people to see and hear but not to understand. However, John stiffens this to read that God has blinded and hardened them. Clearly for John the word of God in Scripture creates a destiny of unbelief. The impediment to belief that Israel's history imposes on the Jews is not just from the power of a linguistic tradition — although we have seen that the latter is considerable. This power of language is intensified for John because the scriptural tradition is regarded as *God's* word. The word that states that God has blinded them is *God's* word and thus is the instrument of God's power, his negative power.

Has destiny now become fate? The Jews are blind because God has blinded them. What choice does one have to understand if God has prevented it? One could argue from the texts just considered (John 9:39; 12:37–40) that faith in this Johannine strand is impossible, impossible as a result of causes quite beyond human willing.

But one could also argue, as I have, that it is still a matter of destiny. I observed that in John 9:39–41 those in the dark are there not only because of Jesus' intention but also because of their own preferential choice. And even though (or just because) the negative intention and causality in 12:37–40 come from *God*, the Jews are still in touch with God. It is destiny shaped by God. Unbelievers have been created by God and are his own and also have been encountered by the divine Word as Jesus. This means that even though the unbelievers have been predisposed to unbelief by destiny, they can be thought to embrace this destiny with a certain freedom. They are God's own, and God is true (*alēthēs* in 3:33; 8:26; *alēthinos* in 7:28; 17:3), and the word by which he creates is truth (*alētheia* in 17:17), as is Jesus (14:6). Since then the truth confers freedom (8:32), even unbelievers have some degree of freedom.

The Fate of Unbelief

In certain Johannine texts we seem to have crossed the border from an adverse destiny that is also chosen to a fate in which there is no real freedom to choose to believe. People could logically assert a recalcitrant will in various ways and be the prey of multiple dimensions of negative destiny and still be regarded as God's own and thus as having some degree of freedom. God's own would both have willfully strayed in freedom and also been victimized. But how can one be God's own and also be not from or of God (John 8:47)?

I begin with the devil motif. Bultmann grants that in John the devil represents the power to whose dominance the world has surrendered itself. But he denies that this power is mythologically conceived as having committed a trespass in primeval times that thereafter has enmeshed human beings in a sinister heritage. Rather the devil is the power that lurks behind each particular instance of rejecting the light (Bultmann 1955c, 17–18, 24–25). Bultmann may be right that the devil is not conceived mythologically, but that does not mean the devil does not represent a power that eliminates freedom.

The Jews claim that God is their father (John 8:41). Jesus retorts that they are rather from their father the devil, and they choose to do his desires (8:44). But how much choice do they have if their source of life (father) is a suprahuman power? The devil does not stand in the truth and is by nature a liar (8:44). The Jews cannot understand or believe the truth (8:43, 45) because they participate in a suprahuman power whose nature is lying. The Jews in fact do not believe in Jesus because he speaks the truth (8:45). Fate has eliminated faith.

Interwoven with the devil theme is the word theme. Jesus' word does not make room for itself in or reach the Jews (John 8:37). Why does it not? In 5:38 Jesus tells the Jews that they do not have God's word abiding in them *because* they do not believe in Jesus, whom God sent. The causal clause here could have two senses.

(1) Not believing in the one God sent is the cause of not having God's word abiding in one. Therefore, the reference to God's word is a reference to the word that Jesus preached. Because they rejected Jesus' preaching of God's word, it does not abide in them. (2) But not believing in Jesus could be taken as evidence for the fact that they do not have God's word already abiding in them. Thus, the reference to the word is to the imprint that creation by the agency of the Word should have left on them. That they do not believe in Jesus is evidence that God's word does not abide in them. That implies that this abiding presence is a prior requisite for believing Jesus' word.

This second interpretation would probably be criticized as idealizing by Käsemann (1969, 143), but there are passages in John that suggest, if they do not require, the interpretation that the creative Logos imprinted himself on human beings in such a way that there should be a predisposition for receiving Jesus' teaching. Otherwise Jesus' *critical* observation that they do not have the word of God abiding in them (John 5:38) or do not know God (7:28; 8:55) prior to Jesus' preaching would have no point. Lacking the abiding word and not knowing God seem to mean the same thing. The absence of the precondition — already knowing God — is the reason why Jesus' word makes no progress in the Jews (8:37). This knowing God or having God's abiding word prior to hearing Jesus' preaching takes on a bit more specificity by means of its association with the propensity to do the truth (3:21). Just as the word of God may abide in people before they hear Jesus' word, so those who intend to have themselves exposed by the light of revelation are already doing the truth before they come to the light. A relationship to the truth is what prompts them toward an intention — that their works might be manifested as accomplished in God — that still lies in front of them.

This line of interpretation is supported by John 8:43, 47. The Jews do not understand what Jesus says because they cannot hear his word. And the reason that they cannot hear Jesus' word is that they are not from God. Thus they do not have the prerequisite for hearing Jesus with understanding. Faith now seems to have become a human impossibility. Since unbelievers are not from God (8:47) but are rather from the devil (8:44), whose very nature is untruth, how can they respond to the truth? They lack the freedom to make an intentional decision in favor of the light. This motif seems to be in conflict with the texts that make both faith and unfaith a free choice. Yet the fact that fate makes faith a *human* impossibility does not necessarily make effective revelation impossible because God's revelation could be thought of as simply overcoming the utter human separation from God. To the extent that believers are also unbelievers they participate in the situation of unbelievers. Yet God has overcome the unbelief of believers and made revelation actual. However, in the case of unbelievers God has not overcome their separation and unbelief but has rather condemned them to eternal punishment (3:18, 36; 5:28–29).

How does this eschatological motif relate to John's understanding of creation? How can the unbelievers be God's own created by the Logos (John 1:3–4, 10–11) and also be *not* from God (8:47)? There is a sharp tension between John's understanding of creation, which makes every single being God's own, and his eschatology, which finally separates the damned from those who gain eternal life. The universalistic import of the understanding of creation is only implicit while the assertion of final lostness for some is quite explicit. The decision of constructive theology between these two will depend on various factors. One other pertinent text may be mentioned here. In 12:32 Jesus states that if he is lifted up from the earth, he will draw *all* (all people if the correct reading is *pantas;* all things, including people, if *panta* is the correct reading) to himself. The fact that the Jews respond negatively to this (12:34–37) does not necessarily mean that "all" includes only believers (as claimed by Meeks 1972, 64). God has overcome the unbelief of believers, so why not of unbelievers? The affirmation that all will be drawn to Jesus may be an ironic "in spite of" in relation to the unfaith of 12:34–40.

I have interpreted 8:44, 47 and related passages in this subsection as being ontological statements of the *cause* of unbelief: the Jews are from the devil, not God, and do not have the word of God abiding in them. I believe the texts treated have a coherence that generates this interpretation, and that is the view that I will take into the next section. However, there are other possibilities. For example, being not from God and lacking God's abiding word could be taken as conclusions of the Johannine Jesus drawn from the behavior of the Jews. In that case this condition should probably be regarded as a part of the adverse destiny and not as asserting fate.

The Constitutive Role of Human Reception

We have observed that there are strands in John in which faith, although it is enabled by God, is also a free, intentional act of human beings. And we have seen that there are strands in which unbelief is a free choice based on human intentions and interests, although it is also prompted or induced by an adverse destiny. When freedom and intentionality are attributed to humankind, there is an implication that we as human have some capacity to receive the word of revelation in a constitutive way. Characters in the story can perform the hermeneutical function of seeing-as. They see Jesus *as* the Lamb of God (John 1:29, 36), *as* the Messiah (1:41), *as* the Mosaic prophet (1:45), *as* the Son of God and King of Israel (1:49). The receivers of revelation do something by employing the tradition.

But how "natural" is this human action? This question can perhaps be illuminated by a comparison between Mark and John. Could we not say that the naturally positive element constitutive of revelation in Mark has only the slightest tie to what might have been given to human beings by God in creation? That is, the way of hearing that some have in themselves and that merges with the word of God to produce greater understanding (Mark 4:20, 24–25, 27–28) has no direct connection in Mark's text with the allusion to the residual goodness in human beings that goes back to the unfallen creation (Mark 10:5–9). At the beginning of creation, before the fall, God's intention was that marriage as a one-flesh union should be unbroken. Therefore, marriage *now* should be indissoluble. Mark's Jesus calls on his hearers to live as in the primordial time before hardness of heart set in. Thus there is an assumption that something of the resources for good given to human beings by God at the beginning is still present. But that capacity, although real, has been deformed by hardness of heart.

Again, Mark makes no textual connection between the natural capacity to hear fruitfully (Mark 4:20, 24–25) and the resources for good given by God in creation (Mark 10:5–9). If a connection is thought plausible, it will be made by the responsive reader. The absence of this connection in the text of Mark promotes the impression that the human capacity to receive the word — so as to shape it productively by means of categories that are independent of the Christian tradition — is indeed *natural*.

I remind the reader that by "natural" I have meant that which is familiar to a person from nature and culture and is independent of the biblical tradition. Biblical writers may make a connection, or identification, between this natural element and what God has conveyed by revelation in creation, which is also independent of the biblical tradition. My point about Mark is that he leaves the connection between the natural and revelation in creation unarticulated and that that lack of connection seems to give the natural a certain foregrounded independence.

In John the life that enlightens all people was implanted in them by creation (John 1:1–4). Since the light is also the eternal Word (1:1, 4), this illumination by the light marks human beings with the abiding word of God, and this abiding word is the necessary prerequisite for receiving the revelation in Jesus (5:38; 7:28; 8:43, 47, 55). Thus in John the "natural" human reception of revelation has a more visible, direct, and programmatic connection to the illumination of humankind by the Word through creation than it does in Mark. Therefore, the reception of the word in John, while genuinely human and free, is not as natural as it is in Mark, and probably in Paul. John and Matthew are closer on this point.

We do not, then, expect John to make a lot of explicit affirmations of the constitutive shaping of revelation by means of human categories that are outside of his own specifically theological discourse. Yet the very writing of the Gospel in the form in which it is written is a tacit affirmation of the constitutive role of the human. And this poetic act has some continuity with John's sanctioning of free human intentionality.

We have also observed that there are strands in John where human beings seem to lack freedom. Those chosen by God cannot be lost; they lack the freedom to disbelieve. And those who are said to belong to the devil rather than God and who lack the abiding word of God are not free to believe. The implication of this motif would seem to be that there is nothing in human beings as human that could make a positive contribution to the constitution of revelation. The actualization of revelation would be a divine overwhelming of human darkness.

The very writing of the Gospel, however, is a deconstruction of this negating of human possibility, for the narrative employs literary and linguistic constructions that do not emanate from the biblical tradition in any exclusive way but are functions of John's individual imagination or are cross-cultural and cross-religious and hence natural. The revelation thus is constituted in part by natural linguistic and literary constructs. If John were confronted by this claim, he would probably say that these contributions result from the role of the Logos in the whole of reality. I turn now to consider several of the natural poetic constructions that in part constitute John's narrative, which intends to elicit faith and confer eternal life and thus understands itself as revelation.

Symbolic and Metaphorical Language

We have observed that John's symbols combine a sensible, phenomenal image with an ambiguous and misinterpretable transcendent meaning (Culpepper 1983, 180–98; D'Sa 1987, 36, 44–46; Koester 1995, 1–4, 7). Here it simply needs to be noted that whatever the Christian specificity of John's theological vocabulary, his symbolic constructions function formally as they do when used in secular literature or the literature of other religions. For example, when the Jesus who comes from above is metaphorically identified with the gate for the sheep and a good shepherd (John 10:7, 11), we have the same semantic tension that exists between subject and qualifier whenever metaphor is used (see Kysar 1991, 92, 96, 99).

Plot

According to Fernando Segovia, John combines the travel motif common to ancient narrative with the threefold plot of ancient biography: (1) the beginning, concerned with origins (John 1:1–18); (2) the middle, portraying the public life (1:19–17:26); and (3) the conclusion, dealing with death and lasting significance (18:1–21:25). John takes the chronological rather than the topical approach but differs from the customary chronological representation by making the *akme* — the most significant and productive period — coincide with the whole public life rather than come just at the end of it (Segovia 1991, 32–38, 45).

Specific Graeco-Roman characteristics are seen in John's Gospel in his dividing the action into scenes, the dramatic irony, his having only two active characters on stage at the same time, and his using groups to function as the Greek chorus (Koester 1995, 22, 36). Jeffrey Staley argues that John uses rhetorical devices in an imaginative way to form the implied reader by means of the temporal reading process. For example, the narrator employs the victimized implied-reader device in order to commit the reader to a certain "fact" — Jesus baptized (John 3:22, 26) — only to force the reader later to recognize his or her misjudgment — Jesus did not really baptize (4:2). The purpose of the victimization and clarification is to force the implied reader to see that despite her knowledge she still does not know everything (Staley 1988, 19–20, 95–98).

Culpepper finds the Fourth Gospel amenable to interpretation by means of categories developed by modern literary critics. With regard to Northrop Frye's classification of genre types — romantic, tragic, comic, ironic, and satiric — the Gospels approximate most closely to romance but only in a qualified way, for in the Gospels the issue of the recognition of Jesus as revealer permeates the plot rather than being a device just for the end (Culpepper 1983, 83–84). Culpepper also employs concepts and terms developed by Gérard Genette (*Narrative Discourse*) to interpret Proust's *A la Recherche du Temps Perdu*. For example, analepses and prolepses in their several subtypes are, respectively, allusions to previous events and anticipations of coming ones. Analepsis may be seen in John's recalling of events in the history of Israel, and prolepsis, in such passages as "John, of course, had not yet been thrown into prison" (John 3:24) and "I lay down my life for the sheep" (10:15; Culpepper 1983, 56–57, 61–63).

The discussion of plot in John prompts me to ask why Bultmann could place John at the center of his canon within the canon while relegating the synoptic Gospels to the periphery precisely because the latter combined the eschatological crisis with an extended chronological narrative. For Bultmann the eschatological crisis is a *moment*, and its intensity is undermined by combining it with a developing story (Bultmann 1955c, 122–27). But John is also a chronological story. Why then does it not dissipate the eschatological crisis? Perhaps, in Bultmann's eyes, it is for such reasons as these. (1) Discourse is prominent in John. (2) There is copious repetition of themes and symbols. (3) Each episode tends to repeat the plot of the whole (Culpepper 1983, 89). (4) The *akme* or focus on Jesus' transcendent significance, the revelation of God's glory, does not come at one point but is dispensed throughout the narrative. All of these features qualify the chronological unfolding of change in John's narrative and perhaps made the story seem to Bultmann like the *same* extended *moment*. For Bultmann it is the moment that can be eschatologically charged.

Irony

This complex cross-cultural phenomenon will receive brief and selective treatment. I will touch on only two types of irony and one characteristic that could attach to either type. First, *verbal irony* occurs when a speaker says something the surface meaning of which must be rejected in favor of another incongruous or higher meaning that must be reconstructed from contextual clues to the speaker or author's real position (Booth 1974, 6, 10–11, 72). Verbal irony is saying one thing and meaning something other. Second, *situational irony* occurs in literature when a character's situation turns out to be other than he or she perceives it to be or other than a reader with an "ordinary" understanding of the work's narrative world would perceive it to be. Situational irony appears when a character who could be expected to understand misinterprets another character's verbal irony (Duke 1985, 25). Verbal irony is stable or fixed when the reconstructed higher meaning of an ironic construct is not superseded, or ironized, by a further reconstruction that produces a still higher meaning (Booth 1974, 6). Situational irony would be stable if the character who uses verbal irony that others may misunderstand never falls victim to misperceiving his or her own situation.

Jesus' statement to Nicodemus that if one is to see the kingdom of God one must be born *anōthen* is verbally ironic, for the key term can mean either "again" or "from above," and Jesus puts the two meanings in opposition (John 3:4–6; Duke 1985, 145). Jesus rejects Nicodemus's assumption of the literal "again" in favor of "from above." However, it does not mean from above in a literal spatial sense but means rather "from the Spirit" (3:5–8). Perhaps we should say that the irony here is not very subtle or problematical for the *reader*, however puzzling it was for Nicodemus, because the wrong meaning is so quickly and definitively corrected. The situation is ironic for Nicodemus because as a teacher of Israel he should not have misunderstood (3:10).

Similarly, Jesus' offer to the Samaritan woman of living water (John 4:10) is verbally ironic because the key term "living water" can have the lower literal meaning of "running or spring water" (4:11) and also the correct higher or spiritual meaning of "source of eternal life" (4:14). The woman takes the physical meaning (4:11), to which Jesus opposes the spiritual (4:13–14). Some interpreters believe that the woman is still on the wrong track when she asks for living water in 4:15 (Duke 1985, 102; O'Day 1986, 64–65), but we must return to that question shortly.

The Samaritan woman's situation also is ironic. From the sociological standpoint perhaps she could not be expected to understand. After all she is a Samaritan and a woman. But from the standpoint of the narrative world created by the text — which is the more immediate and thus the more authoritative context — she could be expected to understand. She is on the superior end — the giving end — of the interaction regarding drinking water (John 4:7, 9). Jesus *needs* to ask for water, and she is *able* to give it. More importantly we might expect more of her since she aggressively assumes the right to question Jesus about whether he thinks too highly of himself (4:12) and in like manner raises a question about the conflicting claims of Jews and Samaritans (4:20). There-fore, her failure to grasp the higher meaning — source of eternal life — is ironic.

According to Gail O'Day the ironic means of presenting reve-lation in John is a part of the word's power, for the indirectness and incongruities of the irony draw the reader into participation in the text and require her to achieve understanding by making judgments about the relative value of competing meanings (O'Day 1986, 30–31, 89–90). It seems to me, however, that since the reader is able to stand above the characters and watch *them* strug-gle (with little success) for the right meaning, which is made rather clear for the reader, the challenge to the reader is minimal in com-parison with the challenge to the characters. At the same time the reader does participate in the same adverse destiny and fate as the characters.

John's verbal irony would be stable if the higher or spiritual meaning of the ironic constructs articulated by Jesus and the im-plied author is consistently maintained and not superseded, or ironized, by a still higher meaning. The situational irony would be stable if Jesus is never victimized by irony or portrayed as inferior to another character. Johannine scholars apparently tend to regard both types of Johannine irony as stable (Culpepper 1983, 168, 178; Duke 1985, 21, 45). O'Day at one point seems to say that the dis-cernment of the irony does *not* consist in seeing the true meaning rather than the false but in grasping the exposure of both at the same time (1986, 24). However, her further discussion seems to indicate that the reader is expected to move through a character's misunderstanding to Jesus' higher level of understanding (61, 65).

In a very provocative way Stephen Moore has challenged this assessment of John's irony as stable. I will summarize in my terms the three basic points of Moore's case. First, in John 19:30 Jesus' giving up of the spirit, anticipating the conferring of the Spirit in 20:22, is dependent on his physical thirst being satisfied with sour wine (19:28–30a). Thus the hierarchical superiority of the spiritual is overturned by the dependence of the spiritual on the physical (Moore 1993, 214–20). Similarly the water that came out of Jesus' side in 19:34 is both physical and symbolic of the Spirit (221–22). Moreover, although Jesus *speaks* as if the physical and spiritual can be separated and the spiritual is superior, he *is* the Son of man who is effectively in heaven and on earth at the same time (1:51; 3:13), and thus he dissolves the partition between heaven and earth (222–23). The superiority of the spiritual in Jesus' verbal irony is then ironized by the inseparable fusion of material and spiritual, and the verbal irony becomes unstable.

Second, Moore argues that in the Samaritan woman's request for living water in order that she might neither thirst nor come to the well to draw water (John 4:15), the water is again both literal (physical) and figurative (spiritual). Thus the woman's language corresponds to what Jesus is but is superior to what he says when he separates physical and spiritual (Moore 1993, 224–25). Jesus' situation is ironized because the Son of man who holds together heaven and earth is bested by the socially disadvantaged Samaritan woman.

Third, according to Moore, even more than Jesus longs for water, he desires that the woman desire the living water that he desires to give her. So deeper than the irony of the woman's not understanding her real need is the irony that Jesus' need is as great as hers (Moore 1993, 207–8, 226–27). This also ironizes Jesus' situation.

My response to Moore concludes this subsection. Jesus' desire and need in this story seem to me to be less than explicit but may be implied in his "If you knew the gift of God and who is the one speaking to you, you would have asked" (my translation; John 4:10). This suggests that he wants her to ask, and in the ancient world there was a widespread precedent for seeing thirst — and Jesus was thirsty — as a metaphor for desire (Koester 1995, 179).

I think the most serious question about Moore's case is whether the water in John 4:15 and 19:34 can be construed without undue strain as merging physical and spiritual. But it does seem to be true that the Son of man combines heaven and earth, and certainly the incarnation of the Logos fuses the eternal and the fleshly. In addition the bread-of-life discourse in John 6 affirms the inseparable fusion of the material and spiritual as necessary for eternal life. As we have seen, this is the overall meaning of the dialectical movement of the chapter, and nowhere is it more succinctly and compactly expressed than in 6:56–58. The *flesh and blood* of the Son of man eaten in the communion *meal* are the bread that came down from *heaven* (6:51, 56–58).

It seems probable to me that the hierarchial superiority of the spiritual level in Jesus' verbal irony as well as Jesus' own situation are somewhat unstable in John. But Jesus is perhaps not as much ironized by the Samaritan woman as by his own language, for example, the bread-of-life discourse and his Son-of-man sayings (John 1:51; 3:13), and by the implied author's interpretation of him as incarnate Logos. As is the case generally with victims of irony, Jesus would be unaware of his victimization. His preference for the spiritual level in the dialogues with Nicodemus and the Samaritan woman would be expressed in forgetfulness of his Son-of-man sayings and in "forgetful" anticipation of what he would say about the union of the material and spiritual in the bread-of-life dialogue, and he would not be aware of the implied author's interpretation of him as divine Logos incarnate. This lack of awareness would be a deconstruction of the unlimited knowledge of human and divine things that Jesus generally claims or is claimed for him (2:24; 6:46; 8:14, 23, 38, 55, 58; 10:15, 30; 13:3; 17:8, 20–24). Similarly his knowledge of his origin from and unity with God would not permit him to recognize that in debate he is no more than the equal of the Samaritan woman. Yet this unawareness of his ironization attests the reality of the *flesh* that the divine Logos became.

In like manner the implied author's representation of Jesus as the victim of irony would be unintentional and unconscious, for his intentional position is Jesus' union with God and unlimited knowledge. The ironization of Jesus would be a deconstruction worked on the implied author by his language and thought, the insertion into his theological point of view of the excluded outside. But again the superior position that ironizes Jesus' preference for the spiritual level and ironizes his own situation is the incarnational principle that Spirit and flesh are inseparable in the one who brings eternal life.

Identity, Synonyms, and Reference

Petersen has offered a stimulating account of John's use of language that I will discuss under three headings.

Petersen's description. John uses language in a "blatantly self-conscious" way, employing everyday vocabulary and grammar in such a different way as to create a special language and to cause everyday speakers of the language to misunderstand (Petersen 1993, 1). In 1:1a–b John differentiates Word and God and relates them by a preposition. But in 1:1c he violates this everyday usage by identifying the entities he had just differentiated (9). Further, in 1:1–4 John makes Word, God, life, and light all synonyms; they refer to the same entity. But in everyday language they refer to different entities (14).

Petersen's critical analysis of John's language. John's use of synonyms to identify entities that are not identical makes reference a problem. We can understand what he is saying but not what he means because he undercuts everyday meanings and we cannot tell what he is referring to (Petersen 1993, 10, 29). All we can say is that for John there is an Other that originated the world and subsequently entered it as Jesus (14). But the language of the Fourth Gospel obscures and blurs the meaning of the Other and what it means to receive the incarnate Other (20, 42, 47, 69, 89). In sum John's use of language renders it opaque to its referent (22).

My critical response. There is no inherent reason why John's language as described by Petersen, whose description seems basically accurate, should lead to Petersen's skeptical and negative conclusions about the nature of the reference. His view of the reference is something that he brings to the Fourth Gospel, not something that he derives from it. John uses the language but does not reflect on how it refers. There are other possibilities, and while the position that I have attributed to Petersen is his major thrust, he occasionally hints at another point of view himself. At times he tacitly seems to acknowledge that religious language necessarily begins with ordinary language and then uses it in a special way. He can say that John uses everyday language to refer to heavenly realities and to say more than everyday things (Petersen 1993, 48, 70, 76, 108), but he denies that the reference is successful.

I want to argue that John's imaginative use of language is a special and specific instance of the way religious language generally and properly works and that its reference is much fuller than Petersen acknowledges. As Ian Ramsey has argued, religious language is grounded in ordinary language. It starts with something familiar (a model) and directs that in an odd way (by a qualifier). The qualifier stretches the model until an awareness of something different — the unseen — emerges. To use a nonreligious example, the model of a polygon is stretched by the qualifier "infinite" until an entity of a different order comes into view — a circle (Ramsey 1957, 68–78).

In the Fourth Gospel *king* or *kingdom* is one of the models that John uses to interpret Jesus, and Jesus' kingdom's not being of this world (18:36) is its qualifier. But the meaning of "King of Israel" (1:49) is not "totally undercut" by "not of this world" (18:36) as Petersen claims (1993, 29). *King* and *kingdom* are used oddly, but that does not mean that we have no idea what John is referring to, as Petersen repeatedly asserts. It is counter to the intuition of most religious people (except those who begin with radically skeptical presuppositions) to hold that they do not know at all what they are referring to when they talk about God or God's revelation.

It is true, however, that when people use religious language, they do not literally or objectively know what they are referring to. As I. M. Crombie persuasively argued years ago, what Ramsey calls "models," when used religiously (e.g., John's use of *kingdom*), must up to a point be understood in their ordinary sense. "Hot" in "hot temper" can be understood figuratively — and not in the ordinary sense of hot as in "hot stove" — because we know what temper means apart from the metaphor "hot temper." But we do not know what God (or John's Jesus) is like apart from the models that are used of the transcendent. Therefore, we in fact do not know what God as referent is like if the models are not taken in their ordinary sense. But the ordinary sense is strained by the qualifiers so that it cannot be taken literally (Crombie 1963, 120–24; 1957, 72). Jesus is not literally the king of Israel since his kingdom is not of this world. But he is still like a king even if he is so oddly. Thus something is known about Jesus beyond the affirmation that he is the Other in the flesh. In similar manner something is communicated by John's tendency to distinguish and identify at the same time and to use synonyms oddly.

Again, Jesus is like bread in the ordinary sense of *bread*. Bread is nurturing, not to mention tasty and the occasion for communal participation. But Jesus is not literally bread because he is the bread from heaven. Jesus' language about himself is both ordinary and odd, and Jesus as the referent of this language is not totally unknown, although the language obscures as well as reveals. And it should be remembered that for John, Jesus' *word* represents Jesus himself and is the source of life (6:63, 68).

All of this means that John's linguistic imagery is no more than translucent in its reference to Jesus, but it is not opaque. The ordinary sense makes the imagery intelligible while the odd logic challenges conventional understanding. John's theology implies that the ordinary sense of his language can no more be completely undercut or divested of its referentiality by its odd qualities than the palpability of flesh/bread can be relinquished as a necessary vehicle for the life-giving spirit (John 6:51c, 53–58, 63).

The examples given in this section show that John has received the gospel tradition by means of his own imaginative and reflective grasp of cross-cultural linguistic and literary constructions — even if John would have attributed these phenomena to the imprint of the eternal Logos.

Chapter 7

CONCLUSION

Revelation in the New Testament

I conclude by redescribing the four constituent elements of the revelation situation and reflecting briefly on some of the interrelationships.

1. The ground of revelation is the word of God that intervenes in human life. This is the linguistic component, and it includes the preaching and teaching of Jesus, the kerygmatic word about Jesus and the Hebrew Scriptures by which he is interpreted. This constituent is the word of God as content — the tradition. Just as the Old Testament was a part of the linguistic component for the earliest church, and still is for the church of today, so the New Testament is the primary element in the linguistic component once canonization has been completed.

2. The second component is the word of God as power. The content is not revelation unless there is power to imprint the word on human existence and shape it according to the content. The power to create faith is a function that Mark and Matthew, by the way they tell the story, attribute to the word itself. At the same time there is also a hint that the power is the Holy Spirit, a suggestion evident in the fact that both Gospels, Matthew a bit more explicitly, attribute Jesus' power to expel demons both to his word and to the Spirit (Matt 8:16; 12:28; Mark 1:25; 3:22, 28–30; 5:8, 13). This suggests that the word is the vehicle of the Spirit. Similarly in the Gospel of John the word itself has power to generate faith and create life (4:41; 5:24–26), or it does these things because it is the vehicle of the Spirit (6:63, 68; 14:16–17, 26; 15:26; 16:12–15; 17:20; 20:22).

Paul, like the Gospel writers, can attribute the power function to the word itself. The gospel is the power of God (Rom 1:16), or the word of the cross is (1 Cor 1:18). But Paul just as explicitly and characteristically can make the spirit the power of his proclamation (1 Cor 2:4; 2 Cor 3:2–3, 6; 1 Thess 1:5).

3. Word as content and power does not become the self-disclosure of God unless it is actively received by human beings

192

through the merging of their specific human understanding of reality with the content of the word. The factor of human reception makes a constitutive contribution to the form and content of the revelation. Human reception is not a clear transparency onto the pure word of God.

4. The word humanly interpreted is revelation only in terms of a particular historical situation. I have dealt with the historical settings of the New Testament texts discussed and have reflected on the role of these situations as constituents of revelation. But what is the New Testament's own position on this point?

It should be observed that the New Testament is quite explicit in referring to the word of God both as content and as power. The role of human reception is stated or assumed with varying degrees of emphasis and explicitness but is never really focalized. The place of the historical context is tacitly assumed in that the New Testament texts are directed to specific historical situations. The force of the historical setting is made manifest in the variations that appear in the Gospel narratives and in Paul's letters. But the New Testament does not reflect on the way in which the historical setting in part shapes human reception and thus itself becomes a constituent of the revelation situation. The New Testament, however, prompts us to make that reflection, for the impact of different historical settings and purposes on variations in content cannot be ignored.

The disclosure of God is real only if it is actively received, and it can be received only by thinking and acting according to a particular cultural location. It is the word as empowered by the Spirit and the word as shaped by this particular situation and as prompting people to act in this particular situation that moves them to receive it by assimilation and action. Or it is the concrete situation as interpreted by the empowered word that prompts people to receive the word in a particular way. At the same time it is the positive contribution of active reception that reshapes the tradition and relates it to the historical situation so that the latter can be seen in a new way. Reception combines individual capabilities with the impact of the historical past and the cultural present.

Notice that the event of revelation in this interpretation of the New Testament material is not an event or events from the past — the history of Israel or the historical ministry of Jesus. Those events have been absorbed in the kerygmatic interpretation of them in the word. Apart from this they remain in the past and do not encounter us in our present. But the historical event of the past as interpreted in texts about it becomes a symbol both of the power of the word to be event and of the present situation to be revelation event. And the event of the past also contributes content and particularity to the language of the gospel.

The revelation event then in the New Testament texts studied is the event of powerful language, or it is the fusion of language with the present situation of the biblical writer. By analogy the revelation situation for us is constituted by Scripture, Spirit, and our historical situation. But this eventful situation becomes revelation in an actualized sense — for the biblical witness or for us — only when it is interpretively received by means of the reflective and imaginative capacities of the reader or hearer. Because human reception has a constitutive role in revelation, I am inclined to question the distinction that Langdon Gilkey, for example, makes between revelation *per se*, or the originating event in Jesus of Nazareth, and the human witnesses to revelation in Scripture, sacrament, preaching, faith, love, theology, and so on. These witnesses are human and fallible and not divine, nor are they themselves directly revealed (Gilkey 1979, 50–53). I do not believe that such a distinction is possible from the New Testament standpoint. There is no such thing as an originating event that is separable from human shaping, and since human shaping is contingent and subject to change, so is revelation, a point that Gilkey implicitly makes in his 1985 article.

The role of human reception in constituting revelation is supported by what the New Testament texts explicitly or implicitly say about the capacity and role of the receiver of the gospel. It is furthermore supported by the fact that the New Testament uses literary forms and sometimes substantive content that appear in secular texts and the texts of other religions. And the human element is undergirded by the fact that open texts with many possible meanings leave the receiver the job of turning the text's potential for meaning into a meaningful work.

These factors require us to reconsider the first element in the revelation situation — the linguistic factor as *word of God* (I thank Frank Crouch for calling my attention to this). If there is no word of God that is not composed of *human* words — structures of human reception — what is the word of God as content? Is it simply and exhaustively the human word understood as empowered by the Spirit? The content of God's word is simply a human content that has shown itself powerful in a particular historical tradition.

The issue is seen neatly in 1 Thess 2:13. Paul is quite convinced that what he has preached to the Thessalonians is the gospel of God (2:2, 8–9) and that what they have received is *God's* word (2:13). Yet he recognizes that they could have received the message as the word of human beings (2:13), which is a tacit acknowledgment that the content was human words. Why was it not simply a human word to the Thessalonians? First, it was not a merely human word because *they* received it *as* word of God. Here there is an allusive and elusive reference to the act of human reception, the hermeneutical move that understands one thing as another, human word as word of God. Second, it was not merely human in Paul's view because the Spirit gives power that imprints the word on the heart and enables understanding (Rom 8:16; 1 Cor 2:4, 10, 12; 2 Cor 3:2–3, 6; 1 Thess 1:5–6).

Does not Paul's view leave us with a word fully human in content empowered by the Spirit? In significant part the answer is yes. But do the New Testament and the Christian tradition prompt us to say something more about the content of God's word as *God's?* Does the word of God have a content that distinguishes it from other meaningful structures as God's?

We could recur to Ronald Thiemann's claim that Christian faith and practice constrain us to attribute to God the initiating role in the divine-human transaction. God's promising and fulfilling are to be distinguished from the human response. The logic of Christian convictions points, not to the epistemological or temporal priority of God, but to God's ontological priority (Thiemann 1985, 69, 72–77, 80, 143–44). I want to agree on the issue of ontological priority, but I have argued throughout that in the New Testament the vocabulary of divine unveiling and human understanding or misunderstanding, as well as the role of language in this interaction, is far too prominent to bracket out epistemological issues. We still have the question of the relationship between the ontological priority of God and the language of the gospel. It could simply be held that God's priority gives power to a certain human language network. God is ontologically prior to the human response, but there is no word or language of God as content that is prior to human language. One cannot identify any linguistic form of God's promise that is not composed of human linguistic forms. Is there any way to contextualize this position further so as to connect a certain content more closely with God?

Two factors in the Christian tradition may justify speaking of the word of God as a content — *in a certain sense.* These factors are (1) specificity and (2) historical experience. The New Testament message as a whole, while not totally self-consistent or without its tensions, has a specificity that is identifiable and not reducible or assimilable to something else. The New Testament's network of varying gospel messages has been experienced over the centuries by countless people in the Christian community as the vehicle of redemptive power, a power that they felt constrained to attribute to God. There is a sense then in which this content is God's. Again, there is no word of God that is not composed of human language and that, therefore, is not always subject to being taken as merely human. But the ongoing experience of this particular human word as redemptive makes it not amiss to claim that God has chosen this human content as God's own word. This is not to claim that God has chosen no other linguistic vehicle.

Within the Christian tradition, then, one can say that the word of God has a content that is expressed in the various forms of the New Testament gospel. One can affirm this, however, only after he or she has experienced that (1) content as (2) power and in terms of a (3) particular historical situation in which it (4) has been received by human imagination, will, and reflection.

Continuing Revelation: The Reception of the New Testament Today

Since in the New Testament revelation occurs when the linguistic tradition is mediated in the power of the Spirit to a person or community that receives it imaginatively and reflectively in terms of a particular situation, then revelation can be plausibly understood as continuing to occur in ever new situations in the life of the Christian community. One contemporary mode of constitutive reception, one fruitful hermeneutical lens, one means of naturalizing the biblical material is the claim of liberation theology that the God of the Bible has a preferential concern for the poor. I want briefly to pursue this possibility. What does the New Testament (or Bible) say when viewed from the location of the oppressed?

J. Severino Croatto has suggested that action vis-à-vis the modern history of oppression, not just the appropriate preunderstanding, enables us to see the depth and scope of the Bible's concern about the poor. A theology born of praxis, for Croatto, is not a Latin American novelty but is the starting point of biblical theology itself (Croatto 1981, vi, 2–3, 11; Thiselton 1980, 110–12). What Croatto sees in the Bible from his vantage point is where God's epiphany actually takes place (Isa 58:2; Jer 21:2; Ezek 14:7;

Hos 10:12; Amos 5:4). The exodus story discloses God's intention to deliver God's people from political and social oppression. God acted violently against the Egyptian king because the situation of the Hebrews admitted no other path. Oppressors do not freely liberate or give up their power. Freedom is a gift of such value that love for those in need of freedom justifies violence (Croatto 1981, v, 18, 23, 29–30).

Jesus establishes a solidarity with the oppressed and marginalized and thereby gives them a value, an affirmation of their authenticity, that is liberating. He conveys to them a new kind of consciousness (Croatto 1981, 49, 51–52, 54, 63). But Jesus, Croatto maintains, was a religious liberator and had no political program. Had he been a political revolutionary his program would have exhausted itself within the horizon of his own time. However, the new symbolic order generated by Jesus' religious movement started a process that should culminate in radical political liberation (62–64).

Jon Sobrino's hermeneutical position is similar. The most important contribution of liberation theology to theology in general, he claims, is to have shifted the basic issue from the content of theology to the precondition for doing theology. Theology can be done only from within the context of praxis. We can understand Jesus only if we practice his way, proclaiming the coming of the kingdom, denouncing injustice, realizing the kingdom in life. But we can follow this practice only if we live in the Spirit that Jesus sends (Sobrino 1984, xxv).

If present praxis gives us insight into the Bible's preference for the marginalized, we can also give reasons deriving from our own situation for why the priority of the oppressed should be acknowledged. Mark Taylor does this in his insightful articulation of a liberation theology for North America. His cultural-political theology wants to keep three categories in dialogue: (1) the lingering force of tradition, (2) the celebration of plurality and difference, and (3) the need to resist dominant centers of power and to prefer the poor (Taylor 1990, ix, 23–26, 30–39). While, as indicated, plurality should be celebrated, that appreciation for differences should not be allowed to produce a "regressive tolerance" that could undermine the opposition to oppression (56, 61).

Taylor give three reasons why the privilege of the oppressed should be recognized. First, in the conversational view of understanding that Taylor advocates, truth is attained by achieving the widest reflective equilibrium of competing arguments. The oppressed have a privileged position because, as those normally excluded from society's conversation, they represent the far limits of the required breadth. Second, the poor have a distinctive insight born of sustained suffering. Third, because they have learned how to survive in the powerless spaces of society, the oppressed know more about the culture of the powerful than the powerful know about those whom they oppress (Taylor 1990, 63–65).

Carlos Mesters has shown that in certain circumstances in Latin America when the common people view their situation and the Bible together, revelation occurs. For these Christians the word of God is not just in the Bible. Rather the Bible functions to enable them to discover the word of God in their real-life situations. They see that God is calling them in the hubbub of real life, and they are not so much trying to interpret the Bible as to interpret life with the help of the Bible. The common people are using the Bible as a mirror to comprehend their own lives and are discovering things in it that other readers do not find (Mesters 1992, 44, 49–52).

Mesters is aware that this communal-life approach can lead to using the Bible simply to confirm one's own ideas (1992, 54–55), but he may not deal with this problem as forthrightly as it needs to be dealt with. The Bible may be used as a mirror of my life situation to the point that it can no longer compel me to question my own life critically. It is very difficult for anyone to tell exactly when that point is reached; therefore, a dialectical approach is needed. Without wanting to deny the legitimacy or fruitfulness of the communal-life approach or to trample on its intuitive insights, we see the need for a dialectical interaction between interpretation in light of the real-life situation, or interpreting the situation in light of the Bible, and critical exegesis that aims to see the Bible in its particularity and otherness from me and thus as capable of confronting me with critical questions about my life and context.

I want to affirm the basic position of liberation theology hermeneutics that the Bible calls for aggressive action against oppression. But sometimes liberation theology manifests a one-dimensionality that causes it to miss other theological issues and claims that I would regard as valid and valuable. Recall that Croatto interpreted Jesus' mission as essentially religious but as also having a political potential. In a way that is formally analogous Dominique Barbé has argued that to identify the church base communities with political movements would be religious catastrophe. The community would lose the religious character that constitutes its energy. And the political party or labor union would become the instrument of a new Christendom (Barbé 1992, 190–91). Both the religious and the political are important, and they should be properly related, but each should be accorded its own integrity. Not all liberation theologians (or social-science exegetes), however, are as circumspect and inclusive as Croatto and Barbé. Sometimes the singular focus on the need for and theological legitimacy of political-cultural liberation causes other issues to be treated with ambiguity, neglect, or plain denial. I respond critically to three such instances.

My first response is to Christopher Rowland and Mark Corner, who in *Liberating Exegesis* argue convincingly that liberation theology is pertinent for First World Christians and countries and that only a change in the international economic structure can deal effectively with poverty and oppression. According to them, Christians must consider that it is this structure that needs to be rearranged, and liberation theology advocates the rejection of this capitalistic system that encroaches on the lives of all (Rowland and Corner 1989, 156–57, 163, 172, 185, 196). Their position is ambiguous, however, with regard to the question of what can be expected — on theological grounds — in the socioeconomic order.

On the one hand, Rowland and Corner state that Judaism and early Christianity expect the consummation of the kingdom of God in this world. The biblical tradition espouses the chiliastic position that the eschatological hope can be fulfilled within the confines of history in a material way, and Jesus is a supreme example of this chiliastic mentality (Rowland and Corner 1989, 92, 116–19, 123). On the other hand, the two scholars maintain that the New Testament, at least in Paul, imposes an eschatological reservation. The present is not devalued but is seen as offering only limited possibilities for the pursuit of the eschaton (125–26).

Rowland and Corner acknowledge that the New Testament Apocalypse displays both a chiliastic and a not so chiliastic point of view. They hold that a text will not generally stand on just one side of an ideological issue. Thus it is the job of the interpreter to lay bare the ambiguities and contradictions in all texts (Rowland and Corner 1989, 149–51). They have apparently not recognized, however, that they have interpreted the biblical tradition as a whole in two different ways. Thus their construal remains ambiguous.

This ambiguity carries over into Rowland and Corner's assessment of the goal of liberation theology. On the one hand, they maintain that liberation theology affirms the Bible's chiliastic expectation (Rowland and Corner 1989, 123). But they also claim that liberation theology has consistently renounced fantastic projects that are unrelated to political circumstances. Most liberation theologians and those with whom they work are engaged in small-scale programs that offer a glimpse of God's eschatological kingdom in the midst of the unjust old order (120). The two scholars themselves at least at one point affirm the reality of the eschatological reservation and acknowledge that no human system can be identified with the kingdom of God (137–38).

We may well agree with Sobrino that the eschatological reservation should not be invoked to curb social projects against oppression that could be understood as mediations of the kingdom of God. But the eschatological reservation should be maintained to remind us that no such project is the last word and that the kingdom is always also ahead of us (Sobrino 1984, xviii, xxv).

My second response is to Elsa Tamez's interesting study of justification by faith in the light of liberation theology. Her work is motivated by the fact that the present understanding of the doctrine, detached as it is from the concrete details of the Latin American reality, has had negative consequences for the process of liberation. She begins from the Latin American experience of struggle against oppression and works to recover the biblical source of justification (Tamez 1993, 13, 15). Tamez has some very insightful things to say about the relevance of liberation theology to the oppressiveness of the international economic order (129, 142), but the treatment of her central theme — justification by faith — creates two troubling problems that I want to address.

For Tamez justification is the revelation of God's justice, which enables human beings to do justice, something that had not been humanly possible prior to God's action (1993, 77, 96, 107–8, 110, 126). The entailments of this new possibility can be further described as people of faith being made subjects of their own history. They become protagonists with God, who can affect the course of history (134, 141, 143).

One of the problems that Tamez's discussion produces is that while justice is her central concept — it comes from God and is what human beings ought to do (1993, 77, 84, 96, 126) — it remains ill defined throughout. The closest she comes to a definition is when she says by reference to Rom 2:6 that God is just and true because there is coherence in God's acts, that God gives to each according to his or her works (101). But this is not integrally connected to the justice of justification, which, however undefined, does *not* have to do with merit (preface, 125, 130). Also she treats love and justice as equivalents (126, 131) but does not explain how this can be so. Her tendency is to give brief, isolated descriptions of justice that may not agree with each other, but she neither deals with the tensions nor pursues a broader concept of justice that might be able to include divergent descriptions. There is no philosophical-theological probing of the nature of justice. She rather seems to assume that its character is self-evident, undebatable, and agreed upon by all.

The second problem is that Tamez tends to exclude the connotation of forgiveness from Paul's understanding of justification. She affirms grace as empowerment (Tamez 1993, 126) but has little to say about it as forgiveness. Quite forthrightly she claims that there are no grounds for affirming that Paul's first concern was the need for human beings to be declared just before God or for their sins to be forgiven. The fundamental problem was rather that not one person was capable of doing the justice necessary to transform the unjust society (107). From the other side of the hermeneutical circle she observes poignantly that it is an irony to tell poor and excluded Latin Americans, so much sinned against, that grace is the forgiveness of their sins (138).

I appreciate this irony. But a circumspect view of both the human condition and Paul's text requires that the forgiveness element — as applicable to all — not be neglected. Tamez's emphasis on the positive side of justification is valuable: it makes people the subjects of their own history and enables them to enact justice. But a conception of justification that does not include the "acceptance of the unacceptable" is insufficiently dialectical and is inadequate to the human and textual realities. It does not do justice to what in Paul's view makes social action possible — faith as response to the God who acquits the guilty, justifies the ungodly.

It should be pointed out, however, that Tamez does rarely refer to justification and grace as forgiveness in a kind of tangential way (1993, 131, 141) and clearly opposes the demands of the economic order that one must achieve merits of production in order to have standing (137). And in a couple of places (143, 153–54) she allusively suggests that justification as enablement of justice and affirmation of life depends on awareness of being a forgiven sinner. But this is not organically integrated into her programmatic interpretation of justification, nor does she do the kind of anthropological analysis that would illuminate *how* the faith of justification can generate social action.

I conclude this discussion by trying to amplify a fruitful suggestion that Tamez makes. She argues that the anguish that diminished
Luther's life because of his insecurity about eternal salvation is
translated today as the anguish experienced by the poor in the face
of hunger, repression, and insignificance. Those who want to be
recognized and thus to save themselves must submit to the law that
demands profitable productivity. There is no grace or faith in this
system, and many are condemned to remain on the outside. Both
oppressor and oppressed are dehumanized (Tamez 1993, 130–31).

Tamez seems to be pushing toward a formulation like this: for
Luther (and, I would add, Paul) those who are uncertain of salvation, because their consciences condemn them for a lack of good
works toward God, are addressed by the gift of justification, for
justification assures people that God accepts them despite a lack of
meritorious works. Translated into the socioeconomic realm, this
would suggest the following: those who are anxious and uncertain, because their lack of economically productive achievements
has marginalized them and rendered them insignificant, are addressed by the gift of justice that assures them of the satisfaction of
their bodily and material needs and accords them dignity despite
their lack of economic power. This translates the theological principle of justification into a principle for social justice. We still need,
however, to analyze how it is that those who have experienced
justification in the theological sense are enabled and prompted to
enact the kind of social justice (the guarantee of needs) that is suggested by — and is a translation of — the theological principle of
justification by grace through faith.

For Paul the light of the gospel shines in our hearts to reveal
Christ to us (2 Cor 4:6) but also to make us see our own hidden
purposes (1 Cor 4:5; 14:25). But whether or not our own conscience condemns us for what we see, our right relationship with
God depends on *God's* judgment (1 Cor 4:4–5). And God does not
count merits but rather acquits the guilty (Rom 3:21–25; 4:5; Phil
3:8–10). Since God accepts us, no other condemnation of us counts
(Rom 8:33–39). Since God does not deal with us on the basis of
our own moral righteousness, we are freed from the compulsive
but impossible task of trying to establish our own righteousness
and from trying to conceal our failure. Being delivered from this
concentration upon ourselves, we are free to embrace the totality
of reality (1 Cor 3:21–23) and free even to relinquish our freedom
for the well-being of the other (1 Cor 9:19–23). We can dispose
ourselves toward the neighbor for his or her advantage, not for our

own (Rom 15:1–2; 1 Cor 10:24, 33; 1 Thess 5:15; Phil 2:4). Thus it is possible to enact in the social realm what we have experienced in the divine-human transaction of justification.

My third response is to William Herzog's discussion of the parable of the workers in the vineyard (Matt 20:1–16), the interpretation of which he revealingly entitles "Blaming the Victims of Oppression" (1994, 79). Herzog begins his approach to Jesus' parables by recognizing that as they stand in the Gospels the parables serve the theological and ethical concerns of the Evangelists. But he proposes to interpret them in the context of the historical Jesus, where they serve a very different purpose (4, 48). Jesus was a political subversive situated in the social world of an agrarian society that belonged to an aristocratic empire. Jesus' parables thus serve the purpose, not of envisioning the glory of the reign of God, but of detailing how oppression promoted the interests of the ruling class (3). Herzog then treats the parables that he interprets in two groups: (1) as codifications of how exploitation worked in Palestine and (2) as codifications of limit situations that suggest courses of action for resisting oppression (7, 51). His method is social scientific, and his hermeneutical orientation is that Jesus' parables functioned as part of the liberation praxis of Jesus' ministry (3–4).

Herzog states that he does not claim to have found the only true way to read the parables and that some of them will not fit his framework (1994, 4). But he then seems to espouse an either/or approach. What if, he asks, the parables were neither theological nor moral stories but political and economic ones (7)? This expresses his real attitude. He will occasionally in passing allude to the possibility of secondary theological purposes (73) or make theological comments when the text makes them absolutely inescapable, as in the case of the Pharisee and the toll collector (192). But the thrust of his hermeneutic is strongly antitheological. Herzog also tacitly acknowledges that the parables have literary qualities, to which he declines to pay much attention (4). But by ignoring the force of literary features (such as plot and metaphorical relationships), he forgets that literary density obscures a text's reference to the real world and prevents Jesus' parables from being the transparencies onto the social order that he takes them to be.

It was Herzog's reflection on the parable of the workers in the vineyard that prompted him to move from the prevailing theological approach to the parables to a social-scientific approach. How could the rich landowner's exploitation of and injustice to the day laborers — equal pay for unequal work — be read as an image of the generosity of God (49–50)? Something other than theology must be going on here.

In my opinion Herzog's mistake is that in his effort to relate the details of the parables to social wholes or gestalts that exist outside of the stories (1994, 48–49), he has dissipated the literary wholeness, the coherence of the narrative, which is the most immediate context of meaning for the details. Herzog has not assimilated the fundamental literary-critical point that the *narrative* world of any significant story will not exactly correspond to the *real* world to which the story may well in some way indirectly refer. The landowner's behavior may indeed be unjust and exploitive — have a negative meaning — when viewed in the context of a real social setting outside of the parable. That does not mean that it will have a negative meaning within the narrative world projected by the parable itself. But Herzog ignores the latter.

According to Herzog's interpretation the vineyard owner is not to be seen as a God figure. Rather the parable is to be divested of its theological investments and read as an encoding of the Palestinian agrarian world (Herzog 1994, 81–82, 84). The landowner belongs to the patron class as is seen from the fact that he owns a vineyard (and produces a luxury product) and has an overseer. Urban elites (such as the owner) generally had retainers perform such visible work as hiring, in order to deflect peasant resentment from themselves. But Jesus has the owner himself do the hiring in order to make visible certain hidden aspects of the social order (85–87). The day laborers who are hired fall into the class of helpless expendables, who could not sustain life on a denarius a day since they worked so seldom (87–90).

Paying first those hired last was contrary to custom and thus was an affront to those first hired. And by paying those hired last a full day's wages, the owner shames those who had worked all day and treats their work as if it were worthless. The parable codifies a confrontation between two social extremes — elites and expendables — in one of the few moments in the economic cycle when the former are dependent on the latter. But the owner conquers the workers by banning and blacklisting the spokesman of their protest. By banishing one the owner intimidates the others and divides them (Herzog 1994, 91–96).

I have three criticisms of Herzog's approach. First, from the standpoint of hermeneutical reflection Herzog denies polyvalence. Although he tacitly gives theoretical recognition to various levels of meaning, in practice he tends to take only one as legitimate. I do not object in principle to social-scientific interpretation, but I do object to reducing parables to this one level of meaning. It is theoretically unjustified (see Crossan 1977, *Polyvalent Narration. Semeia* 9).

Second, removing parables from their context in the Gospels and placing them in a historical Jesus context does not, exegetically speaking, eliminate the religious element in the context. Even if Jesus' proclamation of the kingdom of God was not as central as once thought, it can hardly be totally denied. Moreover, Jesus was broadly speaking an heir of the Jewish religious tradition. His parables cannot be totally disengaged from that context. In addition, it needs to be affirmed that parables *in themselves*, because of their formal trait of interlacing the extraordinary and the realistic, imply a religious meaning. I argued this long ago (Via 1967, 65–66, 104–6, 188), and it was reiterated by Paul Ricoeur. Parable is a religious kind of poetic discourse because it creates oddness or extravagance by mixing the extraordinary and the ordinary. The tension thus created points to an "other" or a "beyond" (see Crossan 1975. *Paul Ricoeur on Biblical Hermeneutics. Semeia* 4, 99).

The plot tells the story of the full-day workers. It moves downward (tragically) from the workers' being given an opportunity to work (20:1–7), through the protest of the full-day workers about the owner's method of payment (20:8–12), to the exclusion of one of the protesters from the presence of a good(?) man (20:13–14a). The fact that there is dissonance between the apparently unjust behavior of the landowner (when viewed from a certain sociological paradigm outside of the parable) and envisioning his action as an image of the grace of God (Herzog 1994, 50) is no argument against reading the parable from a religious perspective and interpreting the vineyard owner's act in theological terms. As a matter of fact, it is precisely the tension between the ordinary social setting — work and pay — and the odd behavior of the landowner — paying the last first and paying them too much — that creates the metaphorical quality that constitutes the parable *as* parable and points to the "beyond."

But if the vineyard owner's conduct can be understood as an image of God's action, how is the latter to be interpreted? Perhaps it is too theologically explicit to say that the parable portrays God's grace, although it may indirectly imply this. But it is not over-interpreting the story to say that "God's" action is surprising and incalculable. It does not fit the expectations generated by everyday quid pro quo justice. But even the theme of the incalculable is not there for its own sake. It must be understood in light of the plot. The real focus is how the full-day workers respond to their encounter with the incalculable. And the suggestion is that in their desire to have life be calculable, they interpret the incalculable as injustice rather than as grace. God in God's incalculability seeks the well-being of humankind. But some human beings in their quest for secure calculability alienate themselves from this possibility.

Is it too much to have expected the full-day workers to see the possibility of freedom in the incalculability? No, it is no more too much than it is to expect the audience of the parable to see the possibility of grace in the apparent injustice of the land-owner's behavior. But in both cases it is a demanding expectation. The biblical tradition teaches us that parable is not a genre that conveys a clear message. Quite the contrary, parables are dark sayings that create misunderstanding (Ps 49:3–4; 78:1–3; Prov 1:6; Mark 4:10–12). It takes a radical act of faith-as-imagination to see through the darkness of the enigma to the light.

A satisfactory interpretation of this parable will maintain a dialectic between consciousness-raising hints about the nature of oppression and allusions to how an encounter with the incalculable might empower one to engage the social reality.

Third, functionally or pragmatically considered Herzog's one-dimensional approach turns out to be counterintuitive when compared with the communal interpretation given by oppressed Latin American peasants who are actually reading the Bible to find out what word God is speaking to them out of their historical situation. Ernesto Cardenal has gathered in several volumes many of the dialogical commentaries on biblical texts that resulted from his work with country people in the Nicaraguan community of Solentiname. One of the texts discussed was our parable.

Cardenal began the discussion by saying that in his opinion the boss was unfair to pay all the workers the same. But Oscar replied that he did not think the boss was unfair because he did not care about the profits the work would bring. The boss rather wanted everyone to have work and to be together. Manuel reiterated that it was not unjust. It is not taking anything from me to do a favor for him (Cardenal 1979, 180–81). Olivia continued that what she sees is the opposite of real life, where the one that makes the most gets the most. Jesus is telling us that in the new society everyone is going to get the same. Laureno adds that people will be paid according to their needs, and everybody has almost the same needs

(181). Felipe turns the discussion in a different direction. The Jews who began to work first for the kingdom were holding to the religious promises that God had given them. Those who come later are not thinking about those promises but are just expecting what is fair. But in the end they are all going to receive the same reward of eternal life (182).

These interpretations are obviously not informed by historical or literary criticism. But as Mesters has pointed out (1992, 48), the dialogical interaction resembles the free association of ideas used by psychoanalysis. These engaged hearers of the parable in Nicaragua spontaneously recognize that the parable is about equality in a new society *and* about eternal life. We can thank Herzog for bringing out the sociopolitical side. But the political and the religious are both potentially available in the parable. Our hermeneutical lens should be wide enough to actualize both of them.

I conclude in brief summary. Liberation theology hermeneutics is a legitimate and fruitful way of receiving the biblical tradition in our situation, in the hope that the Holy Spirit will turn it into word of God. At the same time this mode of reception needs to be contextualized and complemented by other hermeneutical lenses and theological claims. And — at least for those who are biblical scholars or theologians — a critical eye needs to be turned both on the texts to be interpreted and the vantage point of the interpreter.

Throughout this book I have stressed the New Testament's position(s) on the role of human reception — will, reflection, imagination — in constituting the revelation of God. It should also be remembered that the four New Testament writers considered amply attest the obdurate resistance of humankind to God's pressing intervention.

APPENDIX

My intention here is to amplify the discussion of several of the theological issues raised in chapter 1.

The Yale School

Hans Frei argues that the basic conviction of the Christian faith is the unique affirmation that to know the identity of Jesus Christ is to have him present and to speak of Jesus' presence is to speak of the presence of God (Frei 1975, vii, 137, 154). According to Frei Jesus' identity is manifested in the gospel narrative, which he characterizes as realistic and history-like (xiv–xvi).

Identity for Frei is the coalescence of temporal change and continuity in such a way that a person is uniquely who he or she is (1975, 15, 38, 91, 127). It is constituted by an intention-action pattern that answers the question What is he like? and by a self-manifestation pattern that answers the question Who is he? The application of these patterns to the gospel narrative, in Frei's view, imposes nothing on the story that would reflect its significance for us (43–46). Turning to the Gospels Frei finds that Jesus' intention was to obey God for the good of humankind, which he enacted by consenting to what God mandated for him through the course of historical events. Jesus' manifested subject-self is to be the presence of God or life, which is manifested in his embodiment of Israel's history, in his relation to the kingdom of God, and in his individuality, especially as actualized in his resurrection (97, 103, 105, 110–11, 128, 130, 137, 142–45).

According to Frei a realistic narrative like that in the Gospels means literally what it says, contains no gap between representation and meaning. Therefore, the story renders its meaning to interpreters regardless of what significance it may have for them or how they dispose themselves toward the story (Frei 1975, xiv–xvi). Frei claims that his hermeneutical devices, the identity patterns that he uses to capture Jesus' identity, simply bring out the narrative's own meaning and enable us to see what is there (x, xv, 46). Frei then claims that employing the hermeneutical circle, using one's social location and conceptual preunderstanding as an angle of vision for grasping the text's meaning, is unnecessary. It is also wrong-headed, for it distorts the subject matter of the text (xvi–xvii, 89, 138; 1974, 304, 322–23).

George Lindbeck agrees essentially with Frei's claim that the gospel story of Jesus is a realistic narrative rendering Jesus' identity. Its proper meaning is the literal meaning that the church finds in the story and not some meaning behind, beneath, or in front of the text that is suggested by the extrascriptural categories that form the hermeneutical standpoints of the interpreters (Lindbeck 1984, 118–20, 125–26). Lindbeck also claims that all the categories the early Christians possessed for communal self-understanding were derived from their only Scriptures, the Hebrew Bible, and they interpreted this as Jews (1987, 169). In Lindbeck's opinion the present theological crisis caused by disagreements over what the story of Jesus is really about — its historicity, its ethical ideas, its symbolization of a way of being, or what — results from the "liberal" fault of interpreting the narrative in terms of hermeneutical vantage points that shape it in a distorting way (1984, 118–20, 125–26).

At this point I will respond to Frei and Lindbeck. First, it is not the case that Frei's identity patterns are simply there in the narrative and do not express the significance that the narrative has for him. In no way does the narrative itself talk literally about continuity in change, enacting intentions, or Jesus' subject-self as manifesting the presence of God. Frei construes the narrative as expressing these patterns. He employs them because they already are significant for him. Any reading that does not literally repeat the text is a construal from some culturally — and religiously — shaped vantage point. And Frei's own description of his patterns shows that they do carry philosophical presuppositions. They express an anthropology that he brings to the story. For example, he states that intention alone would discount action, which does not merely illustrate but rather constitutes identity. On the other hand, action alone does not pertain to a centered self but only to overt behavior (Frei 1975, 92–93). Identity is to be located at the point at which inward life coming to outward expression meshes into the train of public circumstances (114).

Moreover, it is simply not true that the Jesus story renders its subject matter regardless of the personal disposition of the reader. To claim such ignores the power of preunderstanding or ignores the phenomenon that the refusal to understand may rest on a tacit awareness that to understand would shatter a presently held self-understanding. Anyone who has taught the synoptic Gospels many times has had at least once the vivid experience of getting to know a student's mind well enough to be sure that the student's refusal to understand the narratives about Jesus (or Jesus' narratives) was based on an unwillingness to have his or her own assumptions questioned in the way that these narratives question the reader.

With Frei it is not just that his identity patterns do in fact express the significance that the Jesus narrative has for him. It is also that from these patterns he has actually created the text that he is interpreting. For he does not interpret one or more of the Gospel narratives in its own terms, nor does he attempt to reconstruct critically the story of the historical Jesus. Frei makes use of individual contents from the Gospels, but his narrative *as structure*, as a whole story, is derived from the patterns of identity that belong to his philosophical presuppositions. Therefore, the narrative text that he claims to be interpreting, which he says renders itself literally regardless of the reader's presuppositions and which he claims to be interpreting on *its own* terms, actually exists primarily in *his own* mind. Thus because of his inattention to his hermeneutical standing point, his position is more subjective than that of interpreters who acknowledge the operation of the hermeneutical circle and make themselves critically aware of where they are in it.

With regard to the contention of Lindbeck — that the present lack of consensus about the meaning of the Jesus story is a crisis caused by the liberal proclivity for interpreting Scripture from an external standpoint — it should be said that the present situation is neither more liberal nor more critical than the one that obtained between A.D. 70 and 100. The four canonical Gospels written during that period give divergent interpretations of an already divergent tradition and from different hermeneutical standpoints conditioned by a limited social and cultural location. Lindbeck apparently holds that the New Testament situation was different from ours on the ground that the early Christians used only scriptural interpretive categories (1987, 169), while modern liberals use extrabiblical categories (1984, 118–20). But his position with regard to the New Testament is anything but demonstrable. Consider such "small" forms as parables, proverbs, miracle stories, and pronouncement stories; such "large" forms as tragicomedy, biography, romantic novel, and travelogue; and such versatile forms as metaphor and irony, not to mention such contents as conscience. Moreover, recent theory has shown that forms themselves always imply content (see chap. 2). All of the phenomena just mentioned can be found in nonbiblical religious and/or secular literature. Even if it could be shown that *all* of them also have some degree of manifestation in the Hebrew Scriptures, their appearance outside of the Bible shows that they are not peculiarly or exclusively biblical. Their employment reveals, not the distinctiveness of the Bible, but its continuity with other religious and humanistic interpretations of reality. The biblical writers were not committed to theologizing exclusively within the canon.

And that brings us to Brevard Childs and his contention that biblical interpretation should be a *strictly intra*canonical activity. Childs distinguishes his position in several explicit ways from Lindbeck (Childs 1984, 544–46), but one notes a certain similarity of theological ethos (541). According to Childs the canon — the *whole* canon and not some canon within the canon — is the proper and normative context for the interpretation of Scripture. Biblical interpretation should be canonical from beginning to end. The exegete is free to construe intracanonical relationships in various fresh ways (1970, 99; 1984, 28, 30, 38, 40, 42, 48, 52–53); however, Childs rejects the "liberal hermeneutical presupposition" that one must come to the Bible from a vantage point outside the text. The theological content of the Bible lies within the canon and not in some such category behind the text as salvation history, self-understanding, or the linguisticality of existence (1970, 102).

I shall try to show that Childs's exegetical practice discloses the impossibility of staying strictly within the canon as well as the inevitability of a canon within the canon. If all parts of the canon should be considered in interpreting any one part and if all are authoritative, how does one deal with tensions and contradictions within the canon? Childs suggests that the whole canon is a new context that somehow neutralizes conflicts between the parts (1984, 38, 52–53), but how this actually might occur is very obscure.

Take, for example, the conflicts in the birth stories of Matthew and Luke at the story level. Childs's solution is to say that they have a joint theological witness (hidden and revealed elements in Jesus' birth) that makes unnecessary our having to solve the *historical* problems of Jesus' birth (1984, 162–64). The point about the theological witness is true, and I would want to affirm it. But at least some believers will still want to raise questions and take some kind of position, however tentative, about the historical element. And suppose that there are theological tensions.

An example of a theological conflict that Childs addresses is the synoptic Gospels' portrayal of John the Baptist as Elijah (Matt 3:4; 17:11–13; Mark 1:3; Luke 3:4) while the Fourth Gospel flatly denies this identification (John 1:21). In my view it is not that either the Synoptics or John believes that John the Baptist is literally Elijah. It is rather a question of whether John fulfills the Jewish expectation about the eschatological appearance of Elijah. If John does fulfill the expectation — as in the Synoptics — then Jesus is not as exclusively the eschatological figure as he is in the Fourth Gospel, where John is not Elijah. How is the issue to be adjudicated? Which one is right? Childs agrees that they cannot be reconciled in a precritical harmonistic way. Nor is it an irreconcilable contradiction, as the historical critic says. Canonization offers a third approach. Each part must be seen in light of the whole canonical collection. The Gospels are not to be read on the same level, but rather the Fourth Gospel is the framework from which to interpret the other three. The effect of canonization is to highlight some features and subordinate others (Childs 1984, 170–73). This argument creates three serious problems for Childs.

First, it produces a glaring contradiction, for he has said explicitly that the absence of combination or fusion in the Gospels shows that each has its integrity and none is subordinated to another. Childs pointedly states that the Fourth Gospel is not the interpretive framework for the Synoptics as P is for J and E in the Pentateuch (1984, 153–55). Thus Childs both affirms and denies that the Fourth Gospel is more authoritative than the Synoptics.

Secondly, he seems not to recognize that even if canonization did make the *whole* collection the authoritative horizon for interpretation and theological reflection — a point still to be discussed — that in itself would not say what the relationships are within the canon. It is the interpreter who makes those judgments. Childs deals with theological conflict between the Fourth Gospel and the Synoptics by stating an evaluative preference for the former. And he does this from the standpoint of his own theological perspective and not with precise direction or guidance from the canon itself. Because Childs refuses to acknowledge the noncanonical influences inevitably at work in all interpretation, he attributes to the canon as canon more power than it can have. It cannot tell him that John is to be superordinated over the Synoptics — as he himself recognizes on one side of his contradiction.

Childs's Yale colleague David Kelsey recognizes that interpretations of Scripture are based on a logically prior imaginative judgment (Kelsey 1975, 166–68, 170). Thus he acknowledges the operation of a presuppositional standpoint. This standpoint or discrimen results from the interaction in the Christian community between the community's understanding of the mode of God's presence and the use of Scripture (193). In the face of the diverse range of images offered by the Bible, the interpreter makes a judgment about what is to be chosen as the root metaphor that expresses the meaning of the whole.

Obviously this judgment is strongly guided by the Christian tradition and participation in the community (Kelsey 1975, 170, 193, 205–6). At the same time it is an imaginative, free, and creative decision (206), and there are non-Christian factors involved in it. Once the root metaphor has been chosen, its significance must be capable of being reasonably argued (171, 200). Moreover, social and cultural factors set limits on how God's presence can be seriously imagined (171–72). For Kelsey, then, the construal of biblical texts does not come in an unmediated way from the canonical arrangement itself but is governed by an imaginative, interpretive judgment that is comprised of a diversity of factors.

Thirdly, Childs does not really escape a canon within the canon. He states that the effect of canonization is to highlight some features and subordinate others. But it is the interpreter, or interpretive community, that achieves this effect. The canon does not do it. The highlighted parts are more canonical than the subordinated parts; they are, in fact, a canon within the canon. There is a way to affirm the ancient canonical choices of the church and also to acknowledge forthrightly that there are tensions in the Bible and that only parts of it actually shape the life of individual believers and believing communities — different parts for different believers. The way is to accept the reality of canons within the canon that have actual authority based on experienced impact and to consider the rest of the canon as of potential authority based on the generally reliable witness of the church.

Ronald Thiemann

Here I focus on Thiemann's rejection of foundationalist epistemology in constructing an understanding of revelation. Thiemann declines to identify himself with deconstruction in any thoroughgoing way, but he does repudiate foundationalism, as do deconstruction and postmodernism more broadly, on the ground that it is conceptually incoherent (1987, 22, 26).

According to Thiemann a foundationalist epistemology assumes that in order for a system of thought to be valid it must rest on our ability to demonstrate the necessity of a self-evident and nonreferential sufficient reason or first cause, a set of beliefs not constituted by a relationship to other beliefs, that must be universally accepted as true. The foundation or sufficient reason is independent of the system of thought but is the source of intelligibility for all beliefs in the system. For foundationalism there is an unshakable, incorrigible foundation for knowledge that needs no external illumination but glows with the light of self-illumination (Thiemann 1985, 44–45, 158 n. 20; 1987, 26). Friedrich Schleiermacher's doctrine of revelation was founded, for example, on its being a particular expression of a universal human possibility — the consciousness of being absolutely dependent (Thiemann 1985, 20–29). T. F. Torrance's very different foundationalism claims that Christian theology, like every other scholarly discipline, is a rational objective science because it adheres to the nature of its own object. Its object is different from that of any other science, but it is like other sciences in having a disciplined method appropriate to its object (Thiemann 1985, 35–40).

Thiemann holds that for modern epistemological theories of revelation the problem is how the knowing subject can know the ontologically distinct object — God. How can the ontological gap be bridged? According to foundational epistemologies, to know is to have the subject's representations of the object correspond with that which is given to the subject. The ontological gap is bridged either by the object's causing its nature to be imposed on the subject or by the subject's causing its consciousness to be imposed on the unschematized object. When this causal scheme is applied to theology, it issues in one of two results: (1) God is set outside of our context, and God creates God's own conditions for and content of knowledge: therefore, one cannot say how it is that *we* know God. The integrity of human subjectivity is denied. (2) We bring God within a context dominated by our categories and concepts; therefore, the independent reality of God is denied (Thiemann 1985, 42–43, 81, 96, 151).

Thiemann regards the basic foundationalist assumption as unwarranted and attempts an understanding of revelation that does not see God as an external causal agent (1985, 44–45, 81). His nonfoundational approach does not appeal to God's epistemological or temporal priority but argues that God's reality (ontological priority) is implied by a set of concrete Christian beliefs concerning God's identity. Thiemann's justification of theological claims, then, is specific to Christian faith and bases the validity of theological construction on the internal logic of the several theological themes, and on theology's relationship to the Christian community's own faith and worship, and not on its dependence upon a criterion external to the Christian tradition and universally demonstrable (69, 72–77, 80).

The construction proposed by Thiemann centers upon the gospel as narrated promise and God's identity as the one who promises. The doctrine of revelation should be a subtheme within the doctrine of God. God's identity as the one who creates, promises, and fulfills and the church's identity as a community that remembers, trusts, and hopes necessarily imply a relationship in which God is primary actor and initiator and the church, the primary recipient. God's prevenience is a necessary pragmatic implication of the force and content of the language of Christian practice. The modern doctrine of revelation, founded on the pattern of knowledge and causality, cannot consistently affirm both the priority of God and God's relationship to a human conceptual framework. But Thiemann believes that the notion of narrated promise addresses the central problem and is able to affirm both God's priority and the human theological construction (Thiemann 1985, 101–2, 109, 112, 137).

I want to respond to two aspects of Thiemann's project — its antifoundationalism and its marginalization, if not negation, of epistemological concerns. Since my proposal has been to relate several themes from the New Testament witnesses and not to provide them with a theoretical foundation independent of the New Testament, I suppose that my approach is (or at least might be) nonfoundational. But my project is not programmatically nonfoundational, for I regard the distinction between foundational and nonfoundational approaches as unstable, if not obscure. Thiemann, for example, criticizes a theology's employment of a noninferential philosophical foundation for Christian knowledge of God. Yet he allows — as an (allegedly) nonfoundational move — the theological use of philosophical ideas as long as they are assimilated to the logic of the Christian tradition and are not governed by their own original context (Thiemann 1985, 74–75, 90). My point is that we can never make ourselves totally aware of our (philosophical) presuppositions and how we are using them — or they, us. Moreover, an exegete or theologian has to use some method or methods, and whether the method is historical, literary, analytical, phenomenological, or whatever, it is used also in other disciplines, and it is not conceptually neutral. Thus it is always possible that a nonfoundational theologian may believe that he or she is using a borrowed philosophical concept — or method — in a way that is conformed to the logic of the Christian tradition when in actual fact her or his interpretation of the logic of the Christian tradition is already substantially governed by the philosophical position from which the concept is borrowed. For example, a theologian may believe that a borrowed bit of Aristotle has been assimilated to the logic of the Christian religion. But it will only seem this way because the theologian has already accommodated the logic of the Christian tradition as a whole to Aristotle.

Although Thiemann apparently does not think of himself as a deconstructor, it is the case that antifoundationalism and deconstruction characteristically go together. The point I want to make is that they cannot go together with logical consistency. The reason for this impossibility is that according to deconstruction, thought-in-language always turns against itself. An idea excluded from a discourse and pushed outside will always make its way back in again. Thus in deconstructionist terms, an excluded foundation will always reassert itself.

Regarding the epistemological issue I tried to show concisely in the introduction and throughout the discussion of the New Testament that the categories of revelation, manifestation, and enlightening activity as applied to God and the language of knowing, understanding, seeing, and hearing as applied to human beings are too pervasive in the New Testament to dismiss the question of how knowledge of God is made available. The solution to the problem that Thiemann sees in the modern understanding of revelation (the inability to affirm consistently both the priority of God and the integrity of human subjectivity) is not to abandon or diminish the epistemological dimension of the revelation concept but to look more closely at the implications of the New Testament. My contention has been that the New Testament is concerned with how God is known but in such a way as not to deny either the prior independent reality of God or the material effect of human figuration.

Paul Tillich

My question about Tillich has to do with the precise role of the human factor in constituting revelation. One of Tillich's most famous claims is that while the content of the Christian answer is determined by revelation, the form of the answer is dependent on the question it answers. If the question is how to face the anxiety of finite being, God will be defined as the infinite ground of courage (Tillich 1953, 72). But if God's own self-manifestation is in some part constituted by the human reception of it in changing cultural categories, as Tillich acknowledges (68), then it would seem that the human part in revelation cannot be excluded from content and limited to form. Nor can form and content be separated in actuality, for form has at least an implied content, and content is shaped, not contained, by form.

Tillich also makes a distinction between original and dependent revelation. An *original revelation* is one that occurs in a constellation that did not exist before. Peter knew Jesus as the Christ in an original revelation. Here the objective and subjective sides are joined for the first time. *Dependent revelation* exists in that later generations met the Jesus who had been received as the Christ by Peter and the other apostles. In dependent revelation the receiving side is always changing (Tillich, 1953, 140).

On the objective side of the original revelation Jesus is the medium of a revelation that is as final as it is original. Jesus of Nazareth is the medium of final revelation because he sacrifices everything finite in himself, which could bring people to him as a great personality, to Jesus as the Christ, which is greater than both he and they. He is final revelation only for those who accept him as such. Peter did so accept him; thus, his acceptance is a part of the revelation itself (Tillich 1953, 151–52).

My question is whether an original revelation can be a constellation that did not exist before in a radical sense. We know Peter's revelational experience, not directly, but only through the Gospels in which the Evangelists received the Peter story by contextualizing it within cross-cultural forms that already existed, although the Evangelists undoubtedly gave their materials an original twist. There was hermeneutical work — naturalizing the tradition — on the part of the Gospel writers. And if later readers or hearers receive the gospel story as the revelation of God, these, too, will do hermeneutical work. Tillich probably suggests that we know more about Peter's experience than we can know. But we can know something indirectly — by analogy. We do not know how Peter experienced subjectively his encounter with Jesus. But if the story of his experience is revelation for us, then it is plausible to assume that Peter's experience was in some way analogous to ours, or that the experience of the person or community that created the story was in some way analogous to ours. That is, the eventful process of revelation entails constitutive human reception by hermeneutical work from beginning to end. The distinction between original and dependent revelation is a hazy one.

David Tracy

For Tracy the revelation in Jesus Christ is the manifestation that is normative for Christianity (1991, 233–35) of the holy mystery of the whole that comes to expression in religious classics generally (155, 159, 168–69, 173, 193, 202–3). Does that mean that Tracy's position is foundational in very much the same sense that Schleiermacher's (probably) is? According to Thiemann, Schleiermacher's doctrine of revelation was "founded" on its being the expression of a universal human possibility—the consciousness of being absolutely dependent (Thiemann 1985, 20–29).

According to Schleiermacher the sum total of religion is to feel that our being and living are in and through God (Schleiermacher 1958, 49–50). Or the self-identical essence of piety is the consciousness of being absolutely dependent, which is the same thing as being conscious of being in relation with God (Schleiermacher 1956, 12–13, 16–17). However, the essential oneness of religion spreads itself out in endless variety in the religions of Turks, Indians, Christians, and others (1958, 50–51). What gives Christianity its distinctiveness is that everything is related to the redemption accomplished by Jesus of Nazareth (1956, 52, 58). Schleiermacher knows that historical context governs meaning and generates specificity; therefore, only historical interpretation can do justice to the rootedness of the New Testament authors in their time and place (Schleiermacher 1977, 46, 48, 104, 107, 117).

But despite the various different expressions of religion Schleiermacher is adamant that the feeling of absolute dependence does not vary from person to person but is a universal element of life. It is the same in all persons because it rests, not upon any particular modification of, but upon the absolutely general nature of humankind (Schleiermacher 1956, 133–34). Yet we ask Schleiermacher if the acknowledgment of variety nevertheless deconstructs the affirmation of universal self-identity? It probably does not. Schleiermacher's foundation would remain intact if the universal were conceived in terms of a moderate Aristotelian realism, that is, if the feeling of absolute dependence were understood as *really* present *in* its varied expressions but not as existing independently of them.

At first it might seem as if Tracy's formulation is similarly foundational, for he does regard the Christian revelation as an instance of a structure of meaning and experience that is broader than the Christian tradition and experience (1991, 155, 159, 168–69). But if Tracy's position is relatively foundational, it is not thoroughgoingly so. The widespread experience of the mystery of the other is not a self-evident, self-illuminating, nonreferential first cause (Thiemann 1985, 44–45, 158 n. 20; 1987, 26), not a touchstone located outside the play of relativizing forces (Taylor 1990, 37) and unmodified by them. Rather for Tracy all classics are rooted in their own historicity and display the ambiguities of their traditions. There is no reality and there are no texts that are not conditioned by their differentiated languages and historical situations (Tracy 1987, 36, 61–62, 79, 82, 84, 112; 1991, 102). Thus for Tracy there is no universal — undifferentiated — experience of the holy mystery. There are only specific, limited, ambiguous interpretations of it.

But does Tracy's acknowledgment of a commonality of experience behind all religious classics — the experience of the whole as holy mystery — deconstruct his affirmation of the variety of expression generated by different languages and histories? It probably does not. The differences would remain real if the commonality were understood, not in terms of identity, but in terms of analogy.

In view of Tracy's position on the historicity of all texts it is a little surprising that he makes a distinction between the Christ event itself, which is an adequate and decisive manifestation of God, and the only *relatively* adequate witnesses to the event, the New Testament Scriptures, which are normative although only relatively adequate (1991, 248–49, 259). In response to this it needs to be said that just as there is no universal experience of the holy mystery that transcends the relativizing specifics of languages, cultures, and religions, so there is no manifestation of the God whom Christians worship that stands above the multiplicity of not-altogether-consistent, relatively adequate New Testament witnesses. The fully adequate Christ event is inaccessible either as an object of faith or as the subject matter of theological reflection. We are radically dependent on a fragmented vehicle of revelation. We cannot compare the relatively adequate textual witnesses to the fully adequate (nonexistent) Christ event in order to test the validity of the former. We can only compare the relatively adequate witnesses with each other.

Gordon Kaufman

According to Ronald Thiemann, Kaufman argues that theology should be carried on without recourse to a claim of revelation and rejects any conceivable sense of God's prevenience in relation to theology (Thiemann 1985, 49, 55). It is true that Kaufman rejects revelation as an authoritative given, puts a certain emphasis on the human role in achieving an understanding of God, and regards our sense of God's action as a retrospective interpretation of the historical movement in which we find ourselves (Kaufman 1993, 57–58, 486–87). But we have seen that Kaufman by no means rejects revelation out of hand nor does he deny prevenience. In fact what Christian theology can claim in its retrospective interpretation is that our God-talk is a *response* to God's activity toward us; therefore, that activity is necessarily prior (487).

One may wonder to what extent Kaufman's strong criticism of regarding Christian revelation as an authoritative given reflects the spirit of the age, which, according to Peter Stuhlmacher, "threatens to alienate our entire human existence and renders every claim on the individual — from the tradition, from the present and the environment, or even from transcendence — an imposition or restriction on his right to freedom which he must resist" (1977, 84). Whatever the case may be, I agree that theology — or faith — should not *begin* with the affirmation that the Bible is an authoritative given that legitimates specific theological claims. But *after* certain texts have been interpreted and found meaningful and powerful, believers and believing communities are justified in attributing authority to those texts. And in view of the authority that Kaufman attributes to modern experience (1993, 79, 88), it seems plausible to argue that twenty centuries of the church's *experience* of the Bible as authoritative justifies Christians in claiming that any part of the canon is potentially authoritative.

WORKS CITED

Aristotle. 1935a. *On Sense and Sensible Objects*. Translated by W. S. Hett. Loeb. Cambridge: Harvard University Press.

———. 1935b. *On the Soul*. Translated by W. S. Hett. Loeb. Cambridge: Harvard University Press.

Baillie, John. 1956. *The Idea of Revelation in Recent Thought*. New York: Columbia University Press.

Barbé, Dominique. 1992. "Church Base Communities." In *Liberation Theology*, edited by Curt Cadorette. Maryknoll, N.Y.: Orbis Books.

Barr, James. 1973. *The Bible in the Modern World*. London: SCM.

Barrett, C. K. 1957. *The Gospel according to Saint John*. New York: Macmillan.

———. 1973. *The Second Epistle to the Corinthians*. New York: Harper and Row.

Barth, Gerhard. 1963. "Matthew's Understanding of the Law." In *Tradition and Interpretation in Matthew*, translated by P. Scott. Philadelphia: Westminster.

Barth, Karl. 1949. *The Doctrine of the Word of God*. Translated by G. Thomson. Prolegomena to *Church Dogmatics*, vol. 1, pt. 1. Edinburgh: T. and T. Clark.

———. 1954. "The Christian Understanding of Revelation." In *Against the Stream*, Edited by Ronald Gregor Smith, translated by S. Godman. London: SCM.

———. 1959. *A Shorter Commentary on Romans*. Richmond: John Knox.

Beare, F. W. 1959. *A Commentary on the Epistle to the Philippians*. London: Adam and Charles Black.

Beare, Francis Wright. 1981. *The Gospel according to Matthew*. San Francisco: Harper and Row.

Belleville, Linda L. 1993. "Tradition or Creation? Paul's Use of the Exodus 34 Tradition in 2 Corinthians 3:7–18." In *Paul and the Scriptures of Israel*, edited by C. A. Evans and J. A. Sanders. JSNT Supplement Series 83. Sheffield: JSOT Press.

Bellow, Saul. 1987. *More Die of Heartbreak*. New York: Morrow.

Betz, Hans Dieter. 1985. *Essays on the Sermon on the Mount*. Translated by L. L. Welborn. Philadelphia: Fortress.

Booth, Wayne C. 1974. *A Rhetoric of Irony*. Chicago: University of Chicago Press.

Borg, Marcus J. 1994. *Jesus in Contemporary Scholarship*. Valley Forge, Pa.: Trinity Press International.

Boyarin, Daniel. 1994. *A Radical Jew*. Berkeley: University of California Press.

Bremond, Claude. 1970. "Morphology of the French Folktale." *Semiotica* 2:247–76.

———. 1978. "The Narrative Message." *Semeia* 10:5–55.

Brown, Raymond E. 1981a. *The Gospel according to John (1–12)*. Anchor Bible 29. Garden City, N.Y.: Doubleday. Originally published 1966.

———. 1981b. *The Gospel according to John (13–21)*. Anchor Bible 29a. Garden City, N.Y.: Doubleday. Originally published 1970.

Brunner, Emil. 1946. *Revelation and Reason*. Translated by O. Wyon. Philadelphia: Westminster.

Bultmann, Rudolf. 1951. *Theology of the New Testament*. Vol. 1. Translated by K. Grobel. New York: Scribner.

———. 1955a. "The Problem of Hermeneutics." In *Essays*, translated by J. Greig. New York: Macmillan. Originally published 1950.

———. 1955b. "The Question of Natural Revelation." In *Essays*, translated by J. Greig. New York: Macmillan. Originally published 1941.

———. 1955c. *Theology of the New Testament*. Vol. 2. Translated by K. Grobel. New York: Scribner.

———. 1960. "The Concept of Revelation in the New Testament." In *Existence and Faith*, edited and translated by S. Ogden. New York: Meridian. Originally published 1929.

———. 1962. *Das Verhältnis der urchristlichen Christusbotschaft zum historischen Jesus*. Heidelberg: Carl Winter Universitätsverlag.

———. 1964. "The Primitive Christian Kerygma and the Historical Jesus." In *The Historical Jesus and the Kerygmatic Christ*, edited and translated by C. Braaten and R. Harrisville. Nashville: Abingdon.

———. 1971. *The Gospel of John*. Translated by G. R. Beasley-Murray, R. W. N. Hoare, and J. K. Riches. Philadelphia: Westminster.

———. 1985. *The Second Letter to the Corinthians*. Translated R. Harrisville. Minneapolis: Augsburg.

Cardenal, Ernesto. 1979. *The Gospel in Solentiname*. Vol. 3. Translated by D. Walsh. Maryknoll, N.Y.: Orbis Books.

Childs, Brevard S. 1970. *Biblical Theology in Crisis*. Philadelphia: Westminster.

———. 1974. *The Book of Exodus*. Old Testament Library. Philadelphia: Westminster.

———. 1984. *The New Testament as Canon: An Introduction*. Philadelphia: Fortress.

Clark, Kenneth W. 1947. "The Gentile Bias in Matthew." *Journal of Biblical Literature* 66:165–72.

Coleridge, Samuel Taylor. 1854. *Biographia Literaria*. Vol. 3 of *The Complete Works*. New York: Harper and Brothers.

Cousins, Mark. 1989. "The Practice of Historical Investigation." In *Post-Structuralism and the Question of History*, edited by D. Attridge,

G. Bennington, and R. Young. Cambridge: Cambridge University Press.

Croatto, J. Severino. 1981. *Exodus: A Hermeneutics of Freedom*. Translated by S. Attanasio. Maryknoll, N.Y.: Orbis Books.

Crombie, I. M. 1957. "The Possibility of Theological Statements." In *Faith and Logic*, edited by B. Mitchell. London: Allen and Unwin.

―――. 1963. "Arising from the University Discussion." In *New Essays in Philosophical Theology*, edited by A. Flew and A. MacIntyre. London: SCM.

Crossan, John Dominic, ed. 1975. *Paul Ricoeur on Biblical Hermeneutics*. *Semeia* 4.

―――, ed. 1977. *Polyvalent Narration*. *Semeia* 9.

―――. 1991. *The Historical Jesus*. San Francisco: Harper.

―――. 1994. *Jesus: A Revolutionary Biography*. San Francisco: Harper.

Culler, Jonathan. 1975. *Structuralist Poetics*. Ithaca, N.Y.: Cornell University Press.

―――. 1982. *On Deconstruction*. Ithaca, N.Y.: Cornell University Press.

Cullmann, Oscar. 1959. *The Christology of the New Testament*. Translated by S. C. Guthrie and C. A. M. Hall. London: SCM.

Culpepper, R. Alan. 1983. *Anatomy of the Fourth Gospel*. Philadelphia: Fortress.

Davies, W. D. 1964. *The Setting of the Sermon on the Mount*. Cambridge: Cambridge University Press.

―――. 1981. "Conscience." In *The Interpreters' Dictionary of the Bible*, vol. 1. Nashville: Abingdon.

―――. 1993. "Canon and Christology in Paul." In *Paul and the Scriptures of Israel*, edited by C. A. Evans and J. A. Sanders. JSNT Supplement Series 83. Sheffield: JSOT Press.

Davies, W. D., and Dale C. Allison Jr. 1988. *A Critical and Exegetical Commentary on the Gospel according to Saint Matthew*. Vol. 1. International Critical Commentary. Edinburgh: T. and T. Clark.

Dawson, David. 1992. *Allegorical Readers and Cultural Revision in Ancient Alexandria*. Berkeley: University of California Press.

Derrida, Jacques. 1970. "Structure, Sign, and Play in the Discourse of the Human Sciences." In *The Language of Criticism and the Sciences of Man*, edited by R. Macksey and E. Donato. Baltimore: Johns Hopkins University Press.

―――. 1979a. "Differance." In *Speech and Phenomena*, translated and introduced by D. B. Allison. Evanston, Ill.: Northwestern University Press.

―――. 1979b. "Living On: Border Lines." Translated by J. Hulbert. In *Deconstruction and Criticism*. New York: Seabury.

―――. 1980. *Of Grammatology*. Translated by G. Spivak. Baltimore: Johns Hopkins University Press.

Dodd, C. H. 1953. *The Interpretation of the Fourth Gospel*. Cambridge: Cambridge University Press.

Donahue, John R. 1988. *The Gospel in Parable*. Philadelphia: Fortress.

D'Sa, Francis X. 1987. "The Language of God and the God of Language: The Relation between God, Human Beings, World, and Language in St. John." In *God in Language*, edited by R. Scharlemann and G. Ogutu. New York: Paragon House.

Duke, Paul. 1985. *Irony in the Fourth Gospel*. Atlanta: John Knox.

Dunn, J. D. G. 1970. "2 Cor. 3:17 — 'The Lord Is the Spirit.'" *Journal of Theological Studies*, new series, 21:309–20.

Ebeling, Gerhard. 1963. "Theological Reflexions on Conscience." In *Word and Faith*, translated by J. Leitch. Philadelphia: Fortress.

Elliott, John H. 1988. "The Fear of the Leer: The Evil Eye from the Bible to Li'l Abner." *Forum* 4:42–71.

———. 1994. "The Evil Eye and the Sermon on the Mount." *Biblical Interpretation* 2:51–84.

Fish, Stanley. 1980a. "Interpreting the Variorum." In *Reader-Response Criticism*, edited by J. Tompkins. Baltimore: Johns Hopkins University Press.

———. 1980b. *Is There a Text in This Class?* Cambridge: Harvard University Press.

Forster, E. M. 1954. *Aspects of the Novel*. New York: Harcourt, Brace and World.

Fowler, Robert M. 1981. *Loaves and Fishes*. SBL Dissertation Series 54. Decatur, Ga.: Scholars Press.

———. 1991. *Let the Reader Understand*. Minneapolis: Fortress.

Frei, Hans W. 1974. *The Eclipse of Biblical Narrative*. New Haven and London: Yale University Press.

———. 1975. *The Identity of Jesus Christ*. Philadelphia: Fortress.

Furnish, Victor Paul. 1984. *II Corinthians*. Anchor Bible 32a. Garden City, N.Y.: Doubleday.

Gilkey, Langdon. 1961. "Cosmology, Ontology, and the Travail of Biblical Language." *Journal of Religion* 41:194–205.

———. 1976. *Reaping the Whirlwind*. New York: Seabury.

———. 1979. *Message and Existence*. New York: Seabury.

———. 1985. "Events, Meanings, and the Current Task of Theology." *Journal of the American Academy of Religion* 53 (December): 717–34.

Grant, Robert M. 1954. *The Bible in the Church*. New York: Macmillan.

———. 1957. *The Letter and the Spirit*. London: SPCK.

Green, William Scott. 1987. "Romancing the Tome: Rabbinic Hermeneutics and the Theory of Literature." *Semeia* 40:147–68.

Guelich, Robert A. 1985. *The Sermon on the Mount*. Waco, Tex.: Word Books.

Gundry, Robert H. 1982. *Matthew*. Grand Rapids: Eerdmans.

—. 1991. "A Responsive Evaluation of the Social History of the Matthean Community in Roman Syria." In *Social History of the Matthean Community*, edited by David L. Balch. Minneapolis: Fortress.

Guthke, Karl S. 1966. *Modern Tragicomedy*. New York: Random.

Handelman, Susan A. 1982. *The Slayers of Moses: The Emergence of Rabbinic Interpretation in Modern Literary Theory*. Albany: State University of New York Press.

Hanson, Paul D. 1978. *Dynamic Transcendence*. Philadelphia: Fortress.

Hart, Ray L. 1968. *Unfinished Man and the Imagination*. New York: Herder and Herder.

Hays, Richard B. 1989. *Echoes of Scripture in the Letters of Paul*. New Haven and London: Yale University Press.

—. 1993. "On the Rebound: A Response to Critiques of *Echoes of Scripture in the Letters of Paul*." In *Paul and the Scriptures of Israel*, edited by C. A. Evans and J. A. Sanders. JSNT Supplement Series 83. Sheffield: JSOT Press.

Heidegger, Martin. 1961. *An Introduction to Metaphysics*. Translated by R. Manheim. Garden City, N.Y.: Doubleday/Anchor Books.

—. 1962. *Being and Time*. Translated by J. Macquarrie and E. Robinson. New York: Harper and Row.

Hengel, Martin. 1985. *Studies in the Gospel of Mark*. Translated by J. Bowden. Philadelphia: Fortress.

Herzog, William R., II. 1994. *Parables as Subversive Speech*. Louisville: Westminster/John Knox.

Hill, David. 1972. *The Gospel of Matthew*. NCBC. Grand Rapids: Eerdmans; London: Marshall, Morgan and Scott.

Hodgson, Peter C. 1989. *God in History*. Nashville: Abingdon.

Hoskyns, Edwyn, and Noel Davey. 1931. *The Riddle of the New Testament*. London: Faber and Faber.

Hoskyns, Edwyn, and Francis Noel Davey. 1948. *The Fourth Gospel*. Rev. ed. London: Faber and Faber.

Hoy, David C. 1982. *The Critical Circle*. Berkeley and Los Angeles: University of California Press.

Iser, Wolfgang. 1978. *The Act of Reading*. Baltimore: Johns Hopkins University Press.

Jacobson, Roman. 1972. "Linguistics and Poetics." In *The Structuralists from Marx to Lévi-Strauss*, edited by R. T. De George and F. M. De George. Garden City, N.Y.: Doubleday/Anchor Books.

Jeremias, Joachim. 1963. *The Parables of Jesus*. Translated by S. H. Hooke. New York: Scribner.

—. 1964. *The Problem of the Historical Jesus*. Translated by N. Perrin. Facet Books, Biblical Series 13. Philadelphia: Fortress.

—. 1971. *New Testament Theology*. Translated by J. Bowden. New York: Scribner.

Jewett, Robert. 1971. *Paul's Anthropological Terms*. Leiden: Brill.

Käsemann, Ernst. 1969. *New Testament Questions of Today*. Translated by W. J. Montague. Philadelphia: Fortress.

———. 1971. *Perspectives on Paul*. Translated by M. Kohl. Philadelphia: Fortress.

———. 1973. "The Problem of a New Testament Theology." *New Testament Studies* 19 (April): 235–45.

Kaufman, Gordon D. 1981. *The Theological Imagination*. Philadelphia: Westminster.

———. 1993. *In Face of Mystery*. Cambridge: Harvard University Press.

Kee, Howard Clark. 1977. *Community of the New Age: Studies in Mark's Gospel*. Philadelphia: Westminster.

Kelber, Werner H. 1974. *The Kingdom in Mark: A New Place and a New Time*. Philadelphia: Fortress.

———. 1990. "In the Beginning Were the Words: The Apotheosis and Narrative Displacement of the Logos." *Journal of the American Academy of Religion* 58:69–98.

Kellner, Hans. 1989. *Language and Historical Representation*. Madison: University of Wisconsin Press.

Kelsey, David H. 1975. *The Uses of Scripture in Recent Theology*. Philadelphia: Fortress.

Kermode, Frank. 1979. *The Genesis of Secrecy: On the Interpretation of Narrative*. Cambridge: Harvard University Press.

Kilpatrick, G. D. 1946. *The Origins of the Gospel according to Matthew*. Oxford: Clarendon.

Kingsbury, Jack Dean. 1969. *The Parables of Jesus in Matthew 13*. Richmond: John Knox.

Koester, Craig R. 1995. *Symbolism in the Fourth Gospel*. Minneapolis: Fortress.

Koester, Helmut. 1983. *History and Literature of Early Christianity*. Vol. 2 of *Introduction to the New Testament*. Philadelphia: Fortress; Berlin and New York: Walter de Gruyter.

———. 1992. *Ancient Christian Gospels*. Philadelphia: Trinity Press International; London: SCM.

Kraft, Robert A., ed. 1974. *The Testament of Job*. Missoula, Mont.: Scholars Press.

Kysar, Robert. 1991. "Johannine Metaphor — Meaning and Fiction: A Literary Case Study of John 10:1–18." *Semeia* 53:81–111.

Langer, Susanne. 1965. "The Comic Rhythm." In *Comedy*, edited by Robert W. Corrigan. San Francisco: Chandler.

Levine, Amy-Jill. 1988. *The Social and Ethnic Dimensions of Matthean Salvation History*. Lewiston, N.Y.: Edwin Mellen.

Lindbeck, George A. 1984. *The Nature of Doctrine*. Philadelphia: Westminster.

———. 1987. "The Story-Shaped Church: Critical Exegesis and Theological Interpretation." In *Scriptural Authority and Narrative Interpretation*, edited by G. Green. Philadelphia: Fortress.

Luz, Ulrich. 1989. *Matthew 1–7: A Commentary*. Translated by W. Linss. Minneapolis: Augsburg.

Mack, Burton. 1988. *A Myth of Innocence*. Philadelphia: Fortress.

Martyn, J. Lewis. 1979. *History and Theology in the Fourth Gospel*. Rev. ed. Nashville: Abingdon.

Marxsen, Willi. 1990. *Jesus and Easter*. Translated by V. Furnish. Nashville: Abingdon.

Meeks, Wayne A. 1972. "The Man from Heaven in Johannine Sectarianism." *Journal of Biblical Literature* 91, no. 1:44–72.

Meier, John P. 1979. *The Vision of Matthew*. New York: Paulist Press.

Mesters, Carlos. 1992. "The Use of the Bible in Christian Communities of the Common People." In *Liberation Theology*, edited by Curt Cadorette. Maryknoll, N.Y.: Orbis Books.

Montrose, Louis. 1989. "Professing the Renaissance: The Poetics and Politics of Culture." In *The New Historicism*, edited by H. A. Veeser. New York and London: Routledge.

Moore, Stephen D. 1989. *Literary Criticism and the Gospels*. New Haven: Yale University Press.

———. 1992. *Mark and Luke in Poststructuralist Perspective*. New Haven and London: Yale University Press.

———. 1993. "Are There Impurities in the Living Water That the Johannine Jesus Dispenses? Deconstruction, Feminism, and the Samaritan Woman." *Biblical Interpretation* 1:207–27.

Morgan, Robert. 1987. "The Historical Jesus and New Testament Theology." In *The Glory of Christ in the New Testament*, edited by L. D. Hurst and N. T. Wright. Oxford: Clarendon.

Murphy-O'Connor, Jerome. 1991. *The Theology of the Second Letter to the Corinthians*. Cambridge: Cambridge University Press.

Neusner, Jacob. 1987. *What Is Midrash?* Guides to Biblical Scholarship, New Testament Series. Philadelphia: Fortress.

O'Connor, Flannery. 1966. "Revelation." In *Everything That Rises Must Converge*. New York: Noonday Press.

O'Day, Gail R. 1986. *Revelation in the Fourth Gospel*. Philadelphia: Fortress.

———. 1991. "'I Have Overcome the World' (John 16:33): Narrative Time in John 13–17." *Semeia* 53:153–66.

Oepke, Albrecht. 1965. "Kaluptō, Kalumma." In *Theological Dictionary of the New Testament*, vol. 3, edited by Gerhard Kittel, and translated by G. W. Bromiley. Grand Rapids: Eerdmans.

Ogletree, Thomas W. 1983. *The Use of the Bible in Christian Ethics*. Philadelphia: Fortress.

Ollenburger, Ben C. 1985. "Biblical Theology: Situating the Discipline." In *Understanding the Word*, edited by J. T. Butler, E. W. Conrad, and B. C. Ollenburger. Sheffield: JSOT Press.

Overman, J. Andrew. 1990. *Matthew's Gospel and Formative Judaism*. Minneapolis: Fortress.

Pannenberg, Wolfhart. 1969. *Revelation as History*. Translated by D. Granskou. London: Macmillan.

———. 1988. *Systematic Theology*. Vol. 1. Translated by G. Bromiley. Grand Rapids: Eerdmans, 1988.

Petersen, Norman R. 1993. *The Gospel of John and the Sociology of Light*. Valley Forge, Pa.: Trinity Press International.

Pierce, C. A. 1955. *Conscience in the New Testament*. London: SCM.

Plato. 1942a. *The Republic*. Translated by P. Shorey. Loeb. Cambridge: Harvard University Press.

———. 1942b. *Timaeus*. Translated by R. G. Bury. Loeb. Cambridge: Harvard University Press.

Rahner, Karl. 1994. *Foundations of Christian Faith*. New York: Crossroad.

Räisänen, Heikki. 1990. *Beyond New Testament Theology*. London: SCM; Philadelphia: Trinity Press International.

Ramsey, Ian T. 1957. *Religious Language*. New York: Macmillan.

Ricoeur, Paul. 1971a. "The Model of the Text: Meaningful Action Considered as a Text." *Social Research* 38, no. 3:529–62.

———. 1971b. "What Is a Text? Explanation and Interpretation." In *Mythic-Symbolic Language and Philosophical Anthropology*, edited by D. Rasmussen. The Hague: Martinus Nijhoff.

———. 1976. *Interpretation Theory*. Fort Worth: Texas Christian University Press.

———. 1984. *The Rule of Metaphor*. Translated by R. Czerny. Toronto: University of Toronto Press.

Robinson. J. A. T. 1965. "The Relation of the Prologue to the Gospel of John." In *The Authorship and Integrity of the New Testament*. London: SPCK.

Rowland, Christopher, and Mark Corner. 1989. *Liberating Exegesis*. Louisville: Westminster/John Knox.

Sanders, E. P. 1977. *Paul and Palestinian Judaism: A Comparison of Patterns of Religion*. Philadelphia: Fortress; London: SCM.

Saussure, Ferdinand de. 1966. *Course in General Linguistics*. Translated by W. Baskin. New York: McGraw-Hill.

Schleiermacher, Friedrich. 1956. *The Christian Faith*. Edited by H. R. Mackintosh and J. S. Stewart. Edinburgh: T. and T. Clark.

———. 1958. *On Religion*. Translated by J. Oman. Harper Torchbooks. New York: Harper and Brothers.

———. 1977. *Hermeneutics: The Handwritten Manuscripts*. Translated by J. Duke and J. Forstman. Missoula, Mont.: Scholars Press.

Schoedel, William R. 1991. "Ignatius and the Reception of the Gospel of Matthew in Antioch." In *Social History of the Matthean Community*, edited by David L. Balch. Minneapolis: Fortress.

Scholes, Robert. 1985. *Textual Power*. New Haven: Yale University Press.

Scroggs, Robin. 1988. "Can New Testament Theology Be Saved? The Threat of Contextualism." *Union Seminary Quarterly Review* 42:17–31.

Segal, Alan F. 1991. "Matthew's Jewish Voice." In *Social History of the Matthean Community*, edited by David L. Balch. Minneapolis: Fortress.

Segovia, Fernando F. 1991. "The Journey(s) of the Word of God: A Reading of the Plot of the Fourth Gospel." *Semeia* 53:23–54.

Smith, D. Moody. 1989. "Johannine Studies." In *The New Testament and Its Modern Interpreters*, edited by E. J. Epp and G. W. MacRae. Philadelphia: Fortress; Atlanta: Scholars Press.

———. 1995. *The Theology of the Gospel of John*. Cambridge: Cambridge University Press.

Sobrino, Jon. 1984. *Christology at the Crossroads*. Translated by J. Drury. Maryknoll, N.Y.: Orbis Books.

Soskice, Janet Martin. 1985. *Metaphor and Religious Language*. Oxford: Clarendon.

Stacey, W. David. 1956. *The Pauline View of Man*. London: Macmillan.

Staley, Jeffrey Lloyd. 1988. *The Print's First Kiss*. SBL Dissertation Series 82. Atlanta: Scholars Press.

Stegner, William Richard. 1984. "Romans 9:6–29 — A Midrash." *Journal for the Study of the New Testament* 22:37–52.

Stendahl, Krister. 1963. "The Apostle Paul and the Introspective Conscience of the West." *Harvard Theological Review* 56:199–215.

Stockhausen, Carol K. 1993. "2 Corinthians 3 and the Principles of Pauline Exegesis." In *Paul and the Scriptures of Israel*, edited by C. A. Evans and J. A. Sanders. JSNT Supplement Series 83. Sheffield: JSOT Press.

Stratton, G. M. 1917. *Theophrastus and Greek Physiological Psychology before Aristotle*. London: George Allen and Unwin; New York: Macmillan.

Strecker, Georg. 1971. *Der Weg der Gerechtigkeit*. Göttingen: Vandenhoeck and Ruprecht.

Stuhlmacher, Peter. 1977. *Historical Criticism and Theological Interpretation of Scripture*. Translated by R. Harrisville. Philadelphia: Fortress.

Talbert, Charles H. 1977. *What Is a Gospel?* Philadelphia: Fortress.

Tamez, Elsa. 1993. *The Amnesty of Grace*. Translated by S. Ringe. Nashville: Abingdon.

Taylor, Mark Kline. 1990. *Remembering Esperanza*. Maryknoll, N.Y.: Orbis Books.

Theissen, Gerd. 1991. *The Gospels in Context.* Translated by L. Maloney. Minneapolis: Fortress.

Thiemann, Ronald F. 1985. *Revelation and Theology: The Gospel as Narrated Promise.* Notre Dame, Ind.: University of Notre Dame Press.

————. 1987. "Radiance and Obscurity in Biblical Narrative." In *Scriptural Authority and Narrative Interpretation*, edited by G. Green. Philadelphia: Fortress.

Thiselton, Anthony C. 1980. *The Two Horizons.* Grand Rapids: Eerdmans; Exeter: Paternoster.

Tillich, Paul. 1953. *Systematic Theology.* Vol. 1. London: Nisbet.

Tolbert, Mary Ann. 1989. *Sowing the Gospel.* Minneapolis: Fortress.

Torrance, T. F. 1982. *Reality and Evangelical Theology.* Philadelphia: Westminster.

Tracy, David. 1987. *Plurality and Ambiguity.* San Francisco: Harper and Row.

————. 1991. *The Analogical Imagination.* New York: Crossroad.

Via, Dan O. 1967. *The Parables.* Philadelphia: Fortress.

————. 1971. "Justification and Deliverance: Existential Dialectic." *Studies in Religion/Sciences religieuses* 1:204–12.

————. 1975. *Kerygma and Comedy in the New Testament.* Philadelphia: Fortress.

————. 1985. *The Ethics of Mark's Gospel.* Philadelphia: Fortress.

————. 1990. *Self-Deception and Wholeness in Paul and Matthew.* Minneapolis: Fortress.

————. 1994a. "Matthew's Dark Light and the Human Condition." In *The New Literary Criticism and the New Testament*, edited by E. S. Malbon and E. V. McKnight. Sheffield: Sheffield Academic Press; Valley Forge, Pa.: Trinity Press International.

————. 1994b. "Romans." In *Mercer Commentary on the Bible*, edited by Watson E. Mills. Macon, Ga.: Mercer University Press.

Wheelwright, Philip. 1954. *The Burning Fountain.* Bloomington: Indiana University Press.

————. 1962. *Metaphor and Reality.* Bloomington: Indiana University Press.

White, Hayden. 1978. *Tropics of Discourse.* Baltimore: Johns Hopkins University Press.

————. 1989a. " 'Figuring the Nature of the Times': Literary Theory and Historical Writing." In *The Future of Literary Theory*, edited by Ralph Cohen. New York and London: Routledge.

————. 1989b. "New Historicism: A Comment." In *The New Historicism*, edited by H. A. Veeser. New York and London: Routledge.

————. 1990. *The Content of the Form.* Baltimore: Johns Hopkins University Press.

Wilckens, Ulrich. 1969. "The Understanding of Revelation within the History of Primitive Christianity." In *Revelation as History*, edited by W. Pannenberg, translated by D. Granskou. London: Macmillan.

Wrede, William. 1971. *The Messianic Secret*. Translated by J. C. G. Greig. Greenwood, S.C.: Attic Press.

———. 1973. "The Task and Methods of 'New Testament Theology.' " In *The Nature of New Testament Theology*, edited by Robert Morgan. Studies in Biblical Theology, second series 25. London: SCM.

Wright, G. Ernest. 1952. *God Who Acts*. Studies in Biblical Theology 8. London: SCM.

Wright, N. T. 1992. *The Climax of the Covenant*. Minneapolis: Fortress.

INDEX OF SCRIPTURE REFERENCES

INDEX OF NAMES

INDEX OF SUBJECTS